CRACKNELL'S STA

English Legal System

Edited by
D G Cracknell
LLB, Barrister

Old Bailey Press

OLD BAILEY PRESS LIMITED
200 Greyhound Road, London, W14 9RY

First published 1994
Reprinted 1998

© Old Bailey Press Ltd 1994

ISBN 1 85836 017 X

British Library Cataloguing-in-Publication.

A CIP Catalogue record for this book is available from the British Library.

Printed and bound in Great Britain.

CONTENTS

Preface	v
Alphabetical Table of Statutes	vii
Court of Chancery Act 1851	1
Appellate Jurisdiction Act 1876	2–4
Judicial Committee Act 1881	5
Appellate Jurisdiction Act 1887	6
Judicial Committee Amendment Act 1895	7
Appellate Jurisdiction Act 1908	8
Judicial Committee Act 1915	9
Children and Young Persons Act 1933	10–11
Administration of Justice (Appeals) Act 1934	12
Appellate Jurisdiction Act 1947	13
Judicial Pensions Act 1959	14
Administration of Justice Act 1968	15
Administration of Justice Act 1969	16–19
Courts Act 1971	20–23
Administration of Justice Act 1973	24
Juries Act 1974	25–33
Solicitors Act 1974	34–41
Sex Discrimination Act 1975	42–43
Bail Act 1976	44–61
Race Relations Act 1976	62

Justices of the Peace Act 1979   63–73

Magistrates' Courts Act 1980   74–107

Supreme Court Act 1981   108–159

Criminal Justice Act 1982   160

County Courts Act 1984   161–191

Police and Criminal Evidence Act 1984   192–271

Prosecution of Offences Act 1985   272–276

Coroners Act 1988   277–279

Legal Aid Act 1988   280–283

Courts and Legal Services Act 1990   284–335

Child Support Act 1991   336

Criminal Justice Act 1991   337–338

Bail (Amendment) Act 1993   339–340

PREFACE

ALTHOUGH the English legal system has its roots in a distant past, a large part of it is now governed by relatively modern statutes. Many significant changes were made by the Courts and Legal Services Act 1990.

This book contains provisions from 33 statutes, ranging in terms of time from the Court of Chancery Act 1851 to the Bail (Amendment) Act 1993. Of course, the extent of the relevant material is vast, but it is believed that the provisions included are those to which students will find it most helpful to refer.

Account is taken only of statutes, or particular sections of statutes, which had been brought into force by 1 October 1993, the only exception being s1 of the Bail (Amendment) Act 1993 which was then expected to come into force in the relatively near future. Any amendments or substitutions which were effective on 1 October 1993 have been incorporated in the text, and a note at the end of the particular statute indicates the source of any changes.

As it seems that it will be well into 1994 before the Judicial Pensions and Retirement Act 1993 is brought into force, its important provisions have not been set out or incorporated in this edition.

ALPHABETICAL TABLE OF STATUTES

Administration of Justice Act 1968 s1	15
Administration of Justice Act 1969	16–19
s12	16–17
s13	17–18
s14	18
s15	19
Administration of Justice Act 1973 s12	24
Administration of Justice (Appeals) Act 1934	12
s1	12
s2	12
Appellate Jurisdiction Act 1876	2–4
s3	2
s4	2
s5	2–3
s6	3–4
s25	4
Appellate Jurisdiction Act 1887	6
s3	6
s5	6
Appellate Jurisdiction Act 1908	8
s3	8
s4	8
Appellate Jurisdiction Act 1947 s1	13
Bail Act 1976	44–61
s1	44
s2	44–46
s3	46–48
s4	48–49
s5	49–51
s6	52
s7	53–54

Bail Act 1976 (continued)

s8	54–56
s9	56–57
Schedule 1, Part I	57–59
Schedule 1, Part II	59–60
Schedule 1, Part IIA	60
Schedule 1, Part III	60–61
Bail (Amendment) Act 1993 s1	339–340

Child Support Act 1991 s48	336
Children and Young Persons Act 1933 s34	10–11
Coroners Act 1988	277–279
s2	277
s8	277–279
s9	279
s12	279
s30	279
County Courts Act 1984	161–191
s1	161
s5	161–162
s6	162
s7	163
s8	163
s9	163
s11	164
s15	164
s16	165
s17	165
s18	165
s21	165–166
s23	166–167
s24	167–168
s25	168
s26	168–169
s27	169–170
s32	170
s35	170
s36	170
s37	171
s38	171–172

County Courts Act 1984 (continued)

s40	172–173
s41	173
s42	173–174
s47	175
s58	175
s60	175–176
s61	176
s64	176–177
s66	177–178
s67	178
s69	178–179
s75	180
s76	180
s77	181
s79	182
s80	182
s81	182–183
s82	183
s85	183
s89	184
s93	184
s94	184
s95	184–185
s97	185
s107	185–186
s108	186–187
s112	187–188
s114	188–189
s118	189
s147	189–191
Court of Chancery Act 1851 s16	1
Courts Act 1971	20–23
s16	20
s17	20–21
s21	21
s24	21–22
s29	22–23
s42	23
Schedule 2, Part IA	23

Courts and Legal Services Act 1990   284–335
s1   284–286
s8   286
s9   286–287
s11   287–288
s17   289–290
s18   290
s19   290–292
s20   292
s21   292–293
s22   293–295
s23   295–297
s24   297–298
s25   298–299
s26   299
s27   299–302
s28   302–303
s29   303–304
s30   305
s31   305–307
s32   307–309
s33   309–310
s34   310–311
s35   311–312
s40   312–313
s56   313
s57   314–315
s59   315
s61   316
s62   316
s63   316
s66   316–317
s69   317
s70   317–318
s71   318–319
s72   319
s73   319–320
s74   320
s75   320–321
s76   321

Courts and Legal Services Act 1990 (continued)

s113	321–323
s115	323
s119	323–325
s120	325–326
Schedule 1	326–327
Schedule 2	327
Schedule 3	327–328
Schedule 4, Part I	328–330
Schedule 4, Part II	330–332
Schedule 4, Part III	332–333
Schedule 5	333–334
Schedule 11	334–335
Criminal Justice Act 1982 s37	160
Criminal Justice Act 1991 s53	337–338
Judicial Committee Act 1881 s1	5
Judicial Committee Act 1915 s1	9
Judicial Committee Amendment Act 1895 s1	7
Judicial Pensions Act 1959 s2	14
Juries Act 1974	25–33
s1	25
s11	25–26
s12	26–27
s17	27–28
Schedule 1, Part I, Group A	28
Schedule 1, Part I, Group B	28–30
Schedule 1, Part I, Group C	30
Schedule 1, Part I, Group D	31
Schedule 2, Part II	31–32
Schedule 2, Part III	32–33
Justices of the Peace Act 1979	63–73
s6	63
s7	63–64
s8	64–65
s9	65
s10	65
s13	65–66
s14	66
s25	67

Justices of the Peace Act 1979 (continued)
 s26   67–68
 s28   68–69
 s31   69–70
 s39   70–71
 s40   71
 s44   71–72
 s45   72
 s50   72
 s63   72–73

Legal Aid Act 1988   280–283
 s1   280
 s3   280–281
 s5   281–282
 s6   282–283

Magistrates' Courts Act 1980   74–107
 s1   74–75
 s2   75–76
 s4   76–77
 s6   77–78
 s9   78–79
 s17   79
 s18   79–80
 s19   80–81
 s20   81
 s21   81
 s22   82–83
 s24   83–84
 s27   85
 s29   85–86
 s31   86
 s32   86–88
 s33   88–89
 s36   89
 s37   89
 s38   90
 s40   90–91
 s41   91

Magistrates' Courts Act 1980 (continued)

s42	91
s43	91
s51	92
s52	92
s53	92
s58	92–93
s66	93
s67	94
s69	94–95
s81	95–96
s108	97
s111	97–98
s113	98–99
s115	99
s120	99–100
s121	100–101
s122	102
s144	102
s148	103
s150	103–104
Schedule 1	105–106
Schedule 2	106–107

Police and Criminal Evidence Act 1984

	192–271
s1	192–194
s2	194–196
s3	196–197
s4	197–200
s6	200
s7	200
s8	200–201
s9	201–202
s10	202
s11	202–203
s12	203
s13	204
s14	204–205
s15	205–206
s16	206–207
s17	207–208

Police and Criminal Evidence Act 1984 (continued)

s18	209
s19	210
s20	211
s21	211–212
s22	212–213
s23	213
s24	214–215
s25	215–216
s27	217
s28	217–218
s29	218
s30	218–220
s31	220
s32	220–222
s34	222–223
s35	223
s36	223–225
s37	225–226
s38	226–228
s39	228–229
s40	229–231
s41	231–233
s42	234–235
s43	236–238
s44	238–239
s45	239–240
s46	240–241
s47	241–242
s51	242–243
s53	243
s54	243–244
s55	245–247
s56	247–249
s58	249–252
s61	252–253
s62	253–254
s63	255–256
s64	256–257
s65	257–258

Police and Criminal Evidence Act 1984 (continued)

s66	258–259
s67	259–260
s76	260–261
s77	261–262
s78	262
s82	262–263
s116	264–265
s117	265
s118	265–266
Schedule 1	266–269
Schedule 2	269–270
Schedule 5, Part I	270
Schedule 5, Part II	270–271
Prosecution of Offences Act 1985	272–276
s1	272–273
s2	273
s3	273–274
s4	275
s5	275
s6	276
Race Relations Act 1976 s26A	62
Sex Discrimination Act 1975 s35A	42–43
Solicitors Act 1974	34–41
s1	34
s1A	34
s2	34–35
s3	35–36
s6	36
s10	36–37
s19	37–38
s31	38
s46	38–39
s47	39–41
Supreme Court Act 1981	108–159
s1	108
s2	108–109
s3	109

Supreme Court Act 1981 (continued)

s4	109–110
s5	110–111
s6	111
s7	111–112
s8	112
s9	112–115
s10	115–116
s11	116–117
s13	117–118
s14	118
s15	118–119
s16	119
s17	119
s18	120
s19	120–121
s20	121–123
s25	123
s26	123
s27	124
s28	124
s29	124–125
s30	125
s31	125–127
s32	127
s32A	127–128
s35A	128–129
s37	129–130
s42	130–132
s45	132
s46	133
s48	133–134
s49	134
s50	134
s51	135–136
s53	136–137
s54	137–139
s55	139
s56	140
s61	140–141

Supreme Court Act 1981 (continued)

s62	141
s64	142
s65	142
s66	142
s69	143
s73	143–144
s74	144–145
s75	145
s81	145–149
s83	149
s84	149
s85	149–150
s86	150–151
s127	151
s128	152
s138	153–154
s138A	154
s138B	154–155
s151	155–157
Schedule 1	157–159

COURT OF CHANCERY ACT 1851
(14 & 15 Vict c 83)

16   Quorum of Judicial Committee

No matter shall be heard, nor shall any order, report, or recommendation be made, by the Judicial Committee, in pursuance of any Act, unless in the presence of at least three members of the said committee, exclusive of the Lord President of Her Majesty's Privy Council for the time being.

As amended by the Statute Law Revision Acts 1875 and 1892.

APPELLATE JURISDICTION ACT 1876
(39 & 40 Vict c 59)

3 Cases in which appeal lies to House of Lords

Subject as in this Act mentioned an appeal shall lie to the House of Lords from any order or judgment of any of the courts following; that is to say,

(1) of Her Majesty's Court of Appeal in England; and

(2) of any Court in Scotland from which error or an appeal at or immediately before the commencement of this Act lay to the House of Lords by common law or by statute.

4 Form of appeal to House of Lords

Every appeal shall be brought by way of petition to the House of Lords, praying that the matter of the order or judgment appealed against may be reviewed before Her Majesty the Queen in her Court of Parliament, in order that the said Court may determine what of right, and according to the law and custom of this realm, ought to be done in the subject-matter of such appeal.

5 Attendance of certain number of Lords of Appeal required at hearing and determination of appeals

An appeal shall not be heard and determined by the House of Lords unless there are present at such hearing and determination not less than three of the following persons, in this Act designated Lords of Appeal; that is to say,

(1) the Lord Chancellor of Great Britain for the time being; and

(2) the Lords of Appeal in Ordinary to be appointed as in this Act mentioned; and

(3) such Peers of Parliament as are for the time being holding or have held any of the offices in this Act described as high judicial offices.

6 Appointment of Lords of Appeal in Ordinary by Her Majesty

For the purpose of aiding the House of Lords in the hearing and determination of appeals, Her Majesty may by letters patent appoint qualified persons to be Lords of Appeal in Ordinary.

A person shall not be qualified to be appointed by Her Majesty a Lord of Appeal in Ordinary unless he has been at or before the time of his appointment the holder for a period of not less than two years of some one or more of the offices in this Act described as high judicial offices, or has been at or before such time as aforesaid, for not less than 15 years,

> (a) a person who has a Supreme Court qualification, within the meaning of section 71 of the Courts and Legal Services Act 1990;
>
> (b) an advocate in Scotland, or a solicitor entitled to appear in the Court of Session and the High Court of Justiciary; or
>
> (c) a practising member of the Bar of Northern Ireland

Every Lord of Appeal in Ordinary shall hold his office during good behaviour, but he may be removed from such office on the address of both Houses of Parliament.

Every Lord of Appeal in Ordinary, unless he is otherwise entitled to sit as a member of the House of Lords, shall by virtue and according to the date of his appointment be entitled during his life to rank as a Baron by such style as Her Majesty may be pleased to appoint, and shall be entitled to a writ of summons to attend, and to sit and vote in the House of Lords; his dignity as a Lord of Parliament shall not descend to his heirs.

On any Lord of Appeal in Ordinary vacating his office, by death resignation or otherwise, Her Majesty may fill up the vacancy by the appointment of another qualified person.

A Lord of Appeal in Ordinary shall, if a Privy Councillor, be a member of the Judicial Committee of the Privy Council, and, subject to the due performance by a Lord of Appeal in Ordinary of his duties as to the hearing and determining of appeals in the House of Lords, it shall be his duty, being a Privy Councillor, to sit and act as a member of the Judicial Committee of the Privy Council.

25 Definitions: 'high judicial office': 'superior courts'

In this Act, if not inconsistent with the context, the following expressions have the meaning herein-after respectively assigned to them; that is to say,

'High judicial office' means any of the following offices; that is to say,

The office of Lord Chancellor of Great Britain or of Judge of one of Her Majesty's superior courts of Great Britain and Ireland:

'Superior courts of Great Britain and Ireland' means and includes –

As to England, Her Majesty's High Court of Justice and Her Majesty's Court of Appeal; and

As to Northern Ireland, Her Majesty's High Court of Justice in Northern Ireland and Her Majesty's Court of Appeal in Northern Ireland; and

As to Scotland, the Court of Session.

As amended by the Judicature (Northern Ireland) Act 1978, s122(1), Schedule 5, Pt II; Courts and Legal Services Act 1990, s71(2), Schedule 10, para 1.

JUDICIAL COMMITTEE ACT 1881
(44 & 45 Vict c 3)

**1   Lords Justices of Appeal to be members
of Judicial Committee**

Every person holding or who has held in England the office of a
Lord Justice of Appeal shall, if a member of Her Majesty's Privy
Council in England, be a member of the Judicial Committee of the
Privy Council.

APPELLATE JURISDICTION ACT 1887
(50 & 51 Vict c 70)

3   Amendment of 3 & 4 Will 4 c 41

The Judicial Committee of the Privy Council as formed under the provision of the first section of the Judicial Committee Act 1833 shall include such members of Her Majesty's Privy Council as are for the time being holding or have held any of the offices in the Appellate Jurisdiction Act 1876, and this Act, described as high judicial offices.

5   Amendment of 39 & 40 Vict c 59, s25

The expression 'high judicial office' as defined in the 25th section of the Appellate Jurisdiction Act 1876 shall be deemed to include the office of a Lord of Appeal in Ordinary and the office of a member of the Judicial Committee of the Privy Council.

JUDICIAL COMMITTEE AMENDMENT ACT 1895
(58 & 59 Vict c 44)

1 Provision as to persons being or having been Colonial Chief Justices or Judges

(1) If any person being or having been Chief Justice or a Judge of the Supreme Court of any of the Australasian colonies mentioned in the schedule to this Act, or of any other Superior Court in Her Majesty's Dominions named in that behalf by Her Majesty in Council, is a member of Her Majesty's Privy Council, he shall be a member of the Judicial Committee of the Privy Council.

(3) The provisions of this Act shall be in addition to, and shall not affect, any other enactment for the appointment of or relating to members of the Judicial Committee.

SCHEDULE

New South Wales
New Zealand
Queensland
South Australia
Tasmania
Victoria
Western Australia

As amended by the Appellate Jurisdiction Act 1913, s3; Statute Law (Repeals) Act 1986.

APPELLATE JURISDICTION ACT 1908
(8 Edw 7 c 51)

3 Extension of 58 & 59 Vict c 44

(1) Section one of the Judicial Committee Amendment Act 1895 shall have effect as if the persons named therein included any person being or having been chief justice or a justice of the High Court of Australia.

4 Resignation of members of the Judicial Committee

Any member of the Judicial Committee of the Privy Council may resign his office as member of that Committee by giving notice of his resignation in writing to the Lord President of the Council.

JUDICIAL COMMITTEE ACT 1915
(5 & 6 Geo 5 c 92)

1   Power of Judicial Committee of the Privy Council to sit in more than one division at the same time

(1) The Judicial Committee of the Privy Council may, subject to the approval of the Lord Chancellor and the Lord President of the Council, sit in more than one division at the same time, and in such case anything which may be done to, by or before the Judicial Committee may be done to, by or before any such division of the Judicial Committee.

(2) The power of His Majesty in Council to make rules as to the practice and procedure before the Judicial Committee shall include the power to make orders for the constituting of divisions and the holding of divisional sittings of the Judicial Committee.

CHILDREN AND YOUNG PERSONS ACT 1933
(23 Geo 5 c 12)

34 Attendance at court of parent of child or young person charged with an offence, etc

(2) Where a child or young person is in police detention, such steps as are practicable shall be taken to ascertain the identity of a person responsible for his welfare.

(3) If it is practicable to ascertain the identity of a person responsible for the welfare of the child or young person, that person shall be informed, unless it is not practicable to do so –

(a) that the child or young person has been arrested;

(b) why he has been arrested; and

(c) where he is being detained.

(4) Where information falls to be given under subsection (3) above, it shall be given as soon as it is practicable to do so.

(5) For the purposes of this section the persons who may be responsible for the welfare of a child or young person are –

(a) his parent or guardian; or

(b) any other person who has for the time being assumed responsibility for his welfare.

(6) If it is practicable to give a person responsible for the welfare of the child or young person the information required by subsection (3) above, that person shall be given it as soon as it is practicable to do so.

(7) If it appears that at the time of his arrest a supervision order, as defined in section 11 of the Children and Young Persons Act 1969 or Part IV of the Children Act 1989, is in force in respect of him, the person responsible for his supervision shall also be informed as

described in subsection (3) above as soon as it is reasonably practicable to do so.

(7A) If it appears that at the time of his arrest the child or young person is being provided with accommodation by or on behalf of a local authority under section 20 of the Children Act 1989, the local authority shall also be informed as described in subsection (3) above as soon as it is reasonably practicable to do so.

(8) The reference to a parent or guardian in subsection (5) above is in the case of a child or young person in the care of a local authority, a reference to that authority.

(9) The rights conferred on a child or young person by subsections (2) to (8) above are in addition to his rights under section 56 of the Police and Criminal Evidence Act 1984.

(10) The reference in subsection (2) above to a child or young person who is in police detention includes a reference to a child or young person who has been detained under the terrorism provisions; and in subsection (3) above 'arrest' includes such detention.

(11) In subsection (10) above 'the terrorism provisions' has the meaning assigned to it by section 65 of the Police and Criminal Evidence Act 1984.

As substituted by the Children and Young Persons Act 1963, s25(1) and amended by the Police and Criminal Evidence Act 1984, s57, and the Children Act 1989, s108(5), (7), Schedule 13, paras 2, 6, Schedule 15.

ADMINISTRATION OF JUSTICE (APPEALS) ACT 1934
(24 & 25 Geo 5 c 40)

1 Restrictions on appeals from Court of Appeal to House of Lords

(1) No appeal shall lie to the House of Lords from any order or judgment made or given by the Court of Appeal after the first day of October nineteen hundred and thirty-four, except with the leave of that Court or of the House of Lords.

(2) The House of Lords may by order provide for the hearing and determination by a Committee of that House of petitions for leave to appeal from the Court of Appeal:

Provided that section 5 of the Appellate Jurisdiction Act 1876 shall apply to the hearing and determination of any such petition by a Committee of the House as it applies to the hearing and determination of an appeal by the House.

(3) Nothing in this section shall affect any restriction existing, apart from this section, on the bringing of appeals from the Court of Appeal to the House of Lords.

2 Appeals from county courts

(1) Every appeal from a judgment, direction, decision, decree or order of a judge of a county court given or made after such date as the Lord Chancellor may by order appoint, being an appeal under any of the enactments set out in the first column of the Schedule to this Act, shall lie to the Court of Appeal instead of to the High Court; and accordingly those enactments shall have effect in relation to any such appeal subject to the modifications respectively specified in the second column of that Schedule.

As amended by the County Courts Act 1934, s193, Schedule 5.

APPELLATE JURISDICTION ACT 1947
(10 & 11 Geo 6 c 11)

1   Additional Lords of Appeal

(1) Except in the event of the number of the Lords of Appeal in Ordinary being at any time less than seven, His Majesty shall not be advised to make an appointment to fill any vacancy among them unless the Lord Chancellor, with the concurrence of the Treasury, is satisfied that the state of business requires that the vacancy should be filled.

As amended by the Administration of Justice Act 1968, s1(5), Schedule.

JUDICIAL PENSIONS ACT 1959
(8 & 9 Eliz 2 c 9)

2   Retiring age

(1) A person who holds an office listed in the First Schedule to this Act shall vacate that office on the day on which he attains the age of 75 years.

FIRST SCHEDULE

Lord of Appeal in Ordinary ...

ADMINISTRATION OF JUSTICE
ACT 1968
(1968 c 5)

1 Maximum number of Lords of Appeal in Ordinary and certain other judges

(1) The maximum number –

(a) of Lords of Appeal in Ordinary shall be 11 ...

(2) Her Majesty may by Order in Council from time to time amend the foregoing subsection so as to increase or further increase the maximum number of appointments which may be made to any of the offices therein mentioned.

(3) No recommendation shall be made to Her Majesty in Council to make an Order under this section unless a draft of the Order has been laid before Parliament and approved by resolution of each House of Parliament ...

ADMINISTRATION OF JUSTICE ACT 1969
(1969 c 58)

12 Grant of certificate by trial judge

(1) Where on the application of any of the parties to any proceedings to which this section applies the judge is satisfied –

(a) that the relevant conditions are fulfilled in relation to his decision in those proceedings, and

(b) that a sufficient case for an appeal to the House of Lords under this Part of this Act has been made out to justify an application for leave to bring such an appeal, and

(c) that all the parties to the proceedings consent to the grant of a certificate under this section,

the judge, subject to the following provisions of this Part of this Act, may grant a certificate to that effect.

(2) This section applies to any civil proceedings in the High Court which are either –

(a) proceedings before a single judge of the High Court, or

(c) proceedings before a Divisional Court.

(3) Subject to any Order in Council made under the following provisions of this section, for the purposes of this section the relevant conditions, in relation to a decision of the judge in any proceedings, are that a point of law of general public importance is involved in that decision and that that point of law either –

(a) relates wholly or mainly to the construction of an enactment or of a statutory instrument, and has been fully argued in the proceedings and fully considered in the judgment of the judge in the proceedings, or

(b) is one in respect of which the judge is bound by a decision of the Court of Appeal or of the House of Lords in previous proceedings, and was fully considered in the judgments given by the Court of Appeal or the House of Lords (as the case may be) in those previous proceedings.

(4) Any application for a certificate under this section shall be made to the judge immediately after he gives judgment in the proceedings:

Provided that the judge may in any particular case entertain any such application made at any later time before the end of the period of 14 days beginning with the date on which that judgment is given or such other period as may be prescribed by rules of court.

(5) No appeal shall lie against the grant or refusal of a certificate under this section.

(6) Her Majesty may by Order in Council amend subsection (3) of this section by altering, deleting, or substituting one or more new paragraphs for, either or both of paragraphs (a) and (b) of that subsection, or by adding one or more further paragraphs.

(7) Any Order in Council made under this section shall be subject to annulment in pursuance of a resolution of either House of Parliament.

(8) In this Part of this Act 'civil proceedings' means any proceedings other than proceedings in a criminal cause or matter, and 'the judge', in relation to any proceedings to which this section applies, means the judge referred to in paragraph (a) of subsection (2) of this section, or the Divisional Court referred to in paragraph (c) of that subsection, as the case may be.

13   Leave to appeal to House of Lords

(1) Where in any proceedings the judge grants a certificate under section 12 of this Act, then, at any time within one month from the date on which that certificate is granted or such extended time as in any particular case the House of Lords may allow, any of the parties to the proceedings may make an application to the House of Lords under this section.

(2) Subject to the following provisions of this section, if on such an application it appears to the House of Lords to be expedient to do so, the House may grant leave for an appeal to be brought directly to the House; and where leave is granted under this section –

(a) no appeal from the decision of the judge to which the certificate relates shall lie to the Court of Appeal, but

(b) an appeal shall lie from that decision to the House of Lords.

(3) Applications under this section shall be determined without a hearing.

(4) Any order of the House of Lords which provides for applications under this section to be determined by a committee of the House –

(a) shall direct that the committee shall consist of or include not less than three of the persons designated as Lords of Appeal in accordance with section 5 of the Appellate Jurisdiction Act 1876, and

(b) may direct that the decision of the committee on any such application shall be taken on behalf of the House.

(5) Without prejudice to subsection (2) of this section, no appeal shall lie to the Court of Appeal from a decision of the judges in respect of which a certificate is granted under section 12 of this Act until –

(a) the time within which an application can be made under this section has expired, and

(b) where such an application is made, that application has been determined in accordance with the preceding provisions of this section.

14   Appeal where leave granted

In relation to any appeal which lies to the House of Lords by virtue of subsection (2) of section 13 of this Act –

(a) section 4 of the Appellate Jurisdiction Act 1876 (which provides for the bringing of appeals to the House of Lords by way of petition),

(b) section 5 of that Act (which regulates the composition of the House for the hearing and determination of appeals), and

(c) except in so far as those orders otherwise provide, any orders of the House of Lords made with respect to the matters specified in section 11 of that Act (which relates to the procedure on appeals),

shall have effect as they have effect in relation to appeals under that Act.

15 Cases excluded from s12

(1) No certificate shall be granted under section 12 of this Act in respect of a decision of the judge in any proceedings where by virtue of any enactment, apart from the provisions of this Part of this Act, no appeal would lie from that decision to the Court of Appeal, with or without the leave of the judge or of the Court of Appeal.

(2) No certificate shall be granted under section 12 of this Act in respect of a decision of the judge where –

(b) by virtue of any enactment, apart from the provisions of this Part of this Act, no appeal would (with or without the leave of the Court of Appeal or of the House of Lords) lie from any decision of the Court of Appeal on an appeal from the decision of the judge.

(3) Where by virtue of any enactment, apart from the provisions of this Part of this Act, no appeal would lie to the Court of Appeal from the decision of the judge except with the leave of the judge or of the Court of Appeal, no certificate shall be granted under section 12 of this Act in respect of that decision unless it appears to the judge that apart from the provisions of this Part of this Act it would be a proper case for granting such leave.

(4) No certificate shall be granted under section 12 of this Act where the decision of the judge, or any order made by him in pursuance of that decision, is made in the exercise of jurisdiction to punish for contempt of court.

As amended by the Supreme Court Act 1981, s152(4), Schedule 7.

COURTS ACT 1971
(1971 c 23)

16   Appointment of Circuit judges

(1) Her Majesty may from time to time appoint as Circuit judges, to serve in the Crown Court and county courts and to carry out such other judicial functions as may be conferred on them under this or any other enactment, such qualified persons as may be recommended to Her by the Lord Chancellor.

(2) The maximum number of Circuit judges shall be such as may be determined from time to time by the Lord Chancellor with the concurrence of the Minister for the Civil Service.

(3) No person shall be qualified to be appointed a Circuit judge unless –

    (a) he has a ten year Crown Court or ten year county court qualification within the meaning of section 71 of the Courts and Legal Services Act 1990;

    (b) he is a Recorder; or

    (c) he has held as a full-time appointment for at least three years one of the offices listed in Part 1A of Schedule 2.

(4) Before recommending any person to Her Majesty for appointment as a Circuit judge, the Lord Chancellor shall take steps to satisfy himself that that person's health is satisfactory ...

17   Retirement, removal and disqualification of Circuit judges

(1) Subject to subsections (2) to (4) below, a Circuit judge shall vacate his office at the end of the completed year of service in which he attains the age of 72.

(2) Where the Lord Chancellor considers it desirable in the public interest to retain a Circuit judge in office after the time at which he would otherwise retire in accordance with subsection (1) above,

he may from time to time authorise the continuance in office of that judge until such date, not being later than the date on which the judge attains the age of 75, as he thinks fit ...

(4) The Lord Chancellor may, if he thinks fit, remove a Circuit judge from office on the ground of incapacity or misbehaviour.

21 Appointment of Recorders

(1) Her Majesty may from time to time appoint qualified persons, to be known as Recorders, to act as part-time judges of the Crown Court and to carry out such other judicial functions as may be conferred on them under this or any other enactment.

(2) Every appointment of a person to be a Recorder shall be of a person recommended to Her Majesty by the Lord Chancellor, and no person shall be qualified to be appointed a Recorder unless he has a ten year Crown Court or ten year county court qualification, within the meaning of section 71 of the Courts and Legal Services Act 1990.

(3) The appointment of a person as a Recorder shall specify the term for which he is appointed and the frequency and duration of the occasions during that term on which he will be required to be available to undertake the duties of a Recorder.

(4) Subject to subsection (5) below the Lord Chancellor may, with the agreement of the Recorder concerned, from time to time extend for such period as he thinks appropriate the term for which a Recorder is appointed.

(5) Neither the initial term for which a Recorder is appointed nor any extension of that term under subsection (4) above shall be such as to continue his appointment as a Recorder after the end of the completed year of service in which he attains the age of 72.

(6) The Lord Chancellor may if he thinks fit terminate the appointment of a Recorder on the ground of incapacity or mis-behaviour or of a failure to comply with any requirement specified under subsection (3) above in the terms of his appointment ...

24 Deputy Circuit judges and assistant Recorders

(1) If it appears to the Lord Chancellor it is expedient as a temporary

measure to make an appointment under this section in order to facilitate the disposal of business in the Crown Court or a county court or official referees' business in the High Court, he may –

(a) appoint to be a deputy Circuit judge, during such period or on such occasions as he thinks fit, any person who has held office as a judge of the Court of Appeal or of the High Court or as a Circuit judge; or

(b) appoint to be an assistant Recorder, during such period or on such occasions as he thinks fit, any person who has a ten year Crown Court or ten year county court qualification, within the meaning of section 71 of the Courts and Legal Services Act 1990.

(2) Except as provided by subsection (3) below, during the period or on the occasions for which a deputy Circuit judge or assistant Recorder is appointed under this section he shall be treated for all purposes as, and accordingly may perform any of the functions of, a Circuit judge or a Recorder, as the case may be.

(3) A deputy Circuit judge appointed under this section shall not be treated as a Circuit judge for the purpose of any provision made by or under any enactment and relating to the appointment, retirement, removal or disqualification of Circuit judges, the tenure of office and oaths to be taken by such judges, or the remuneration, allowances or pensions of such judges; and section 21 of this Act shall not apply to an assistant Recorder appointed under this section.

(4) Notwithstanding the expiry of any period for which a person is appointed under this section a deputy Circuit judge or an assistant Recorder, he may attend at the Crown Court or a county court or, in the case of a deputy Circuit judge, as regards official referees' business, at the High Court for the purpose of continuing to deal with, giving judgment in, or dealing with any ancillary matter relating to, any case which may have been begun before him when sitting as a deputy Circuit judge or an assistant Recorder, and for that purpose and for the purpose of any proceedings subsequent thereon he shall be treated as a Circuit judge or a Recorder, as the case may be ...

29   Accommodation in City of London

(1) The courthouse and accommodation which up to the appointed day have been respectively known as the Central Criminal Court and the Mayor's and City of London Court shall continue to be

known by those names, and it shall be the duty of the Common Council of the City of London (in this section referred to as 'the Common Council') to continue to make the said premises available for use for the sittings and business of those courts respectively ...

42 Local court for City of London ...

(2) For the purpose of establishing a court to exercise so much of the jurisdiction previously exercised by the Mayor's and City of London Court as is appropriate to a county court and for exercising any other jurisdiction which may hereafter be conferred on a county court, the City of London shall, by virtue of this section, become a county court district and accordingly the enactments relating to county courts shall apply in relation to the county court for the City of London as they apply in relation to a county court for any other county court district.

(3) Without prejudice to subsection (1) above, the county court for the district constituted by subsection (2) above shall be known as the Mayor's and City of London Court and the Circuit judge assigned to that district under section 20(1) of this Act shall be known as the judge of the Mayor's and City of London Court.

SCHEDULE 2

PART IA

Social Security Commissioner appointed under section 97 of the Social Security Act 1975.

President of Social Security Appeal Tribunals and Medical Appeal Tribunals or chairman of such a tribunal appointed under Schedule 10 to that Act ...

Coroner appointed under section 2 of the Coroners Act 1988.

Master of the Queen's Bench Division ...

Taxing Master of the Supreme Court ...

District judge.

Stipendiary magistrate.

As amended by the Supreme Court Act 1981, s146; Courts and Legal Services Act 1990, s71(2), Schedule 10, para 31(1), (2), 32(2).

ADMINISTRATION OF JUSTICE ACT 1973

(1973 c 15)

12 Retirement of higher judiciary in event of incapacity

(1) Where the Lord Chancellor is satisfied by means of a medical certificate that a person holding office as Lord of Appeal in Ordinary ... is disabled by permanent infirmity from the performance of the duties of his office but is for the time being incapacitated from resigning it, then subject to subsection (2) ... below the Lord Chancellor may by instrument under his hand declare that person's office to have been vacated, and the instrument shall have the like effect for all purposes as if that person had on the date of the instrument resigned his office.

(2) A declaration under this section with respect to a Lord of Appeal in Ordinary shall be of no effect unless it is made with the concurrence of the senior of the Lords of Appeal or, if made with respect to him, with that of the next senior of them.

JURIES ACT 1974
(1974 c 23)

1 Qualification for jury service

Subject to the provisions of this Act, every person shall be qualified to serve as a juror in the Crown Court, the High Court and county courts and be liable accordingly to attend for jury service when summoned under this Act, if –

(a) he is for the time being registered as a parliamentary or local government elector and is not less than 18 nor more than 70 years of age; and

(b) he has been ordinarily resident in the United Kingdom, the Channel Islands or the Isle of Man for any period of at least five years since attaining the age of thirteen,

but not if he is for the time being ineligible or disqualified for jury service; and the persons who are ineligible, and those who are disqualified, are those respectively listed in Parts I and II of Schedule 1 to this Act.

11 The ballot and swearing of jurors

(1) The jury to try an issue before a court shall be selected by ballot in open court from the panel, or part of the panel, of jurors summoned to attend at the time and place in question.

(2) The power of summoning jurors under section 6 of this Act may be exercised after balloting has begun, as well as earlier, and if exercised after balloting has begun the court may dispense with balloting for persons summoned under that section.

(3) No two or more members of a jury to try an issue in a court shall be sworn together.

(4) Subject to subsection (5) below, the jury selected by any one ballot shall try only one issue (but any juror shall be liable to be selected on more than one ballot).

(5) Subsection (4) above shall not prevent –

(a) the trial of two or more issues by the same jury if the trial of the second or last issue begins within 24 hours from the time when the jury is constituted, or

(b) in a criminal case, the trial of fitness to plead by the same jury as that by whom the accused is being tried, if that is so directed by the court under section 4(4)(b) of the Criminal Procedure (Insanity) Act 1964, or

(c) in a criminal case beginning with a special plea, the trial of the accused on the general issue by the jury trying the special plea.

(6) In the cases within subsection (5)(a), (b) and (c) above the court may, on the trial of the second or any subsequent issue, instead of proceeding with the same jury in its entirety, order any juror to withdraw, if the court considers he could be justly challenged or excused, or if the parties to the proceedings consent, and the juror to replace him shall, subject to subsection (2) above, be selected by ballot in open court.

12   Challenge

(1) In proceedings for the trial of any person for an offence on indictment –

(a) that person may challenge all or any of the jurors for cause, and

(b) any challenge for cause shall be tried by the judge before whom that person is to be tried.

(2) Any party to county court proceedings to be tried by a jury shall have the same right of challenge to all or any of the jurors as he would have in the High Court.

(3) A challenge to a juror in any court shall be made after his name has been drawn by ballot (unless the court, pursuant to section 11(2) of this Act, has dispensed with balloting for him) and before he is sworn.

(4) The fact that a person summoned to serve on a jury is not qualified to serve shall be a ground of challenge for cause; but subject to that, and to the foregoing provisions of this section, nothing in this Act affects the law relating to challenge of jurors.

(5) In section 29 of the Juries Act 1825 (challenges to jurors by the Crown) the words 'the Crown Court' shall continue to be substituted for the words 'any of the courts hereinbefore mentioned', notwithstanding the repeal by this Act of paragraph 3(2) of Schedule 4 to the Courts Act 1971 and of the entries relating to the said Act in Schedule 5 to the Criminal Justice Act 1972.

(6) Without prejudice to subsection (4) above, the right of challenge to the array, that is to say the right of challenge on the ground that the person responsible for summoning the jurors in question is biased or has acted improperly, shall continue to be unaffected by the fact that, since the coming into operation of section 31 of the Courts Act 1971 (which is replaced by this Act), the responsibility for summoning jurors for service in the Crown Court, the High Court and county courts has lain with the Lord Chancellor.

17 Majority verdicts

(1) Subject to subsections (3) and (4) below, the verdict of a jury in proceedings in the Crown Court or the High Court need not be unanimous if –

(a) in a case where there are not less than 11 jurors, ten of them agree on the verdict; and

(b) in a case where there are ten jurors, nine of them agree on the verdict.

(2) Subject to subsection (4) below, the verdict of a jury (that is to say a complete jury of eight) in proceedings in a county court need not be unanimous if seven of them agree on the verdict.

(3) The Crown Court shall not accept a verdict of guilty by virtue of subsection (1) above unless the foreman of the jury has stated in open court the number of jurors who respectively agreed to and dissented from the verdict.

(4) No court shall accept a verdict by virtue of subsection (1) or (2) above unless it appears to the court that the jury have had such period of time for deliberation as the court thinks reasonable having regard to the nature and complexity of the case; and the Crown Court shall in any event not accept such a verdict unless it appears to the court that the jury have had at least two hours for deliberation.

(5) This section is without prejudice to any practice in civil proceedings by which a court may accept a majority verdict with the consent of the parties, or by which the parties may agree to proceed in any case with an incomplete jury.

SCHEDULE 1

INELIGIBILITY AND DISQUALIFICATION FOR AND EXCUSAL FROM JURY SERVICE

PART I

PERSONS INELIGIBLE

GROUP A

The Judiciary

Holders of high judicial office within the meaning of the Appellate Jurisdiction Act 1876.

Circuit judges and Recorders.

Masters of the Supreme Court.

Registrars and assistant registrars of any court.

Metropolitan and other stipendiary magistrates.

Justices of the peace.

The Chairman or President, the Vice-Chairman or Vice-President, and the registrar and assistant registrar of any Tribunal.

A person who has at any time been a person falling within any description specified above in this Group.

GROUP B

Others concerned with administration of justice

Barristers and solicitors, whether or not in actual practice as such.

Solicitors' articled clerks.

Barristers' clerks and their assistants.

Any person who is not a barrister or solicitor but who is an authorised advocate or authorised litigator (as defined by section 119(1) of the Courts and Legal Services Act 1990) and –

(a) any legal executive or person corresponding to a legal executive; or

(b) any person corresponding to a barristers' clerk or assistant clerk,

who is employed by such an authorised advocate or authorised litigator.

Legal executives in the employment of solicitors.

Public notaries.

The Director of Public Prosecutions and members of his staff.

Officers employed under the Lord Chancellor and concerned wholly or mainly with the day-to-day administration of the legal system or any part of it.

Officers and staff of any court, if their work is wholly or mainly concerned with the day-to-day administration of the court.

Coroners, deputy coroners and assistant coroners.

Justices' clerks and their assistants.

Clerks and other officers appointed under section 15 of the Administration of Justice Act 1964 (Inner London magistrates courts administration).

Active Elder Brethren of the Corporation of Trinity House of Deptford Strond.

A shorthandwriter in any court.

Governors, chaplains, medical officers and other officers of penal establishments; members of boards of visitors for penal establishments.

('Penal establishment' for this purpose means any establishment regulated by the Prison Act 1952.)

The warden or a member of the staff of a probation home, probation hostel or bail hostel (within the meaning of the Powers of Criminal Courts Act 1973).

Probation officers and persons appointed to assist them.

Members of the Parole Board; members of local review committees established under the Criminal Justice Act 1967.

A member of any police force (including a person on central service under section 43 of the Police Act 1964); special constables; a member of any constabulary maintained under statute; a person employed in any capacity by virtue of which he has the powers and privileges of a constable.

A member of a police authority within the meaning of the Police Act 1964; a member of any body (corporate or other) with responsibility for appointing members of a constabulary maintained under statute.

Inspectors of Constabulary appointed by Her Majesty; assistant inspectors of constabulary appointed by the Secretary of State.

Civilians employed for police purposes under section 10 of the Police Act 1964, members of the metropolitan civil staffs within the meaning of section 15 of the Superannuation (Miscellaneous Provisions) Act 1967 (persons employed under the Commissioner of Police of the Metropolis, Inner London justices' clerks, etc.)

A person in charge of, or employed in, any forensic science laboratory.

Court security officers.

Prisoner custody officers.

A person who at any time within the last ten years has been a person falling within any description specified above in this Group.

GROUP C

The clergy, etc

A man in holy orders; a regular minister of any religious denomination.

A vowed member of any religious order living in a monastery, convent or other religious community.

GROUP D

Mentally disordered persons

A person who suffers or has suffered from mental illness, psychopathic disorder, mental handicap or severe mental handicap and on account of that condition either –

(a) is resident in a hospital or other similar institution; or

(b) regularly attends for treatment by a medical practitioner.

A person for the time being in guardianship under section 7 of the Mental Health Act 1983.

A person who, under Part VII of that Act, has been determined by a judge to be incapable, by reason of mental disorder, of managing and administering his property and affairs.

(In this Group –

(a) 'mental handicap' means a state of arrested or incomplete development of mind (not amounting to severe mental handicap) which includes significant impairment of intelligence and social functioning;

(b) 'severe mental handicap' means a state of arrested or incomplete development of mind which includes severe impairment of intelligence and social functioning;

(c) other expressions are to be construed in accordance with the said Act of 1983.)

PART II

PERSONS DISQUALIFIED

A person who has at any time been sentenced in the United Kingdom, the Channel Islands or the Isle of Man –

(a) to imprisonment for life, custody for life or to a term of imprisonment or youth custody of five years or more, or

(b) to be detained during Her Majesty's pleasure, during the pleasure of the Secretary of State or during the pleasure of the Governor of Northern Ireland.

A person who at any time in the last ten years has, in the United Kingdom or the Channel Islands or the Isle of Man –

(a) served any part of a sentence of imprisonment, youth custody or detention; or

(b) been detained in a Borstal institution; or

(c) had passed on him or (as the case may be) made in respect of him a suspended sentence of imprisonment or order for detention; or

(d) had made in respect of him a community service order.

A person who at any time in the last five years has, in the United Kingdom or the Channel Islands or the Isle of Man, been placed on probation.

PART III

PERSONS EXCUSABLE AS OF RIGHT

General

Persons more than 65 years of age.

Parliament

Peers and peeress entitled to receive writs of summons to attend the House of Lords.

Members of the House of Commons.

Officers of the House of Lords.

Officers of the House of Commons.

European Parliament

Representatives to the Parliament of the European Communities.

The Forces

Full-time serving members of any of Her Majesty's naval, military or air forces.

(A person excusable under this head shall be under no obligation to attend in pursuance of a summons for jury service if his commanding officer certifies to the officer issuing the summons that it would be prejudicial to the efficiency of the service if the person were required to be absent from duty.)

Medical and other similar professions

The following, if actually practising their profession and registered (including provisionally or temporarily registered), enrolled or certified under the enactments relating to that profession –

medical practitioners,

dentists,

nurses,

midwives,

veterinary surgeons and veterinary practitioners,

pharmaceutical chemists.

As amended by the Criminal Law Act 1977, s65, Schedule 12; European Assembly Elections Act 1978, s5(1); Criminal Justice Act 1982, s77, Schedule 14, para 35(b)(i); Mental Health (Amendment) Act 1982, s65(1), Schedule 3, Pt I; Mental Health Act 1983, s148, Schedule 4, para 37; Juries (Disqualification) Act 1984, s1(1); Criminal Justice Act 1988, ss119(1), (2), 170(2), Schedule 16, s123(6), Schedule 8, Pt I, para 8; Courts and Legal Services Act 1990, s125(2), (3), Schedule 17, para 7, Schedule 18, para 5; Criminal Justice Act 1991, s100, Schedule 11, para 18.

SOLICITORS ACT 1974
(1974 c 47)

1 Qualifications for practising as solicitor

No person shall be qualified to act as a solicitor unless –

(a) he has been admitted as a solicitor, and

(b) his name is on the roll, and

(c) he has in force a certificate issued by the Society in accordance with the provisions of this Part authorising him to practise as a solicitor (in this Act referred to as a 'practising certificate').

1A Practising certificates: employed solicitors

A person who has been admitted as a solicitor and whose name is on the roll shall, if he would not otherwise be taken to be acting as a solicitor, be taken for the purposes of this Act to be so acting if he is employed in connection with the provision of any legal services –

(a) by any person who is qualified to act as a solicitor;

(b) by any partnership at least one member of which is so qualified; or

(c) by a body recognised by the Council of the Law Society under section 9 of the Administration of Justice Act 1985 (incorporated practices).

2 Training regulations

(1) The Society, with the concurrence of the Lord Chancellor, the Lord Chief Justice and the Master of the Rolls, may make regulations (in this Act referred to as 'training regulations') about education and training for persons seeking to be admitted or to practise as solicitors

(3) Training regulations –

(a) may prescribe –

(i) the education and training, whether by service under articles or otherwise, to be undergone by persons seeking admission as solicitors;

(ii) any education or training to be undergone by persons who have been admitted as solicitors;

(iii) the examinations or other tests to be undergone by persons seeking admission as solicitors or who have been admitted;

(iv) the qualifications and reciprocal duties and responsibilities of persons undertaking to give education or training for the purposes of the regulations or undergoing such education or training; and

(v) the circumstances in which articles may be discharged or education or training under the regulations may be terminated;

(b) may require persons who have been admitted as solicitors to hold practising certificates while they are undergoing education or training under the regulations;

(c) may include provision for the charging of fees by the Society and the application of fees which the Society receives;

(d) may make different provision for different classes of persons and different circumstances.

(4) Where, under Schedule 4 to the Courts and Legal Services Act 1990 (approval of certain regulations in connection with the grant of rights of audience or rights to conduct litigation), the Lord Chancellor, the Lord Chief Justice or the Master of the Rolls approves any regulation made under this section he shall be taken, for the purposes of this section, to have concurred in the making of that regulation.

(5) Subsection (4) shall have effect whether or not the regulation required to be approved under Schedule 4 to the Act of 1990.

3 Admission as solicitor

(1) Subject to section 4 and to section 20(3) of the Justices of the Peace Act 1949 (which relates to the admission as solicitors of

certain persons who have served as assistant to a justices' clerk), no person shall be admitted as a solicitor unless he has obtained a certificate from the Society that the Society –

(a) is satisfied that he has complied with training regulations, and

(b) is satisfied as to his character and his suitability to be a solicitor.

(2) Any person who has obtained a certificate that the Society is satisfied as mentioned in subsection (1) may apply to the Master of the Rolls to be admitted as a solicitor; and if any such person so applies, the Master of the Rolls shall, unless cause to the contrary is shown to his satisfaction, in writing, and in such manner and form as the Master of the Rolls may from time to time think fit, admit that person to be a solicitor.

6 Keeping of the roll

(1) The Society shall continue to keep a list of all solicitors of the Supreme Court, called 'the roll'.

(2) The roll may be kept by means of a computer.

(3) If the roll is kept by means of a computer, the Society shall make any entry available for inspection in legible form during office hours, without payment, by any person who applies to inspect it.

(4) If the roll is not kept by means of a computer, any person may inspect it during office hours without payment.

10 Issue of practising certificates

(1) Subject to sections 11 and 12, the Society shall issue a practising certificate to a person who applies for one, if it is satisfied, within 21 days of receipt of his application, –

(a) that his name is on the roll; and

(b) that he is not suspended from practice; and

(c) that his application complies with any regulations under section 28; and

(d) that he is complying with such training regulations (if any) as apply to him; and

(e) that he is complying with any indemnity rules or is exempt from them.

(2) At any time when regulations under section 28 specify a training condition or training conditions, any practising certificate issued to an applicant by the Society shall be issued subject to that condition or one of those conditions if it appears to the Society that training regulations will apply to him at the end of 21 days from the Society's receipt of his application.

(3) At any time when regulations under section 28 specify an indemnity condition or indemnity conditions, any practising certificate issued to an applicant by the Society shall be issued subject to that condition or one of those conditions if it appears to the Society that he will be exempt from indemnity rules at the end of 21 days from the Society's receipt of his application.

19   Rights of practising and rights of audience

(1) Subject to subsection (2), every person qualified in accordance with section 1 may practise as a solicitor –

(a) in the Supreme Court;

(b) in any county court;

(c) in all courts and before all persons having jurisdiction in ecclesiastical matters; and

(d) in all matters relating to applications to obtain notarial faculties,

and shall be entitled to all the rights and privileges, and may exercise and perform all the powers and duties, formerly appertaining to the office or profession of a proctor in the provincial, diocesan or other jurisdictions in England and Wales.

(2) Nothing in subsection (1) shall affect the provisions of section 94 of the Supreme Court Act 1981, section 13 or 60 of the County Courts Act 1984 or any other enactment in force at the commencement of this Act which restricts the right of any solicitor to practise as such in any court.

(3) Nothing subsection (1) or (2) shall prejudice or affect any right of practising or being heard in, before or by any court, tribunal or other body which immediately before the commencement of this Act was enjoyed by virtue of any enactment, rule, order or

regulation or by custom or otherwise by persons qualified to act as solicitors.

31 Rules as to professional practice, conduct and discipline

(1) Without prejudice to any other provision of this Part the Council may, if they think fit, make rules, with the concurrence of the Master of the Rolls, for regulating in respect of any matter the professional practice, conduct and discipline of solicitors.

(2) If any solicitor fails to comply with rules made under this section, any person may make a complaint in respect of that failure to the Tribunal.

(3) Where, under Schedule 4 to the Courts and Legal Services Act 1990 (approval of certain rules in connection with the grant of rights of audience or rights to conduct litigation), the Master of the Rolls approves any rule made under this section he shall be taken, for the purposes of this section, to have concurred in the making of that rule.

(4) Subsection (3) shall have effect whether or not the rule required to be approved under Schedule 4 to the Act of 1990.

46 Solicitors Disciplinary Tribunal

(1) Applications and complaints made by virtue of any provision of this Act shall be made, except so far as other provision is made by this Act or by any regulations under it, to the tribunal known as the 'Solicitors Disciplinary Tribunal'.

(2) The Master of the Rolls shall appoint the members of the Tribunal.

(3) The Tribunal shall consist –

(a) of practising solicitors of not less than ten years' standing (in this section referred to as 'solicitor members'); and
(b) of persons who are neither solicitors nor barristers (in this section referred to as 'lay members').

(4) A member of the Tribunal shall hold and vacate his office in accordance with the terms of his appointment and shall, on ceasing to hold office, be eligible for re-appointment.

(5) There shall be paid to the lay members out of money provided by Parliament such fees and allowances as the Lord Chancellor may, with the approval of the Minister for the Civil Service, determine.

(6) Subject to subsections (7) and (8), the Tribunal shall be deemed to be properly constituted if –

(a) at least three members are present; and

(b) at least one lay member is present; and

(c) the number of solicitor members present exceeds the number of lay members present.

(7) For the purpose of hearing and determining applications and complaints the Tribunal shall consist of not more than three members.

(8) A decision of the Tribunal on an application or complaint may be announced by a single member ...

47 Jurisdiction and powers of Tribunal

(1) Any application –

(a) to strike the name of a solicitor off the roll;

(b) to require a solicitor to answer allegations contained in an affidavit;

(c) to require a former solicitor whose name has been removed from or struck off the roll to answer allegations contained in an affidavit relating to a time when he was a solicitor;

(d) by a solicitor who has been suspended from practice for an unspecified period, by order of the Tribunal, for the termination of that suspension;

(e) by a former solicitor whose name has been struck off the roll to have his name restored to the roll;

(f) by a former solicitor in respect of whom a direction has been given under subsection (2)(g) to have his name restored to the roll,

shall be made to the Tribunal; but nothing in this subsection shall affect any jurisdiction over solicitors exercisable by the Master of the Rolls, or by any judge of the High Court, by virtue of section 50.

(2) Subject to subsection (3) and to section 54, on the hearing of any application or complaint made to the Tribunal under this Act, other

than an application under section 43, the Tribunal shall have power to make such order as it may think fit, and any such order may in particular include provision for any of the following matters –

(a) the striking off the roll of the name of the solicitor to whom the application or complaint relates;

(b) the suspension of that solicitor from practice indefinitely or for a specified period;

(c) the payment by that solicitor or former solicitor of a penalty not exceeding £5,000, which shall be forfeit to Her Majesty;

(d) in the circumstances referred to in subsection (2A), the exclusion of that solicitor from legal aid work (either permanently or for a specified period);

(e) the termination of that solicitor's unspecified period of suspension from practice;

(f) the restoration to the roll of the name of a former solicitor whose name has been struck off the roll and to whom the application relates;

(g) in the case of a former solicitor whose name has been removed from the roll, a direction prohibiting the restoration of his name to the roll except by order of the Tribunal;

(h) in the case of an application under subsection (1)(f), the restoration of the applicant's name to the roll;

(i) the payment by any party of costs or a contribution towards costs of such amount as the Tribunal may consider reasonable.

(2A) An order of the Tribunal may make provision for the exclusion of a solicitor from legal aid work as mentioned in subsection (2)(d) where the Tribunal determines that there is good reason for doing so arising out of –

(a) his conduct in connection with the giving of advice or assistance under Part I of the Legal Aid Act 1974;

(b) his conduct in connection with the provision of services for any persons receiving legal aid under that Part of that Act;

(c) his conduct in connection with the provision of services for any legally assisted person in pursuance of Part II of that Act; or

(d) his conduct in connection with the provision of advice and representation pursuant to section 1 of the Legal Aid Act 1982 (duty solicitors); or

(e) his professional conduct generally;

and the reference in each of paragraphs (b) and (c) to the provision of services for any such person as is there mentioned includes the provision of services for any such person in the capacity of agent for that person's solicitor.

(2B) Where the Tribunal makes any such order as is re-referred to in subsection (2A) in the case of a solicitor who is a member of a firm of solicitors, the Tribunal may, if it thinks fit, order that any other person who is for the time being a member of the firm shall be excluded (either permanently or for a specified period) from legal aid work.

(2C) The Tribunal shall not make an order under subsection (2B) excluding any person from legal aid work unless an opportunity is given to him to show cause why the order should not be made.

(2D) Any person excluded from legal aid work by an order under this section may make an application to the Tribunal for an order terminating his exclusion from such work.

(3) On proof of the commission of an offence with respect to which express provision is made by any section of this Act, the Tribunal shall, without prejudice to its power of making an order as to costs, impose the punishment, or one of the punishments, specified in that section.

(3A) Where, on the hearing of any application or complaint under this Act, the Tribunal is satisfied that more than one allegation is proved against the person to whom the application or complaint relates it may impose a separate penalty (by virtue of subsection (2)(c)) with respect to each such allegation ...

As amended by the Supreme Court Act 1981, s152(1), Schedule 5; County Courts Act 1984, s148(1), Schedule 2, Pt V, para 49; Administration of Justice Act 1985, s44; Courts and Legal Services Act 1990, ss85, 92(1)-(4), 125(2), (7), Schedule 17, paras 8, 10, Schedule 20.

SEX DISCRIMINATION ACT 1975
(1975 c 65)

35A Discrimination by, or in relation to, barristers

(1) It is unlawful for a barrister or barrister's clerk, in relation to any offer of a pupillage or tenancy, to discriminate against a woman –

(a) in the arrangements which are made for the purpose of determining to whom it should be offered;

(b) in respect of any terms on which it is offered; or

(c) by refusing, or deliberately omitting, to offer it to her.

(2) It is unlawful for a barrister or barrister's clerk, in relation to a woman who is a pupil or tenant in the chambers in question, to discriminate against her –

(a) in respect of any terms applicable to her as a pupil or tenant;

(b) in the opportunities for training, or gaining experience, which are afforded or denied to her;

(c) in the benefits, facilities or services which are afforded or denied to her; or

(d) by terminating her pupillage or by subjecting her to any pressure to leave the chambers or other detriment.

(3) It is unlawful for any person, in relation to the giving, withholding or acceptance of instructions to a barrister, to discriminate against a woman.

(4) In this section –

'barrister's clerk' includes any person carrying out any of the functions of a barrister's clerk; and

'pupil', 'pupillage', 'tenancy' and 'tenant' have the meanings commonly associated with their use in the context of a set of barristers' chambers.

(5) Section 3 applies for the purposes of this section as it applies for the purposes of any provision of Part II ...

As inserted by the Courts and Legal Services Act 1990, s64(1).

BAIL ACT 1976
(1976 c 63)

1 Meaning of 'bail in criminal proceedings'

(1) In this Act 'bail in criminal proceedings' means –

(a) bail grantable in or in connection with proceedings for an offence to a person who is accused or convicted of the offence, or

(b) bail grantable in connection with an offence to a person who is under arrest for the offence or for whose arrest for the offence a warrant (endorsed for bail) is being issued.

(2) In this Act 'bail' means bail grantable under the law (including common law) for the time being in force.

(3) Except as provided by section 13(3) of this Act, this section does not apply to bail in or in connection with proceedings outside England and Wales.

(4) This section does not apply to bail granted before the coming into force of this Act.

(5) This section applies –

(a) whether the offence was committed in England or Wales or elsewhere, and

(b) whether it is an offence under the law of England and Wales, or of any other country or territory.

(6) Bail in criminal proceedings shall be granted (and in particular shall be granted unconditionally or conditionally) in accordance with this Act.

2 Other definitions

(1) In this Act, unless the context otherwise requires, 'conviction' includes –

(a) a finding of guilt,

(b) a finding that a person is not guilty by reason of insanity,

(c) a finding under section 30(1) of the Magistrates' Courts Act 1980 (remand for medical examination) that the person in question did the act or made the omission charged, and

(d) a conviction of an offence for which an order is made placing the offender on probation or discharging him absolutely or conditionally,

and 'convicted' shall be construed accordingly.

(2) In this Act, unless the context otherwise requires –

'bail hostel' and 'probation hostel' have the same meanings as in the Powers of Criminal Courts Act 1973,

'child' means a person under the age of 14,

'court' includes a judge of a court or a justice of the peace and, in the case of a specified court, includes a judge or (as the case may be) justice having powers to act in connection with proceedings before that court,

'Courts-Martial Appeal rules' means rules made under section 49 of the Courts-Martial (Appeals) Act 1968,

'Crown Court rules' means rules made under section 15 of the Courts Act 1971,

'magistrates' courts rules' means rules made under section 15 of the Justices of the Peace Act 1949,

'offence' includes an alleged offence,

'proceedings against a fugitive offender' means proceeding under the Extradition Act 1989 or section 2(1) or 4(3) of the Backing of Warrants (Republic of Ireland) Act 1965,

'Supreme Court rules' means rules made under section 99 of the Supreme Court of Judicature (Consolidation) Act 1925,

'surrender to custody' means, in relation to a person released on bail, surrendering himself into the custody of the court or of the constable (according to the requirements of the grant of bail) at the time and place for the time being appointed for him to do so,

'vary', in relation to bail, means imposing further conditions after bail is granted, or varying or rescinding conditions,

'young person' means a person who has attained the age of 14 and is under the age of 17.

(3) Where an enactment (whenever passed) which relates to bail in criminal proceedings refers to the person bailed appearing before a court it is to be construed unless the context otherwise requires as referring to his surrendering himself into the custody of the court.

(4) Any reference in this Act to any other enactment is a reference thereto as amended, and includes a reference thereto as extended or applied, by or under any other enactment, including this Act.

3   General provisions

(1) A person granted bail in criminal proceedings shall be under a duty to surrender to custody, and that duty is enforceable in accordance with section 6 of this Act.

(2) No recognizance for his surrender to custody shall be taken from him.

(3) Except as provided by this section –

(a) no security for his surrender to custody shall be taken from him,

(b) he shall not be required to provide a surety or sureties for his surrender to custody, and

(c) no other requirement shall be imposed on him as a condition of bail.

(4) He may be required, before release on bail, to provide a surety or sureties to secure his surrender to custody.

(5) If it appears that he is unlikely to remain in Great Britain until the time appointed for him to surrender to custody, he may be required, before release on bail, to give security for his surrender to custody.

The security may be given by him or on his behalf.

(6) He may be required (but only by a court) to comply, before release on bail or later, with such requirements as appear to the court to be necessary to secure that –

(a) he surrenders to custody,

(b) he does not commit an offence while on bail,

(c) he does not interfere with witnesses or otherwise obstruct the course of justice whether in relation to himself or any other person,

(d) he makes himself available for the purpose of enabling inquiries or a report to be made to assist the court in dealing with him for the offence.

(6ZA) Where he is required under subsection (6) above to reside in a bail hostel or probation hostel, he may also be required to comply with the rules of the hostel.

(6A) In the case of a person accused of murder the court granting bail shall, unless it considers that satisfactory reports on his mental condition have already been obtained, impose as conditions of bail –

(a) a requirement that the accused shall undergo examination by two medical practitioners for the purpose of enabling such reports to be prepared; and

(b) a requirement that he shall for that purpose attend such an institution or place as the court directs and comply with any other directions which may be given to him for that purpose by either of those practitioners.

(6B) Of the medical practitioners referred to in subsection (6A) above at least one shall be a practitioner approved for the purposes of section 12 of the Mental Health Act 1983.

(7) If a parent or guardian of a child or young person consents to be surety for the child or young person for the purposes of this subsection, the parent or guardian may be required to secure that the child or young person complies with any requirement imposed on him by virtue of subsection (6) or (6A) above but –

(a) no requirement shall be imposed on the parent or the guardian of a young person by virtue of this subsection where it appears that the young person will attain the age of 17 before the time to be appointed for him to surrender to custody; and

(b) the parent or guardian shall not be required to secure compliance with any requirement to which his consent does not extend and shall not, in respect of those requirements to which his consent does extend, be bound in a sum greater than £50.

(8) Where a court has granted bail in criminal proceedings that court or, where that court has committed a person on bail to the Crown Court for trial or to be sentenced or otherwise dealt with, that court or the Crown Court may on application –

(a) by or on behalf of the person to whom bail was granted, or

(b) by the prosecutor or a constable,

vary the conditions of bail or impose conditions in respect of bail which has been granted unconditionally.

(8A) Where a notice of transfer is given under section 4 of the Criminal Justice Act 1987, subsection (8) above shall have effect in relation to a person in relation to whose case the notice is given as if he had been committed on bail to the Crown Court for trial.

(9) This section is subject to subsection (2) of section 30 of the Magistrates' Courts Act 1980 (conditions of bail on remand for medical examination).

(10) Where a custody time limit has expired this section shall have effect as if –

(a) subsections (4) and (5) (sureties and security for his surrender to custody) were omitted;

(b) in subsection (6) (conditions of bail) for the words 'before release on bail or later' there were substituted the words 'after release on bail'.

4 General right to bail of accused persons and others

(1) A person to whom this section applies shall be granted bail except as provided in Schedule 1 to this Act.

(2) This section applies to a person who is accused of an offence when –

(a) he appears or is brought before a magistrates' court or the Crown Court in the course of or in connection with proceedings for the offence, or

(b) he applies to a court for bail in connection with the proceedings.

This subsection does not apply as respects proceedings on or after a person's conviction of the offence or proceedings against a fugitive offender for the offence.

(3) This section also applies to a person who, having been convicted of an offence, appears or is brought before a magistrates' court to be dealt with under Part II of Schedule 2 to the Criminal Justice Act 1991 (breach of requirement of probation, community service, combination or curfew order)

(4) This section also applies to a person who has been convicted of an offence and whose case is adjourned by the court for the purpose of enabling inquiries or a report to be made to assist the court in dealing with him for the offence.

(5) Schedule 1 to this Act also has effect as respects conditions of bail for a person to whom this section applies.

(6) In Schedule 1 to this Act 'the defendant' means a person to whom this section applies and any reference to a defendant whose case is adjourned for inquiries or a report is a reference to a person to whom this section applies by virtue of subsection (4) above.

(7) This section is subject to section 41 of the Magistrates' Courts Act 1980 (restriction of bail by magistrates' court in cases of treason).

(8) Where a custody time limit has expired this section shall have effect as if, in subsection (1), the words 'except as provided in Schedule 1 to this Act' were omitted.

5 Supplementary provisions about decisions on bail

(3) Where a magistrates' court or the Crown Court –

(a) withholds bail in criminal proceedings, or

(b) imposes conditions in granting bail in criminal proceedings, or

(c) varies any conditions of bail or imposes conditions in respect of bail in criminal proceedings,

and does so in relation to a person to whom section 4 of this Act applies, then the court shall, with a view to enabling him to consider making an application in the matter to another court, give reasons for withholding bail or for imposing or varying the conditions.

(4) A court which is by virtue of subsection (3) above required to give reasons for its decision shall include a note of those reasons in the record of its decision and shall (except in a case where, by virtue of subsection (5) below, this need not be done) give a copy of that note to the person in relation to whom the decision was taken.

(5) The Crown Court need not give a copy of the note of the reasons for its decision to the person in relation to whom the decision was taken where that person is represented by counsel or a solicitor unless his counsel or solicitor requests the court to do so.

(6) Where a magistrates' court withholds bail in criminal proceedings from a person who is not represented by counsel or a solicitor, the court shall –

(a) if it is committing him for trial to the Crown Court, or if it issues a certificate under subsection (6A) below, inform him that he may apply to the High Court or to the Crown Court to be granted bail;

(b) in any other case, inform him that he may apply to the High Court for that purpose.

(6A) Where in criminal proceedings –

(a) a magistrates' court remands a person in custody under any of the following provisions of the Magistrates' Courts Act 1980 –

(i) section 5 (adjournment of inquiry into offence);

(ii) section 10 (adjournment of trial);

(iii) section 18 (initial procedure on information against adult for offence triable either way); or

(iv) section 30 (remand for medical examination),

after hearing full argument on an application for bail from him; and

(b) either –

(i) it has not previously heard such argument on an application for bail from him in those proceedings; or

(ii) it has previously heard full argument from him on such an application but it is satisfied that there has been a change in his circumstances or that new considerations have been placed before it,

it shall be the duty of the court to issue a certificate in the prescribed form that they heard full argument on his application for bail before they refused the application.

(6B) Where the court issues a certificate under subsection (6A) above in a case to which paragraph (b)(ii) of that subsection applies, it shall state in the certificate the nature of the change of circumstances or the new considerations which caused it to hear a further fully argued bail application.

(6C) Where a court issues a certificate under subsection (6A) above it shall cause the person to whom it refuses bail to be given a copy of the certificate.

(7) Where a person has given security in pursuance of section 3(5) above and a court is satisfied that he failed to surrender to custody then, unless it appears that he had reasonable cause for his failure, the court may order the forfeiture of the security.

(8) If a court orders the forfeiture of a security under subsection (7) above, the court may declare that the forfeiture extends to such amount less than the full value of the security as it thinks fit to order.

(8A) An order under subsection (7) above shall, unless previously revoked, take effect at the end of 21 days beginning with the day on which it is made.

(8B) A court which has ordered the forfeiture of a security under subsection (7) above may, if satisfied on an application made by or on behalf of the person who gave it that he did after all have reasonable cause for his failure to surrender to custody, by order remit the forfeiture or declare that it extends to such amount less than the full value of the security as it thinks fit to order.

(8C) An application under subsection (8B) above may be made before or after the order for forfeiture has taken effect, but shall not be entertained unless the court is satisfied that the prosecution was given reasonable notice of the applicant's intention to make it.

(9) A security which has been ordered to be forfeited by a court under subsection (7) above shall, to the extent of the forfeiture –

(a) if it consists of money, be accounted for and paid in the same manner as a fine imposed by that court would be;

(b) if it does not consist of money, be enforced by such magistrates' court as may be specified in the order.

(9A) Where an order is made under subsection (8B) above after the order for forfeiture of the security in question has taken effect, any money which would have fallen to be repaid or paid over to the person who gave the security if the order under subsection (8B) had been made before the order for forfeiture took effect shall be repaid or paid over to him.

(10) In this section 'prescribed' means, in relation to the decision of a court or an officer of a court, prescribed by Supreme Court rules, Courts-Martial Appeal rules, Crown Court rules or magistrates' courts rules, as the case requires or, in relation to a decision of a constable, prescribed by direction of the Secretary of State.

6   Offence of absconding by person released on bail

(1) If a person who has been released on bail in criminal proceedings fails without reasonable cause to surrender to custody he shall be guilty of an offence.

(2) If a person who –

(a) has been released on bail in criminal proceedings, and

(b) having reasonable cause therefor, has failed to surrender to custody,

fails to surrender to custody at the appointed place as soon after the appointed time as is reasonably practicable he shall be guilty of an offence.

(3) It shall be for the accused to prove that he had reasonable cause for his failure to surrender to custody.

(4) A failure to give to a person granted bail in criminal proceedings a copy of the record of the decision shall not constitute a reasonable cause for that person's failure to surrender to custody.

(5) An offence under subsection (1) or (2) above shall be punishable either on summary conviction or as if it were a criminal contempt of court.

(6) Where a magistrates' court convicts a person of an offence under subsection (1) or (2) above the court may, if it thinks –

(a) that the circumstances of the offence are such that greater punishment should be inflicted for that offence than the court has power to inflict, or

(b) in a case where it commits that person for trial to the Crown Court for another offence, that it would be appropriate for him to be dealt with for the offence under subsection (1) or (2) above by the court before which he is tried for the other offence,

commit him in custody or on bail to the Crown Court for sentence.

(7) A person who is convicted summarily of an offence under subsection (1) or (2) above and is not committed to the Crown Court for sentence shall be liable to imprisonment for a term not exceeding three months or to a fine not exceeding level 5 on the standard scale or to both and a person who is so committed for sentence or is dealt with as for such a contempt shall be liable to imprisonment for a term not exceeding 12 months or to a fine or to both ...

7 Liability to arrest for absconding or breaking conditions of bail

(1) If a person who has been released on bail in criminal proceedings and is under a duty to surrender into the custody of a court fails to surrender to custody at the time appointed for him to do so the court may issue a warrant for his arrest.

(2) If a person who has been released on bail in criminal proceedings absents himself from the court at any time after he has surrendered into the custody of the court and before the court is ready to begin or to resume the hearing of the proceedings, the court may issue a warrant for his arrest; but no warrant shall be issued under this subsection where that person is absent in accordance with leave given to him by or on behalf of the court.

(3) A person who has been released on bail in criminal proceedings and is under a duty to surrender into the custody of a court may be arrested without warrant by a constable –

(a) if the constable has reasonable grounds for believing that that person is not likely to surrender to custody;

(b) if the constable has reasonable grounds for believing that that person is likely to break any of the conditions of his bail or has reasonable grounds for suspecting that that person has broken any of those conditions; or

(c) in a case where that person was released on bail with one or more surety or sureties, if a surety notifies a constable in writing that that person is unlikely to surrender to custody and that for that reason the surety wishes to be relieved of his obligations as a surety.

(4) A person arrested in pursuance of subsection (3) above –

(a) shall, except where he was arrested within 24 hours of the time appointed for him to surrender to custody, be brought as soon as practicable and in any event within 24 hours after his arrest before a justice of the peace for the petty sessions area in which he was arrested; and

(b) in the said excepted case shall be brought before the court at which he was to have surrendered to custody.

In reckoning for the purposes of this subsection any period of 24 hours, no account shall be taken of Christmas Day, Good Friday or any Sunday.

(5) A justice of the peace before whom a person is brought under subsection (4) above may, subject to subsection (6) below, if of the opinion that that person –

(a) is not likely to surrender to custody, or

(b) has broken or is likely to break any condition of his bail,

remand him in custody or commit him to custody, as the case may require, or alternatively, grant him bail subject to the same or to different conditions, but if not of that opinion shall grant him bail subject to the same conditions (if any) as were originally imposed.

(6) Where the person so brought before the justice is a child or young person and the justice does not grant him bail, subsection (5) above shall have effect subject to the provisions of section 23 of the Children and Young Persons Act 1969 (remands to the care of local authorities).

(7) Where a custody time limit has expired this section shall have effect as if, in subsection (3), paragraphs (a) and (c) were omitted.

8 Bail with sureties

(1) This section applies where a person is granted bail in criminal proceedings on condition that he provides one or more surety or sureties for the purpose of securing that he surrenders to custody.

(2) In considering the suitability for that purpose of a proposed surety, regard may be had (amongst other things) to –

(a) the surety's financial resources;

(b) his character and any previous convictions of his; and

(c) his proximity (whether in point of kinship, place of residence or otherwise) to the person for whom he is to be surety.

(3) Where a court grants a person bail in criminal proceedings on such a condition but is unable to release him because no surety or no suitable surety is available, the court shall fix the amount in which the surety is to be bound and subsection (4) and (5) below, or in a case where the proposed surety resides in Scotland subsection (6) below, shall apply for the purpose of enabling the recognizance of the surety to be entered into subsequently.

(4) Where this subsection applies the recognizance of the surety may be entered into before such of the following persons or descriptions

of persons as the court may by order specify or, if it makes no such order, before any of the following persons, that is to say —

(a) where the decision is taken by a magistrates' court, before a justice of the peace, a justices' clerk or a police officer who either is of the rank of inspector or above or is in charge of a police station or, if magistrates' courts rules so provide, by a person of such other description as is specified in the rules;

(b) where the decision is taken by the Crown Court, before any of the persons specified in paragraph (a) above or, if Crown Court rules so provide, by a person of such other description as is specified in the rules;

(c) where the decision is taken by the High Court or the Court of Appeal, before any of the persons specified in paragraph (a) above or, if Supreme Court rules so provide, by a person of such other description as is specified in the rules;

(d) where the decision is taken by the Courts-Martial Appeal Court, before any of the persons specified in paragraph (a) above or, if Courts-Martial Appeal rules so provide, by a person of such other description as is specified in the rules;

and Supreme Court rules, Crown Court rules, Courts-Martial Appeal rules or magistrates' courts rules may also prescribe the manner in which a recognizance which is to be entered into before such a person is to be entered into and the persons by whom and the manner in which the recognizance may be enforced.

(5) Where a surety seeks to enter into his recognizance before any person in accordance with subsection (4) above but that person declines to take his recognizance because he is not satisfied of the surety's suitability, the surety may apply to —

(a) the court which fixed the amount of the recognizance in which the surety was to be bound, or

(b) a magistrates' court for the petty sessions area in which he resides,

for that court to take his recognizance and that court shall, if satisfied of his suitability, take his recognizance.

(6) Where this subsection applies, the court, if satisfied of the suitability of the proposed surety, may direct that arrangements be made for the recognizance of the surety to be entered into in Scotland before any constable, within the meaning of the Police (Scotland) Act 1967, having charge at any police office or station in

like manner as the recognizance would be entered into in England or Wales.

(7) Where, in pursuance of subsection (4) or (6) above, a recognizance is entered into otherwise than before the court that fixed the amount of the recognizance, the same consequences shall follow as if it had been entered into before that court.

9 Offence of agreeing to indemnify sureties in criminal proceedings

(1) If a person agrees with another to indemnify that other against any liability which that other may incur as a surety to secure the surrender to custody of a person accused or convicted of or under arrest for an offence, he and that other person shall be guilty of an offence.

(2) An offence under subsection (1) above is committed whether the agreement is made before or after the person to be indemnified becomes a surety and whether or not he becomes a surety and whether the agreement contemplates compensation in money or in money's worth.

(3) Where a magistrates' court convicts a person of an offence under subsection (1) above the court may, if it thinks –

(a) that the circumstances of the offence are such that greater punishment should be inflicted for that offence than the court has power to inflict, or

(b) in a case where it commits that person for trial to the Crown Court for another offence, that it would be appropriate for him to be dealt with for the offence under subsection (1) above by the court before which he is tried for the other offence,

commit him in custody or on bail to the Crown Court for sentence.

(4) A person guilty of an offence under subsection (1) above shall be liable –

(a) on summary conviction, to imprisonment for a term not exceeding 3 months or to a fine not exceeding the prescribed sum or to both; or

(b) on conviction on indictment or if sentenced by the Crown Court on committal for sentence under subsection (3) above, to imprisonment for a term not exceeding 12 months or to a fine or to both.

(5) No proceedings for an offence under subsection (1) above shall be instituted except by or with the consent of the Director of Public Prosecutions.

SCHEDULE 1

PERSONS ENTITLED TO BAIL: SUPPLEMENTARY PROVISIONS

PART I

DEFENDANTS ACCUSED OR CONVICTED OF IMPRISONABLE OFFENCES

1. Where the offence or one of the offences of which the defendant is accused or convicted in the proceedings is punishable with imprisonment the following provisions of this Part of this Schedule apply.

2. The defendant need not be granted bail if the court is satisfied that there are substantial grounds for believing that the defendant, if released on bail (whether subject to conditions or not), would –

(a) fail to surrender to custody, or

(b) commit an offence while on bail, or

(c) interfere with witnesses or otherwise obstruct the course of justice, whether in relation to himself or any other person.

3. The defendant need not be granted bail if the court is satisfied that the defendant should be kept in custody for his own protection or, if he is a child or young person, for his own welfare.

4. The defendant need not be granted bail if he is in custody in pursuance of the sentence of a court or of any authority acting under any of the Services Acts.

5. The defendant need not be granted bail where the court is satisfied that it has not been practicable to obtain sufficient information for the purpose of taking the decisions required by this Part of this Schedule for want of time since the institution of the proceedings against him.

6. The defendant need not be granted bail if, having been released on bail in or in connection with the proceedings for the offence, he has been arrested in pursuance of section 7 of this Act.

7. Where his case is adjourned for inquiries or a report, the defendant need not be granted bail if it appears to the court that it would be impracticable to complete the inquiries or make the report without keeping the defendant in custody.

8. (1) Subject to sub-paragraph (3) below, where the defendant is granted bail, no conditions shall be imposed under subsections (4) to (7) (except subsection (6)(d)) of section 3 of this Act unless it appears to the court that it is necessary to do so for the purpose of preventing the occurrence of any of the events mentioned in paragraph 2 of this Part of this Schedule.

(1A) No condition shall be imposed under section 3(6)(d) of this Act unless it appears to be necessary to do so for the purpose of enabling inquiries or a report to be made.

(2) Sub-paragraphs (1) and (1A) above also apply on any application to the court to vary the conditions of bail or to impose conditions in respect of bail which has been granted unconditionally.

(3) The restriction imposed by sub-paragraph (1A) above shall not apply to the conditions required to be imposed under section 3(6A) of this Act or operate to override the direction in section 30(2) of the Magistrates' Courts Act 1980 to a magistrates' court to impose conditions of bail under section 3(6)(d) of this Act of the description specified in the said section 30(2) in the circumstances so specified.

9. In taking the decisions required by paragraph 2 of this Part of this Schedule, the court shall have regard to such of the following considerations as appear to it to be relevant, that is to say –

   (a) the nature and seriousness of the offence or default (and the probable method of dealing with the defendant for it),

   (b) the character, antecedents, associations and community ties of the defendant,

   (c) the defendant's record as respects the fulfilment of his obligations under previous grants of bail in criminal proceedings,

   (d) except in the case of a defendant whose case is adjourned for inquiries or a report, the strength of the evidence of his having committed the offence or having defaulted,

as well as to any others which appear to be relevant.

9A. (1) If –

(a) the defendant is charged with an offence to which this paragraph applies; and

(b) representations are made as to any of the matters mentioned in paragraph 2 of this Part of this Schedule; and

(c) the court decides to grant him bail,

the court shall state the reasons for its decision and shall cause those reasons to be included in the record of the proceedings.

(2) The offences to which this paragraph applies are –

(a) murder;

(b) manslaughter;

(c) rape;

(d) attempted murder; and

(e) attempted rape.

9B. Where the court is considering exercising the power conferred by section 128A of the Magistrates' Courts Act 1980 (power to remand in custody for more than eight clear days), it shall have regard to the total length of time which the accused would spend in custody if it were to exercise the power.

PART II

DEFENDANTS ACCUSED OR CONVICTED OF NON-IMPRISONABLE OFFENCES

1. Where the offence or every offence of which the defendant is accused or convicted in the proceedings is one which is not punishable with imprisonment the following provisions of this Part of this Schedule apply.

2. The defendant need not be granted bail if –

(a) it appears to the court that, having been previously granted bail in criminal proceedings, he has failed to surrender to custody in accordance with his obligations under the grant of bail; and

(b) the court believes, in view of that failure, that the defendant, if released on bail (whether subject to conditions or not) would fail to surrender to custody.

3. The defendant need not be granted bail if the court is satisfied that the defendant should be kept in custody for his own protection or, if he is a child or young person, for his own welfare.

4. The defendant need not be granted bail if he is in custody in pursuance of the sentence of a court or of any authority acting under any of the Services Acts.

5. The defendant need not be granted bail if, having been released on bail in or in connection with the proceedings for the offence, he has been arrested in pursuance of section 7 of this Act.

PART IIA

DECISIONS WHERE BAIL REFUSED ON PREVIOUS HEARING

1. If the court decides not to grant the defendant bail, it is the court's duty to consider, at each subsequent hearing while the defendant is a person to whom section 4 above applies and remains in custody, whether he ought to be granted bail.

2. At the first hearing after that at which the court decided not to grant the defendant bail he may support an application for bail with any argument as to fact or law that he desires (whether or not he has advanced that argument previously).

3. At subsequent hearings the court need not hear arguments as to fact or law which it has heard previously.

PART III

INTERPRETATION

1. For the purposes of this Schedule the question whether an offence is one which is punishable with imprisonment shall be determined without regard to any enactment prohibiting or restricting the imprisonment of young offenders or first offenders.

2. References in this Schedule to previous grants of bail in criminal proceedings include references to bail granted before the coming into force of this Act.

3. References in this Schedule to a defendant's being kept in custody or being in custody include (where the defendant is a child or young person) references to his being kept or being in the care of a local authority in pursuance of a warrant of commitment under section 23(1) of the Children and Young Persons Act 1969.

4. In this Schedule –

'court', in the expression 'sentence of a court', includes a service court as defined in section 12(1) of the Visiting Forces Act 1952 and 'sentence', in that expression, shall be construed in accordance with that definition;

'default', in relation to the defendant, means the default for which he is to be dealt with under section 6 or section 16 of the Powers of Criminal Courts Act 1973;

'the Services Acts' means the Army Act 1955, the Air Force Act 1955 and the Naval Discipline Act 1957.

Note. Sections 3(10), 4(8) and 7(7) apply to certain proceedings covered by the Prosecution of Offences (Custody Time Limits) Regulations 1987, as amended.

As amended by the Criminal Law Act 1977, s65(4), Schedule 12; Magistrates' Courts Act 1980, ss32(2), 154(1), Schedule 7, paras 143, 144, 145, 146; Criminal Justice Act 1982, ss38, 46, 60(2), (3); Mental Health (Amendment) Act 1982, s34(2), (3), (4); Mental Health Act 1983, s148, Schedule 4, para 46; Criminal Justice Act 1987, s15, Schedule 2, para 9; Criminal Justice Act 1988, ss131(1), (2), 153, 154, 155(2), 170(1), Schedule 15, para 52; Extradition Act 1989, s36(3); Criminal Justice Act 1991, ss100, 101(2), Schedule 11, paras 21, 22, Schedule 13.

RACE RELATIONS ACT 1976
(1976 c 74)

26A Discrimination by, or in relation to, barristers

(1) It is unlawful for a barrister or barrister's clerk, in relation to any offer of a pupillage or tenancy, to discriminate against a person –

(a) in the arrangements which are made for the purpose of determining to whom it should be offered;

(b) in respect of any terms on which it is offered; or

(c) by refusing, or deliberately omitting, to offer it to him.

(2) It is unlawful for a barrister or barrister's clerk, in relation to a pupil or tenant in the chambers in question, to discriminate against him –

(a) in respect of any terms applicable to him as a pupil or tenant;

(b) in the opportunities for training, or gaining experience which are afforded or denied to him;

(c) in the benefits, facilities or services which are afforded or denied to him; or

(d) by terminating his pupillage or by subjecting him to any pressure to leave the chambers or other detriment.

(3) It is unlawful for any person, in relation to the giving, withholding or acceptance of instructions to a barrister, to discriminate against any person.

(4) In this section –

'barrister's clerk' includes any person carrying out any of the functions of a barrister's clerk; and

'pupil', 'pupillage', 'tenancy' and 'tenant' have the meanings commonly associated with their use in the context of a set of barristers' chambers.

As inserted by the Courts and Legal Services Act 1990, s64(2).

JUSTICES OF THE PEACE ACT 1979
(1979 c 55)

6 Appointment and removal of justices of the peace

(1) Subject to the following provisions of this Act, justices of the peace for any commission area shall be appointed by the Lord Chancellor by instrument on behalf and in the name of Her Majesty, and a justice so appointed may be removed from office in like manner.

(2) The preceding subsection does not apply to stipendiary magistrates and shall be without prejudice to the position of the Lord Mayor and aldermen as justices for the City of London by virtue of the charters of the City.

7 Residence qualification

(1) Subject to the provisions of this section, a person shall not be appointed as a justice of the peace for a commission area in accordance with section 6 of this Act, nor act as a justice of the peace by virtue of any such appointment, unless he resides in or within 15 miles of that area.

(2) If the Lord Chancellor is of opinion that it is in the public interest for a person to act as a justice of the peace for a particular area though not qualified to do so under subsection (1) above, he may direct that, so long as any conditions specified in the direction are satisfied, that subsection shall not apply in relation to that person's appointment as a justice of the peace for the area so specified.

(3) Where a person appointed as a justice of the peace for a commission area in accordance with section 6 of this Act is not qualified under the preceding provisions of this section to act by virtue of the appointment, he shall be removed from office as a justice of the peace in accordance with section 6 of this Act if the Lord Chancellor is of opinion that the appointment ought not to continue having regard to the probable duration and other circumstances of the want of qualification.

(4) No act or appointment shall be invalidated by reason only of the disqualification or want of qualification under this section of the person acting or appointed.

8 Supplemental list for England and Wales

(1) There shall be kept in the office of the Clerk of the Crown in Chancery a supplemental list for England and Wales as provided for by this Act (in this Act referred to as 'the supplemental list').

(2) Subject to the following provisions of this section, there shall be entered in the supplemental list –

(a) the name of any justice of the peace who is of the age of 70 years or over and neither holds nor has held high judicial office within the meaning of the Appellate Jurisdiction Act 1876, and

(b) the name of any justice of the peace who holds or has held such office and is of the age of 75 years or over.

(3) A person who on the date when his name falls to be entered in the supplemental list in accordance with subsection (2) above holds office as chairman of the justices in a petty sessions area (whether by an election made, or having effect as if made, under section 17 of this Act, or, in the City of London, as Chief Magistrate or acting Chief Magistrate) shall have his name so entered on the expiry or sooner determination of the term for which he holds office on that date.

(4) The Lord Chancellor may direct that the name of a justice of the peace for any area shall be entered in the supplemental list if the Lord Chancellor is satisfied either –

(a) that by reason of the justice's age or infirmity or other like cause it is expedient that he should cease to exercise judicial functions as a justice for that area, or

(b) that the justice declines or neglects to take a proper part in the exercise of those functions.

(5) On a person's appointment as a justice of the peace for any area the Lord Chancellor may direct that his name shall be entered in the supplemental list, if that person is appointed a justice for that area on ceasing to be a justice for some other area.

(6) The name of a justice of the peace shall be entered in the supplemental list if he applies for it to be so entered and the application is approved by the Lord Chancellor.

(7) Nothing in this section shall apply to a person holding office as stipendiary magistrate.

9   Removal of name from supplemental list

(1) A person's name shall be removed from the supplemental list if he ceases to be a justice of the peace.

(2) The name of any person, if not required to be entered in the supplemental list by subsection (2) or subsection (3) of section 8 of this Act, shall be removed from the list if so directed by the Lord Chancellor.

10   Effect of entry of name in supplemental list

(1) Subject to the following subsections, a justice of the peace for any area, while his name is entered in the supplemental list, shall not by reason of being a justice for that area be qualified as a justice to do any act or to be a member of any committee or other body.

(2) Subsection (1) above shall not preclude a justice from doing all or any of the following acts as a justice, that is to say –

(a) signing any document for the purpose of authenticating another person's signature;

(b) taking and authenticating by his signature any written declaration not made on oath; and

(c) giving a certificate of facts within his knowledge or of his opinion as to any matter.

(3) The entry of a person's name in the supplemental list shall also not preclude him, if so authorised by the Lord Chancellor, from acting as a judge of the Crown Court so long as he has not attained the age of 72 years.

(4) No act or appointment shall be invalidated by reason of the disqualification under this section of the person acting or appointed.

13   Appointment and removal of stipendiary magistrates

(1) It shall be lawful for Her Majesty to appoint a person who has a seven year general qualification within the meaning of section 71 of the Courts and Legal Services Act 1990 to be, during Her

Majesty's pleasure, a whole-time stipendiary magistrate in any commission area or areas outside the inner London area and the City of London, and to appoint more than one such magistrate in the same area or areas.

(2) A person so appointed to be a magistrate in any commission area shall by virtue of his office be a justice of the peace for that area.

(3) Any appointment of a stipendiary magistrate under this section shall be of a person recommended to Her Majesty by the Lord Chancellor, and a stipendiary magistrate appointed under this section shall not be removed from office except on the Lord Chancellor's recommendation.

(4) The number of stipendiary magistrates appointed under this section shall not at any time exceed forty or such larger number as Her Majesty may from time to time by Order in Council specify.

(5) Her Majesty shall not be recommended to make an Order in Council under subsection (4) above unless a draft of the Order has been laid before Parliament and approved by resolution of each House.

14   Retirement of stipendiary magistrates

(1) A stipendiary magistrate appointed on or after 25 October 1968 shall vacate his office at the end of the completed year of service in the course of which he attains the age of 70:

Provided that where the Lord Chancellor considers it desirable in the public interest to retain him in office after that time, the Lord Chancellor may from time to time authorise him to continue in office up to such age not exceeding 72 as the Lord Chancellor thinks fit.

(2)A stipendiary magistrate appointed before 25 October 1968 shall vacate his office at the end of the completed year of service in the course of which he attains the age of 72:

Provided that where the Lord Chancellor considers it desirable in the public interest to retain him in office after that time, the Lord Chancellor may from time to time authorise him to continue in office up to such age not exceeding 75 as the Lord Chancellor thinks fit.

25   Appointment and removal of justices' clerks

(1) Justices' clerks shall be appointed by the magistrates' courts committee and shall hold office during the pleasure of the committee; and a magistrates' courts committee may appoint more than one justices' clerk for any area.

(2) The approval of the Secretary of State shall be required –

(a) for any decision to increase the number of justices' clerks in a petty sessions area or to have more than one justices' clerk in a new petty sessions area;

(b) for any appointment of justices' clerk;

(c) for the removal of the justices' clerk for a petty sessional division where the magistrates for the division do not consent to the removal.

(3) A magistrates' courts committee shall consult the magistrates for any petty sessional division on the appointment or removal of a justices' clerk for the division; and the Secretary of State, before approving the appointment or removal of a justices' clerk for such a division, shall consider any representations made to him by the magistrates for the division, and before approving the removal of any such clerk shall consider any representations made to him by the clerk.

(4) The magistrates' courts committee shall inform the Secretary of State of the age, qualifications and experience of any person proposed to be appointed a justices' clerk and, if the Secretary of State so requires, of any other person offering himself for the appointment.

(5) Subsections (1) to (4) above shall not apply to the inner London area.

26   Qualifications for appointment as justices' clerk

(1) Except as provided by this section, no person shall be appointed as justices' clerk of any class or description unless either –

(a) at the time of appointment he has a five year magistrates' court qualification, within the meaning of section 71 of the Courts and Legal Services Act 1990, and is within any limit of age prescribed for appointment to a clerkship of that class or description, or

(b) he then is or has previously been a justices' clerk.

(2) A lower as well as an upper limit of age may be prescribed under subsection (1) above for appointments to any class or description of clerkship.

(3) A person not having the qualification as barrister or solicitor which is required by subsection (1)(a) above may be appointed a justices' clerk –

(a) if at the time of appointment he is a barrister or solicitor and has served for not less than five years in service to which this subsection applies, or

(b) if before 1 January 1960 he had served for not less than ten years in service to which this subsection applies and, in the opinion of the magistrates' courts committee and of the Secretary of State, there are special circumstances making the appointment a proper one.

(4) Subsection (3) above applies to service in any one or more of the following capacities, that is to say, service as assistant to a justices' clerk and service before 1 February 1969 –

(a) as clerk to a stipendiary magistrate;

(b) as clerk to a magistrates' court for the inner London area or as clerk to a metropolitan stipendiary court;

(c) as clerk at one of the justice rooms of the City of London; or

(d) as assistant to any such clerk as is mentioned in paragraphs (a) to (c) above.

(5) A person may be appointed a justices' clerk notwithstanding that he is over the upper limit of age mentioned in subsection (1) of this section if he has served continuously in service to which subsection (3) above applies from a time when he was below that limit to the time of appointment.

28   General powers and duties of justices' clerks

(1) Rules made in accordance with section 144 of the Magistrates' Courts Act 1980 may (except in so far as any enactment passed after 25 October 1968 otherwise directs) make provision enabling things authorised to be done by, to or before a single justice of the peace to be done instead by, to or before a justices' clerk.

(1A) Such rules may also make provision enabling things authorised to be done by, to or before a justices' clerk (whether by virtue of subsection (1) above or otherwise) to be done instead by, to or before –

(a) a person appointed by a magistrates' courts committee to assist him;

(b) where he is a part-time justices' clerk, any member of his staff who has been appointed by the magistrates' courts committee to assist him in his duties as such;

(c) any officer appointed by the committee of magistrates to be his deputy or to assist him.

(2) Any enactment (including any enactment contained in this Act) or any rule of law regulating the exercise of any jurisdiction or powers of justices of the peace, or relating to things done in the exercise or purported exercise of any such jurisdiction or powers, shall apply in relation to the exercise or purported exercise thereof by virtue of subsection (1) above by the clerk to any justices as if he were one of those justices.

(3) It is hereby declared that the functions of a justices' clerk include the giving to the justices to whom he is clerk or any of them, at the request of the justices or justice, of advice about law, practice or procedure on questions arising in connection with the discharge of their or his functions, including questions arising when the clerk is not personally attending on the justices or justice, and that the clerk may, at any time when he thinks he should do so, bring to the attention of the justices or justice any point of law, practice or procedure that is or may be involved in any question so arising.

In this subsection the reference to the functions of justices or a justice is a reference to any of their or his functions as justices or a justice of the peace, other than functions as a judge of the Crown Court.

(4) The enactment of subsection (3) above shall not be taken as defining or in any respect limiting the powers and duties belonging to a justices' clerk or the matters on which justices may obtain assistance from their clerk.

31 Appointment, removal and retirement of metropolitan stipendiary magistrates

(1) Metropolitan stipendiary magistrates shall be appointed by Her Majesty, and Her Majesty shall from time to time appoint such

number of persons as is necessary; but the number of metropolitan stipendiary magistrates shall not at any time exceed 60 or such larger number as Her Majesty may from time to time by Order in Council specify.

(2) A person shall not be qualified to be appointed a metropolitan stipendiary magistrate unless he has a seven year general qualification within the meaning of section 71 of the Courts and Legal Services Act 1990.

(3) The Lord Chancellor shall designate one of the metropolitan stipendiary magistrates to be the chief metropolitan stipendiary magistrate.

(4) The following provisions shall apply to each metropolitan stipendiary magistrate, that is to say –

(a) he shall by virtue of his office be a justice of the peace for each of the London commission areas and for the counties of Essex, Hertfordshire, Kent and Surrey;

(c) he may be removed from office by the Lord Chancellor for inability or misbehaviour.

(5) A metropolitan stipendiary magistrate who is by virtue of his office a justice of the peace for any area mentioned in subsection (4) above shall not, by reason only of his being a justice of the peace for that area by virtue of that office, be qualified to be chosen under section 17(1) of this Act as chairman or deputy chairman of the justices for a petty sessional division of that area or to vote under that subsection at the election of any such chairman or deputy chairman.

(6) Section 14 of this Act shall apply to metropolitan stipendiary magistrates as well as to other stipendiary magistrates in England or Wales.

(7) Her Majesty shall not be recommended to make an Order in Council under subsection (1) above unless a draft of the Order has been laid before Parliament and approved by resolution of each House.

39 Ex officio and appointed justices

(1) The Lord Mayor and aldermen of the City shall by virtue of the charter granted by His late Majesty King George II dated 25 August 1741 continue to be justices of the peace for the City:

Provided that any of them may be excluded by the Lord Chancellor from the exercise of his functions as a justice.

(2) The persons holding office as justices of the peace for the City shall constitute a single body of justices, without distinction between those holding office by virtue of the charter and those appointed; and the jurisdiction and powers of the Lord Mayor and aldermen as justices by virtue of the charter shall be the same in all respects as those of appointed justices.

(3) The establishment of the City as a separate commission area shall not be taken to have constituted new courts for the City; and the jurisdiction and powers of the justices of the peace for the City are in continuation of those formerly belonging exclusively to the justices holding office by virtue of the charter.

(4) In this Part of this Act 'the City' means the City of London.

40   Chairman and deputy chairmen of justices

(1) The Lord Mayor for the time being, if not disqualified, shall be chairman of the justices, with the style of Chief Magistrate, instead of a chairman being elected under section 17(1) of this Act; and, subject to subsection (3) below, the aldermen who have been Lord Mayor and are not disqualified (or, if there are more than eight such aldermen, the eight who were last Lord Mayor) shall be deputy chairmen in addition to any deputy chairmen elected under section 17(1) above.

(2) For the purposes of this section a Lord Mayor or alderman is disqualified at any time while his name is entered in the supplemental list.

(3) In the event of a Lord Mayor being disqualified, then during his mayoralty the senior of the aldermen designated as deputy chairmen in subsection (1) above shall, instead of being a deputy chairman, be chairman of the justices as acting Chief Magistrate ...

44   Immunity for acts within jurisdiction

No action shall lie against any justice of the peace or justices' clerk in respect of any act or omission of his –

   (a) in the execution of his duty –

   (i) as such a justice; or

(ii) as such a clerk exercising, by virtue of any statutory provision, any of the functions of a single justice; and

(b) with respect to any matter within his jurisdiction.

45 Immunity for certain acts beyond jurisdiction

An action shall lie against any justice of the peace or justices' clerk in respect of any act or omission of his –

(a) in the purported execution of his duty –

(i) as such a justice; or
(ii) as such a clerk exercising, by virtue of any statutory provision, any of the functions of a single justice; but

(b) with respect to a matter which is not within his jurisdiction,

if, but only if, it is proved that he acted in bad faith.

50 Where action prohibited, proceedings may be set aside

If any action is brought in circumstances in which this Part of this Act provides that no action is to be brought, a judge of the court in which the action is brought may, on the application of the defendant and upon an affidavit as to the facts, set aside the proceedings in the action, with or without costs, as the judge thinks fit.

63 Courses of instruction

(1) It shall be the duty of every magistrates' courts committee, in accordance with arrangements approved by the Lord Chancellor, to make and administer schemes providing for courses of instruction for justices of the peace of their area.

(2) It shall be the duty of the committee of magistrates, in accordance with arrangements approved by the Lord Chancellor, to make and administer schemes providing for courses of instruction for justices of the peace of the inner London area.

(3) There may be paid out of moneys provided by Parliament any expenses incurred by the Lord Chancellor in providing courses of instruction for justices of the peace.

(4) If courses of instruction are not provided for justices of the peace of any area as required by subsection (1) or subsection (2) above, then any expenses incurred by the Lord Chancellor in providing courses of instruction to make good the default shall be recoverable by him from the magistrates' courts committee or committee of magistrates in default; and any sums recovered by the Lord Chancellor under this subsection shall be paid into the Consolidated Fund.

(5) The Secretary of State may provide courses of instruction for justices' clerks and their staffs.

(6) In this section 'justices' clerk' includes a clerk of special sessions.

As amended by the Magistrates' Courts Act 1980, s154, Schedule 7, para 194; Administration of Justice Act 1982, s65; Courts and Legal Services Act 1990, ss71(2), 108(1), (2), (3), 117, Schedule 10, paras 44(1), (2), 45, Schedule 20.

MAGISTRATES' COURTS ACT 1980
(1980 c 43)

PART I

CRIMINAL JURISDICTION AND PROCEDURE

1   Issue of summons to accused or warrant for his arrest

(1) Upon an information being laid before a justice of the peace for an area to which this section applies that any person has, or is suspected of having, committed an offence, the justice may, in any of the events mentioned in subsection (2) below, but subject to subsections (3) to (5) below, –

(a) issue a summons directed to that person requiring him to appear before a magistrates' court for the area to answer to the information, or

(b) issue a warrant to arrest that person and bring him before a magistrates' court for the area or such magistrates' court as is provided in subsection (5) below.

(2) A justice of the peace for an area to which this section applies may issue a summons or warrant under this section –

(a) if the offence was committed or is suspected to have been committed within the area, or

(b) if it appears to the justice necessary or expedient, with a view to the better administration of justice, that the person charged should be tried jointly with, or in the same place as, some other person who is charged with an offence, and who is in custody, or is being or is to be proceeded against, within the area, or

(c) if the person charged resides or is, or is believed to reside or be, within the area, or

(d) if under any enactment a magistrates' court for the area has jurisdiction to try the offence, or

(e) if the offence was committed outside England and Wales and, where it is an offence exclusively punishable on summary conviction, if a magistrates' court for the area would have jurisdiction to try the offence if the offender were before it.

(3) No warrant shall be issued under this section unless the information is in writing and substantiated on oath.

(4) No warrant shall be issued under this section for the arrest of any person who has attained the age of 18 years unless –

(a) the offence to which the warrant relates is an indictable offence or is punishable with imprisonment, or

(b) the person's address is not sufficiently established for a summons to be served on him.

(5) Where the offence charged is not an indictable offence –

(a) no summons shall be issued by virtue only of paragraph (c) of subsection (2) above, and

(b) any warrant issued by virtue only of that paragraph shall require the person charged to be brought before a magistrates' court having jurisdiction to try the offence.

(6) Where the offence charged is an indictable offence, a warrant under this section may be issued at any time notwithstanding that a summons has previously been issued.

(7) A justice of the peace may issue a summons or warrant under this section upon an information being laid before him notwithstanding any enactment requiring the information to be laid before two or more justices.

(8) The areas to which this section applies are any county, any London commission area and the City of London.

2 Jurisdiction to deal with charges

(1) A magistrates' court for a county, a London commission area or the City of London shall have jurisdiction to try all summary offences committed within the county, the London commission area or the City (as the case may be).

(2) Where a person charged with a summary offence appears or is brought before a magistrates' court in answer to a summons issued under paragraph (b) of section 1(2) above, or under a warrant issued

under that paragraph, the court shall have jurisdiction to try the offence.

(3) A magistrates' court for a county, a London commission area or the City of London shall have jurisdiction as examining justices over any offence committed by a person who appears or is brought before the court, whether or not the offence was committed within the county, the London commission area or the City (as the case may be).

(4) Subject to sections 18 to 22 below and any other enactment (wherever contained) relating to the mode of trial of offences triable either way, a magistrates' court shall have jurisdiction to try summarily an offence triable either way in any case in which under subsection (3) above it would have jurisdiction as examining justices.

(5) A magistrates' court shall, in the exercise of its powers under section 24 below, have jurisdiction to try summarily an indictable offence in any case in which under subsection (3) above it would have jurisdiction as examining justices.

(6) A magistrates' court for any area by which a person is tried for an offence shall have jurisdiction to try him for any summary offence for which he could be tried by a magistrates' court for any other area.

(7) Nothing in this section shall affect any jurisdiction over offences conferred on a magistrates' court by an enactment not contained in this Act.

4   General nature of committal proceedings

(1) The functions of examining justices may be discharged by a single justice.

(2) Examining justices shall sit in open court except where any enactment contains an express provision to the contrary and except where it appears to them as respects the whole or any part of committal proceedings that the ends of justice would not be served by their sitting in open court.

(3) Subject to subsection (4) below and section 102 below, evidence given before examining justices shall be given in the presence of the accused, and the defence shall be at liberty to put questions to any witness at the inquiry.

(4) Examining justices may allow evidence to be given before them in the absence of the accused if –

(a) they consider that by reason of his disorderly conduct before them it is not practicable for the evidence to be given in his presence, or

(b) he cannot be present for reasons of health but is represented by a legal representative and has consented to the evidence being given in his absence.

6   Discharge or committal for trial

(1) Subject to the provisions of this and any other Act relating to the summary trial of indictable offences, if a magistrates' court inquiring into an offence as examining justices is of opinion, on consideration of the evidence and of any statement of the accused, that there is sufficient evidence to put the accused on trial by jury for any indictable offence, the court shall commit him for trial; and, if it is not of that opinion, it shall, if he is in custody for no other cause than the offence under inquiry, discharge him.

(2) A magistrates' court inquiring into an offence as examining justices may, if satisfied that all the evidence before the court (whether for the prosecution or the defence) consists of written statements tendered to the court under section 102 below, with or without exhibits, commit the accused for trial for the offence without consideration of the contents of those statements, unless –

(a) the accused or one of the accused has no legal representative acting for him in the case (whether present in court or not);

(b) a legal representative for the accused or one of the accused, as the case may be, has requested the court to consider a submission that the statements disclose insufficient evidence to put that accused on trial by jury for the offence;

and subsection (1) above shall not apply to a committal for trial under this subsection.

(3) Subject to section 4 of the Bail Act 1976 and section 41 below, the court may commit a person for trial –

(a) in custody, that is to say, by committing him to custody there to be safely kept until delivered in due course of law, or

(b) on bail in accordance with the Bail Act 1976, that is to say, by directing him to appear before the Crown Court for trial;

and where his release on bail is conditional on his providing one or more surety or sureties and, in accordance with section 8(3) of the Bail Act 1976, the court fixes the amount in which the surety is to be bound with a view to his entering into his recognizance subsequently in accordance with subsections (4) and (5) or (6) of that section the court shall in the meantime commit the accused to custody in accordance with paragraph (a) of this subsection.

(4) Where the court has committed a person to custody in accordance with paragraph (a) of subsection (3) above, then, if that person is in custody for no other cause, the court may, at any time before his first appearance before the Crown Court, grant him bail in accordance with the Bail Act 1976 subject to a duty to appear before the Crown Court for trial.

(5) Where a magistrates' court acting as examining justices commits any person for trial or determines to discharge him, the clerk of the court shall, on the day on which the committal proceedings are concluded or the next day, cause to be displayed in a part of the court house to which the public have access a notice –

(a) in either case giving that person's name, address, and age (if known);

(b) in a case where the court so commits him, stating the charge or charges on which he is committed and the court to which he is committed;

(c) in a case where the court determines to discharge him, describing the offence charged and stating that it has so determined;

but this subsection shall have effect subject to section 4 of the Sexual Offences (Amendment) Act 1976 (anonymity of complainant in rape, etc cases).

(6) A notice displayed in pursuance of subsection (5) above shall not contain the name or address of any person under the age of 18 years unless the justices in question have stated that in their opinion he would be mentioned in the notice apart from the preceding provisions of this subsection and should be mentioned in it for the purpose of avoiding injustice to him.

9   Procedure on trial

(1) On the summary trial of an information, the court shall, if the accused appears, state to him the substance of the information and ask him whether he pleads guilty or not guilty.

(2) The court, after hearing the evidence and the parties, shall convict the accused or dismiss the information.

(3) If the accused pleads guilty, the court may convict him without hearing evidence.

17   Certain offences triable either way

(1) The offences listed in Schedule 1 to this Act shall be triable either way.

(2) Subsection (1) above is without prejudice to any other enactment by virtue of which any offence is triable either way.

18   Initial procedure on information against adult for offence triable either way

(1) Sections 19 to 23 below shall have effect where a person who has attained the age of 18 years appears or is brought before a magistrates' court on an information charging him with an offence triable either way.

(2) Without prejudice to section 11(1) above, everything that the court is required to do under sections 19 to 22 below must be done before any evidence is called and, subject to subsection (3) below and section 23 below, with the accused present in court.

(3) The court may proceed in the absence of the accused in accordance with such of the provisions of sections 19 to 22 below as are applicable in the circumstances if the court considers that by reason of his disorderly conduct before the court it is not practicable for the proceedings to be conducted in his presence; and subsections (3) to (5) of section 23 below, so far as applicable, shall have effect in relation to proceedings conducted in the absence of the accused by virtue of this subsection (references in those subsections to the person representing the accused being for this purpose read as references to the person, if any, representing him).

(4) A magistrate' court proceeding under sections 19 to 23 below may adjourn the proceedings at any time, and on doing so on any occasion when the accused is present may remand the accused, and shall remand him if –

(a) on the occasion on which he first appeared, or was brought, before the court to answer to the information he was in custody or, having been released on bail, surrendered to the custody of the court; or

(b) he has been remanded at any time in the course of proceedings on the information;

and where the court remands the accused, the time fixed for the resumption of the proceedings shall be that at which he is required to appear or be brought before the court in pursuance of the remand or would be required to be brought before the court but for section 128(3A) below.

(5) The functions of a magistrates' court under sections 19 to 23 below may be discharged by a single justice, but the foregoing provision shall not be taken to authorise the summary trial of an information by a magistrates' court composed of less than two justices.

19 Court to begin by considering which mode of trial appears more suitable

(1) The court shall consider whether, having regard to the matters mentioned in subsection (3) below and any representations made by the prosecutor or the accused, the offence appears to the court more suitable for summary trial or for trial on indictment.

(2) Before so considering, the court –

(a) shall cause the charge to be written down, if this has not already been done, and read to the accused; and

(b) shall afford first the prosecutor and then the accused an opportunity to make representations as to which mode of trial would be more suitable.

(3) The matters to which the court is to have regard under subsection (1) above are the nature of the case; whether the circumstances make the offence one of serious character; whether the punishment which a magistrates' court would have power to inflict for it would be adequate; and any other circumstances which appear to the court to make it more suitable for the offence to be tried in one way rather than the other.

(4) If the prosecution is being carried on by the Attorney General, the Solicitor General or the Director of Public Prosecutions and he applies for the offence to be tried on indictment, the preceding provisions of this section and sections 20 and 21 below shall not

apply, and the court shall proceed to inquire into the information as examining justices.

(5) The power of the Director of Public Prosecutions under subsection (4) above to apply for an offence to be tried on indictment shall not be exercised except with the consent of the Attorney General.

20 Procedure where summary trial appears more suitable

(1) If, where the court has considered as required by section 19(1) above, it appears to the court that the offence is more suitable for summary trial, the following provisions of this section shall apply (unless excluded by section 23 below).

(2) The court shall explain to the accused in ordinary language –

(a) that it appears to the court more suitable for him to be tried summarily for the offence, and that he can either consent to be so tried or, if he wishes, be tried by a jury; and

(b) that if he is tried summarily and is convicted by the court, he may be committed for sentence to the Crown Court under section 38 below if the convicting court is of such opinion as is mentioned in subsection (2) of that section.

(3) After explaining to the accused as provided by subsection (2) above the court shall ask him whether he consents to be tried summarily or wishes to be tried by a jury, and –

(a) if he consents to be tried summarily, shall proceed to the summary trial of the information;

(b) if he does not so consent, shall proceed to inquire into the information as examining justices.

21 Procedure where trial on indictment appears more suitable

If, where the court has considered as required by section 19(1) above, it appears to the court that the offence is more suitable for trial on indictment, the court shall tell the accused that the court has decided that it is more suitable for him to be tried for the offence by a jury, and shall proceed to inquire into the information as examining justices.

22 Certain offences triable either way to be tried summarily if value involved is small

(1) If the offence charged by the information is one of those mentioned in the first column of Schedule 2 to this Act (in this section referred to as 'scheduled offences') then, subject to subsection (7) below, the court shall, before proceeding in accordance with section 19 above, consider whether, having regard to any representations made by the prosecutor or the accused, the value involved (as defined in subsection (10) below) appears to the court to exceed the relevant sum.

For the purposes of this section the relevant sum is £2,000.

(2) If, where subsection (1) above applies, it appears to the court clear that, for the offence charged, the value involved does not exceed the relevant sum, the court shall proceed as if the offence were triable only summarily, and sections 19 to 21 above shall not apply.

(3) If, where subsection (1) above applies, it appears to the court clear that, for the offence charged, the value involved exceeds the relevant sum, the court shall thereupon proceed in accordance with section 19 above in the ordinary way without further regard to the provisions of this section.

(4) If, where subsection (1) above applies, it appears to the court for any reason not clear whether, for the offence charged, the value involved does or does not exceed the relevant sum, the provisions of subsections (5) and (6) below shall apply.

(5) The court shall cause the charge to be written down, if this has not already been done, and read to the accused, and shall explain to him in ordinary language –

(a) that he can, if he wishes, consent to be tried summarily for the offence and that if he consents to be so tried, he will definitely be tried in that way; and

(b) that if he is tried summarily and is convicted by the court, his liability to imprisonment or a fine will be limited as provided in section 33 below.

(6) After explaining to the accused as provided by subsection (5) above the court shall ask him whether he consents to be tried summarily and –

(a) if he so consents, shall proceed in accordance with subsection (2) above as if that subsection applied;

(b) if he does not so consent, shall proceed in accordance with subsection (3) above as if that subsection applied.

(8) Where a person is convicted by a magistrates' court of a scheduled offence, it shall not be open to him to appeal to the Crown Court against the conviction on the ground that the convicting court's decision as to the value involved was mistaken.

(9) If, where subsection (1) above applies, the offence charged is one with which the accused is charged jointly with a person who has not attained the age of 18 years, the reference in that subsection to any representations made by the accused shall be read as including any representations made by the person under 18.

(10) In this section 'the value involved', in relation to any scheduled offence, means the value indicated in the second column of Schedule 2 to this Act, measured as indicated in the third column of that Schedule; and in that Schedule 'the material time' means the time of the alleged offence.

(11) Where –

(a) the accused is charged on the same occasion with two or more scheduled offences and it appears to the court that they constitute or form part of a series of two or more offences of the same or a similar character; or

(b) the offence charged consists in incitement to commit two or more scheduled offences,

this section shall have effect as if any reference in it to the value involved were a reference to the aggregate of the values involved.

(12) Subsection (8) of section 12A of the Theft Act 1968 (which determines when a vehicle is recovered) shall apply for the purposes of paragraph 3 of Schedule 2 to this Act as it applies for the purposes of that section.

24 Summary trial of information against child or young person for indictable offence

(1) Where a person under the age of 18 years appears or is brought before a magistrates' court on an information charging him with

indictable offence other than homicide, he shall be tried summarily unless –

(a) he has attained the age of 14 and the offence is such as is mentioned in subsection (2) of section 53 of the Children and Young Persons Act 1933 (under which young persons convicted on indictment of certain grave crimes may be sentenced to be detained for long periods) and the court considers that if he is found guilty of the offence it ought to be possible to sentence him in pursuance of that subsection; or

(b) he is charged jointly with a person who has attained the age of 18 years and the court considers it necessary in the interest of justice to commit them both for trial;

and accordingly in a case falling within paragraph (a) or (b) of this subsection the court shall commit the accused for trial if either it is of opinion that there is sufficient evidence to put him on trial or it has power under section 6(2) above so to commit him without consideration of the evidence.

(2) Where, in a case falling within subsection (1)(b) above, a magistrates' court commits a person under the age of 18 years for trial for an offence with which he is charged jointly with a person who has attained that age, the court may also commit him for trial for any other indictable offence with which he is charged at the same time (whether jointly with the person who has attained that age or not) if that other offence arises out of circumstances which are the same as or connected with those giving rise to the first-mentioned offence.

(3) If on trying a person summarily in pursuance of subsection (1) above the court finds him guilty, it may impose a fine of an amount not exceeding £1,000 or may exercise the same powers as it could have exercised if he had been found guilty of an offence for which, but for section 1(1) of the Criminal Justice Act 1982, it could have sentenced him to imprisonment for a term not exceeding –

(a) the maximum term of imprisonment for the offence on conviction on indictment; or

(b) six months,

whichever is the less.

(4) In relation to a person under the age of 14 subsection (3) above shall have effect as if for the words £1,000 there were substituted the words £250.

27 Effect of dismissal of information for offence triable either way

Where on the summary trial of an information for an offence triable either way the court dismisses the information, the dismissal shall have the same effect as an acquittal on indictment.

29 Power of magistrates' court to remit a person under 17 for trial to a youth court in certain circumstances

(1) Where –

(a) a person under the age of 18 years ('the juvenile') appears or is brought before a magistrates' court other than a youth court on an information jointly charging him and one or more other persons with an offence; and

(b) that other person, or any of those other persons, has attained that age,

subsection (2) below shall have effect notwithstanding proviso (a) in section 46(1) of the Children and Young Persons Act 1933 (which would otherwise require the charge against the juvenile to be heard by a magistrates' court other than a youth court).

In the following provisions of this section 'the older accused' means such one or more of the accused as have attained the age of 18 years.

(2) If –

(a) the court proceeds to the summary trial of the information in the case of both or all of the accused, and the older accused or each of the older accused pleads guilty; or

(b) the court –

(i) in the case of the older accused or each of the older accused, proceeds to inquire into the information as examining justices and either commits him for trial or discharges him; and

(ii) in the case of the juvenile, proceeds to the summary trial of the information,

then, if in either situation the juvenile pleads not guilty, the court may before any evidence is called in his case remit him for trial to a youth court acting for the same place as the remitting court or for the place where he habitually resides.

(3) A person remitted to a youth court under subsection (2) above shall be brought before and tried by a youth court accordingly.

(4) Where a person is so remitted to a youth court –

(a) he shall have no right of appeal against the order of remission; and

(b) the remitting court may give such directions as appear to be necessary with respect to his custody or for his release on bail until he can be brought before the youth court.

(5) The preceding provisions of this section shall apply in relation to a corporation as if it were an individual who has attained the age of 18 years.

31 General limit on power of magistrates' court to impose imprisonment

(1) Without prejudice to section 133 below, a magistrates' court shall not have power to impose imprisonment or a sentence of detention in a young offender institution for more than 6 months in respect of any one offence.

(2) Unless expressly excluded, subsection (1) above shall apply even if the offence in question is one for which a person would otherwise be liable on summary conviction to imprisonment or a sentence of detention in a young offender institution for more than 6 months.

(3) Any power of a magistrates' court to impose a term of imprisonment for non-payment of a fine, or for want of sufficient distress to satisfy a fine, shall not be limited by virtue of subsection (1) above.

(4) In subsection (3) above 'fine' includes a pecuniary penalty but does not include a pecuniary forfeiture or pecuniary compensation.

32 Penalties on summary conviction for offences triable either way

(1) On summary conviction of any of the offences triable either way listed in Schedule 1 to this Act a person shall be liable to imprisonment for a term not exceeding 6 months or to a fine not exceeding the prescribed sum or both, except that –

(a) a magistrates' court shall not have power to impose imprisonment for an offence so listed if the Crown Court would not have that power in the case of an adult convicted of it on indictment;

(b) on summary conviction of an offence consisting in the incitement to commit an offence triable either way a person shall not be liable to any greater penalty than he would be liable to on summary conviction of the last-mentioned offence.

(2) For any offence triable either way which is not listed in Schedule 1 to this Act, being an offence under a relevant enactment, the maximum fine which may be imposed on summary conviction shall by virtue of this subsection be the prescribed sum unless the offence is one for which by virtue of an enactment other than this subsection a larger fine may be imposed on summary conviction.

(3) Where, by virtue of any relevant enactment, a person summarily convicted of an offence triable either way would, apart from this section, be liable to a maximum fine of one amount in the case of a first conviction and of a different amount in the case of a second or subsequent conviction, subsection (2) above shall apply irrespective of whether the conviction is a first, second or subsequent one.

(4) Subsection (2) above shall not affect so much of any enactment as (in whatever words) makes a person liable on summary conviction to a fine not exceeding a specified amount for each day on which a continuing offence is continued after conviction or the occurrence of any other specified event.

(5) Subsection (2) above shall not apply on summary conviction of any of the following offences –

(a) offences under section 5(2) of the Misuse of Drugs Act 1971 (having possession of a controlled drug) where the controlled drug in relation to which the offence was committed was a Class B or Class C drug;

(b) offences under the following provisions of that Act, where the controlled drug in relation to which the offence was committed was a Class C drug, namely –

(i) section 4(2) (production, or being concerned in the production, of a controlled drug);

(ii) section 4(3) (supplying or offering a controlled drug or being concerned in the doing of either activity by another);

(iii) section 5(3) (having possession of a controlled drug with intent to supply it to another);

(iv) section 8 (being the occupier, or concerned in the management, of premises and permitting or suffering certain activities to take place there);

(v) section 12(6) (contravention of direction prohibiting practitioner, etc from possessing, supplying, etc controlled drugs); or

(vi) section 13(3) (contravention of direction prohibiting practitioner, etc from prescribing, supplying, etc controlled drugs).

(6) Where, as regards any offence triable either way, there is under any enactment (however framed or worded) a power by subordinate instrument to restrict the amount of the fine which on summary conviction can be imposed in respect of that offence –

(a) subsection (2) above shall not affect that power or override any restriction imposed in the exercise of that power; and

(b) the amount to which that fine may be restricted in the exercise of that power shall be any amount less than the maximum fine which could be imposed on summary conviction in respect of the offence apart from any restriction so imposed.

(8) In subsection (5) above 'controlled drug', 'Class B drug' and 'Class C drug' have the same meaning as in the Misuse of Drugs Act 1971.

(9) In this section –

'fine' includes a pecuniary penalty but does not include a pecuniary forfeiture or pecuniary compensation;

'the prescribed sum' means £5,000 or such sum as is for the time being substituted in this definition by an order in force under section 143(1) below;

'relevant enactment' means an enactment contained in the Criminal Law Act 1977 or in any Act passed before, or in the same Session as, that Act.

33 Maximum penalties on summary conviction in pursuance of section 22

(1) Where in pursuance of subsection (2) of section 22 above a magistrates' court proceeds to the summary trial of an information, then, if the accused is summarily convicted of the offence –

(a) subject to subsection (3) below the court shall not have power to impose on him in respect of that offence imprisonment for more than 3 months or a fine greater than level 4 on the standard scale; and

(b) section 38 below shall not apply as regards that offence.

(2) In subsection (1) above 'fine' includes a pecuniary penalty but does not include a pecuniary forfeiture or pecuniary compensation.

(3) Paragraph (a) of subsection (1) above does not apply to an offence under section 12A of the Theft Act 1968 (aggravated vehicle-taking).

36 Restriction on fines in respect of young persons

(1) Where a person under 18 years of age is found guilty by a magistrates' court of an offence for which, apart from this section, the court would have power to impose a fine of an amount exceeding £1,000, the amount of any fine imposed by the court shall not exceed £1,000

(2) In relation to a person under the age of 14 subsection (1) above shall have effect as if for the words '£1,000', in both the places where they occur, there were substituted the words '£250'.

37 Committal to Crown Court with a view to sentence of detention in a young offender institution

(1) Where a person who is not less than 15 but under 18 years old is convicted by a magistrates' court of an offence punishable on conviction on indictment with a term of imprisonment exceeding six months, then, if the court is of opinion that he should be sentenced to a greater term of detention in a young offender institution than it has power to impose, the court may commit him in custody or on bail to the Crown Court for sentence.

(2) A person committed in custody under subsection (1) above shall be committed –

(a) if the court has been notified by the Secretary of State that a remand centre is available for the reception, from that court, of persons of the class or description of the person committed, to a remand centre;

(b) if the court has not been so notified, to a prison. .

38 Committal for sentence on summary trial of offence triable either way

(1) This section applies where on the summary trial of an offence triable either way (not being an offence as regards which this section is excluded by section 33 above) a person who is not less than 18 years old is convicted of the offence.

(2) If the court is of opinion –

(a) that the offence or the combination of the offence and other offences associated with it was so serious that greater punishment should be inflicted for the offence than the court has power to impose; or

(b) in the case of a violent or sexual offence committed by a person who is not less than 21 years old, that a sentence of imprisonment for a term longer than the court has power to impose is necessary to protect the public from serious harm from him,

the court may, in accordance with section 56 of the Criminal Justice Act 1967, commit the offender in custody or on bail to the Crown Court for sentence in accordance with the provisions of section 42 of the Powers of Criminal Courts Act 1973.

(3) Paragraphs (a) and (b) of subsection (2) above shall be construed as if they were contained in Part I of the Criminal Justice Act 1991.

(4) The preceding provisions of this section shall apply in relation to a corporation as if –

(a) the corporation were an individual who is not less than 18 years old; and

(b) in subsection (2) above, paragraph (b) and the words 'in custody or on bail' were omitted.

40 Restriction on amount payable under compensation order of magistrates' court

(1) The compensation to be paid under a compensation order made by a magistrates' court in respect of any offence of which the court has convicted the offender shall not exceed £5,000; and the compensation or total compensation to be paid under a compensation order or compensation orders made by a magistrates' court in respect of any offence or offences taken into consideration in determining sentence shall not exceed the difference (if any)

between the amount or total amount which under the preceding provisions of this subsection is the maximum for the offence or offences of which the offender has been convicted and the amount or total amounts (if any) which are in fact ordered to be paid in respect of that offence or those offences.

(2) In subsection (1) above 'compensation order' has the meaning assigned to it by section 35(1) of the Powers of Criminal Courts Act 1973.

41 Restriction on grant of bail in treason

A person charged with treason shall not be granted bail except by order of a judge of the High Court or the Secretary of State.

42 Restriction on justices sitting after dealing with bail

(1) A justice of the peace shall not take part in trying the issue of an accused's guilt on the summary trial of an information if in the course of the same proceedings the justice has been informed, for the purpose of determining whether the accused shall be granted bail, that he has one or more previous convictions.

(2) For the purposes of this section any committal proceedings from which the proceedings on the summary trial arose shall be treated as part of the trial.

43 Bail on arrest

(1) Where a person has been granted bail under the Police and Criminal Evidence Act 1984 subject to a duty to appear before a magistrates' court, the court before which he is to appear may appoint a later time as the time at which he is to appear and may enlarge the recognizances of any sureties for him at that time.

(2) The recognizance of any surety for any person granted bail subject to a duty to attend at a police station may be enforced as if it were conditioned for his appearance before a magistrates' court for the petty sessions area in which the police station named in the recognizance is situated.

PART II

CIVIL JURISDICTION AND PROCEDURE

51   Issue of summons on complaint

Subject to the provisions of this Act, where a complaint is made to a justice of the peace acting for any petty sessions area upon which a magistrates' court acting for that area has power to make an order against any person, the justice may issue a summons directed to that person requiring him to appear before a magistrates' court acting for that area to answer to the complaint.

52   Jurisdiction to deal with complaints

Where no express provision is made by any Act or the rules specifying what magistrates' courts shall have jurisdiction to hear a complaint, a magistrates' court shall have such jurisdiction if the complaint relates to anything done within the commission area for which the court is appointed or anything left undone that ought to have been done there, or ought to have been done either there or elsewhere, or relates to any other matter arising within that area.

In this section 'commission area' has the same meaning as in the Justices of the Peace Act 1979.

53   Procedure on hearing

(1) On the hearing of a complaint, the court shall, if the defendant appears, state to him the substance of the complaint.

(2) The court, after hearing the evidence and the parties, shall make the order for which the complaint is made or dismiss the complaint.

(3) Where a complaint is for an order for the payment of a sum recoverable summarily as a civil debt, or for the variation of the rate of any periodical payments ordered by a magistrates' court to be made, or for such other matter as may be prescribed, the court may make the order with the consent of the defendant without hearing evidence.

58   Money recoverable summarily as civil debt

(1) A magistrates' court shall have power to make an order on

complaint for the payment of any money recoverable summarily as a civil debt.

(2) Any sum payment of which may be ordered by a magistrates' court shall be recoverable summarily as a civil debt except –

(a) a sum recoverable on complaint for a magistrates' court maintenance order; or

(b) a sum that may be adjudged to be paid by a summary conviction or by an order enforceable as if it were a summary conviction.

66 Composition of magistrates' courts for family proceedings: general

(1) Subject to the provisions of this section, a magistrates' court when hearing family proceedings shall be composed of not more than three justices of the peace, including, so far as practicable, both a man and a woman.

(2) Subsection (1) above shall not apply to a magistrates' court for an inner London petty sessions area, and, notwithstanding anything in section 67 below, for the purpose of exercising jurisdiction to hear family proceedings such a court shall be composed of –

(a) a metropolitan stipendiary magistrate as chairman and one or two lay justices who are members of the family panel for that area; or

(b) two or three lay justices who are members of that panel;

or, if it is not practicable for such a court to be so composed, the court shall for that purpose be composed of a metropolitan stipendiary magistrate sitting alone.

(3) Where in pursuance of subsection (2) above a magistrates' court includes lay justices it shall, so far as practicable, include both a man and woman.

(4) In the preceding provisions of this section 'lay justices' means justices of the peace for the inner London area who are not metropolitan stipendiary magistrates.

(5) In this section 'inner London petty sessions area' means the City of London or any petty sessional division of the inner London area.

67 Family proceedings courts and family panels

(1) Magistrates' courts constituted in accordance with the provisions of this section and sitting for the purpose of hearing family proceedings shall be known as family proceedings courts.

(2) A justice shall not be qualified to sit as a member of a family proceedings court unless he is a member of a family panel, that is to say a panel of justices specially appointed to deal with family proceedings ...

(7) A stipendiary magistrate who is a member of a family panel may, notwithstanding anything in section 66(1) above, hear and determine family proceedings when sitting alone.

(8) Nothing in this section shall require the formation of a family panel for the City of London.

69 Sittings of magistrates' courts for family proceedings

(1) The business of magistrates' courts shall, so far as is consistent with the due dispatch of business, be arranged in such manner as may be requisite for separating the hearing and determination of family proceedings from other business.

(2) In the case of family proceedings in a magistrates' court other than proceedings under the Adoption Act 1976, no person shall be present during the hearing and determination by the court of the proceedings except –

   (a) officers of the court;

   (b) parties to the case before the court, their legal representatives, witnesses and other persons directly concerned in the case;

   (c) representatives of newspapers or new agencies;

   (d) any other person whom the court may in its discretion permit to be present, so, however, that permission shall not be withheld from a person who appears to the court to have adequate grounds for attendance.

(3) In relation to any family proceedings under the Adoption Act 1976, subsection (2) above shall apply with the omission of paragraphs (c) and (d).

(4) When hearing family proceedings, a magistrates' court may, if it thinks it necessary in the interest of the administration of justice or of public decency, direct that any persons, not being officers of the court or parties to the case, the parties' legal representatives, or other persons directly concerned in the case, be excluded during the taking of any indecent evidence.

(5) The powers conferred on a magistrates' court by this section shall be in addition and without prejudice to any other powers of the court to hear proceedings in camera.

(6) Nothing in this section shall affect the exercise by a magistrates' court of the power to direct that witnesses shall be excluded until they are called for examination.

PART III

SATISFACTION AND ENFORCEMENT

81 Enforcement of fines imposed on young offenders

(1) Where a magistrates' court would, but for section 1 of the Criminal Justice Act 1982, have power to commit to prison a person under the age of 18 for a default consisting in failure to pay, or want of sufficient distress to satisfy, a sum adjudged to be paid by a conviction, the court may, subject to the following provisions of this section, make –

(a) an order requiring the defaulter's parent or guardian to enter into a recognizance to ensure that the defaulter pays so much of that sum as remains unpaid; or

(b) an order directing so much of that sum as remains unpaid to be paid by the defaulter's parent or guardian instead of by the defaulter.

(2) An order under subsection (1) above shall not be made in respect of a defaulter –

(a) in pursuance of paragraph (a) of that subsection, unless the parent or guardian in question consents;

(b) in pursuance of paragraph (b) of that subsection, unless the court is satisfied in all the circumstances that it is reasonable to make the order.

(3) None of the following orders, namely –

(a) an order under section 17(1) of the Criminal Justice Act 1982 for attendance at an attendance centre; or

(b) any order under subsection (1) above,

shall be made by a magistrates' court in consequence of a default of a person under the age of 18 years consisting in failure to pay, or want of sufficient distress to satisfy, a sum adjudged to be paid by a conviction unless the court has since the conviction inquired into the defaulter's means in his presence on at least one occasion.

(4) An order under subsection (1) above shall not be made by a magistrates' court unless the court is satisfied that the defaulter has, or has had since the date on which the sum in question was adjudged to be paid, the means to pay the sum or any instalment of it on which he has defaulted, and refuses or neglects or, as the case may be, has refused or neglected, to pay it.

(5) An order under subsection (1) above may be made in pursuance of paragraph (b) of that subsection against a parent or guardian who, having been required to attend, has failed to do so; but, save as aforesaid, an order under that subsection shall not be made in pursuance of that paragraph without giving the parent or guardian an opportunity of being heard.

(6) A parent or guardian may appeal to the Crown Court against an order under subsection (1) above made in pursuance of paragraph (b) of that subsection.

(7) Any sum ordered under subsection (1)(b) above to be paid by a parent or guardian may be recovered from him in like manner as if the order had been made on the conviction of the parent or guardian of an offence.

(8) In this section –

'guardian', in relation to a person under the age of 18, means a person appointed, according to law, to be his guardian, or by order of a court of competent jurisdiction;

'sum adjudged to be paid by a conviction' means any fine, costs, compensation or other sum adjudged to be paid by an order made on a finding of guilt, including an order made under section 35 of the Powers of Criminal Courts Act 1973 (compensation orders).

PART V

APPEAL AND CASE STATED

108 Right of appeal to the Crown Court

(1) A person convicted by a magistrates' court may appeal to the Crown Court –

(a) if he pleaded guilty, against his sentence;

(b) if he did not, against the conviction or sentence.

(1A) Section 13 of the Powers of Criminal Courts Act 1973 (under which a conviction of an offence for which an order for conditional or absolute discharge is made is deemed not to be a conviction except for certain purposes) shall not prevent an appeal under this section, whether against conviction or otherwise.

(2) A person sentenced by a magistrates' court for an offence in respect of which a probation order or an order for conditional discharge has been previously made may appeal to the Crown Court against the sentence.

(3) In this section 'sentence' includes any order made on conviction by a magistrates' court, not being –

(b) an order for the payment of costs;

(c) an order under section 2 of the Protection of Animals Act 1911 (which enables a court to order the destruction of an animal); or

(d) an order made in pursuance of any enactment under which the court has no discretion as to the making of the order or its terms;

and also includes a declaration of relevance under the Football Spectators Act 1989.

111 Statement of case by magistrates' court

(1) Any person who was a party to any proceeding before a magistrates' court or is aggrieved by the conviction, order, determination or other proceeding of the court may question the proceeding on the ground that it is wrong in law or is in excess of jurisdiction by applying to the justices composing the court to state

a case for the opinion of the High Court on the question of law or jurisdiction involved; but a person shall not make an application under this section in respect of a decision against which he has a right of appeal to the High Court or which by virtue of any enactment passed after 31 December 1879 is final.

(2) An application under subsection (1) above shall be made within 21 days after the day on which the decision of the magistrates' court was given.

(3) For the purpose of subsection (2) above, the day on which the decision of the magistrates' court is given shall, where the court has adjourned the trial of an information after conviction, be the day on which the court sentences or otherwise deals with the offender.

(4) On the making of an application under this section in respect of a decision any right of the applicant to appeal against the decision to the Crown Court shall cease.

(5) If the justices are of opinion that an application under this section is frivolous, they may refuse to state a case, and, if the applicant so requires, shall give him a certificate stating that the application has been refused; but the justices shall not refuse to state a case if the application is made by or under the direction of the Attorney General.

(6) Where justices refuse to state a case, the High Court may, on the application of the person who applied for the case to be stated, make an order of mandamus requiring the justices to state a case.

113 Bail on appeal or case stated

(1) Where a person has given notice of appeal to the Crown Court against the decision of a magistrates' court or has applied to a magistrates' court to state a case for the opinion of the High Court, then, if he is in custody, the magistrates' court may grant him bail.

(2) If a person is granted bail under subsection (1) above, the time and place at which he is to appear (except in the event of the determination in respect of which the case is stated being reversed by the High Court) shall be –

    (a) if he has given notice of appeal, the Crown Court at the time appointed for the hearing of the appeal;

    (b) if he has applied for the statement of a case, the magistrates' court at such time within 10 days after the judgment of the High

Court has been given as may be specified by the magistrates' court;

and any recognizance that may be taken from him or from any surety for him shall be conditioned accordingly.

(3) Subsection (1) above shall not apply where the accused has been committed to the Crown Court for sentence under section 37 or 38 above.

(4) Section 37(6) of the Criminal Justice Act 1948 (which relates to the currency of a sentence while a person is released on bail by the High Court) shall apply to a person released on bail by a magistrates' court under this section pending the hearing of a case stated as it applies to a person released on bail by the High Court under section 22 of the Criminal Justice Act 1967.

PART VI

RECOGNIZANCES

115 Binding over to keep the peace or be of good behaviour

(1) The power of a magistrates' court on the complaint of any person to adjudge any other person to enter into a recognizance, with or without sureties, to keep the peace or to be of good behaviour towards the complainant shall be exercised by order on complaint.

(2) Where a complaint is made under this section, the power of the court to remand the defendant under subsection (5) of section 55 above shall not be subject to the restrictions imposed by subsection (6) of that section.

(3) If any person ordered by a magistrates' court under subsection (1) above to enter into a recognizance, with or without sureties, to keep the peace or to be of good behaviour fails to comply with the order, the court may commit him to custody for a period not exceeding six months or until he sooner complies with the order.

120 Forfeiture of recognizance

(1) Where a recognizance to keep the peace or to be of good behaviour has been entered into before a magistrates' court or any recognizance is conditioned for the appearance of a person before a magistrates' court or for his doing any other thing connected with a

proceeding before a magistrates' court, and the recognizance appears to the court to be forfeited, the court may, subject to subsection (2) below, declare the recognizance to be forfeited and adjudge the persons bound thereby, whether as principal or sureties, or any of them, to pay the sum in which they are respectively bound.

(2) Where a recognizance is conditioned to keep the peace or to be of good behaviour, the court shall not declare it forfeited except by order made on complaint.

(3) The court which declares the recognizance to be forfeited may, instead of adjudging any person to pay the whole sum in which he is bound, adjudge him to pay part only of the sum or remit the sum.

(4) Payment of any sum adjudged to be paid under this section, including any costs awarded against the defendant, may be enforced, and any such sum shall be applied, as if it were a fine and as if the adjudication were a summary conviction of an offence not punishable with imprisonment and so much of section 85(1) above as empowers a court to remit fines shall not apply to the sum but so much thereof as relates to remission after a term of imprisonment has been imposed shall so apply; but at any time before the issue of a warrant of commitment to enforce payment of the sum, or before the sale of goods under a warrant of distress to satisfy the sum, the court may remit the whole or any part of the sum either absolutely or on such conditions as the court thinks just.

(5) A recognizance such as is mentioned in this section shall not be enforced otherwise than in accordance with this section, and accordingly shall not be transmitted to the Crown Court nor shall its forfeiture be certified to that Court.

PART VII

MISCELLANEOUS AND SUPPLEMENTARY

121 Constitution and place of sitting of court

(1) A magistrates' court shall not try an information summarily or hear a complaint except when composed of at least two justices unless the trial or hearing is one that by virtue of any enactment may take place before a single justice.

(2) A magistrates' court shall not hold an inquiry into the means of an offender for the purposes of section 82 above or determine under

that section at a hearing at which the offender is not present whether to issue a warrant of commitment except when composed of at least two justices.

(3) A magistrates' court shall not –

(a) try summarily an information for an indictable offence or hear a complaint except when sitting in a petty-sessional court-house;

(b) try an information for a summary offence or hold an inquiry into the means of an offender for the purposes of section 82 above, or impose imprisonment, except when sitting in a petty-sessional court-house or an occasional court-house.

(4) Subject to the provisions of any enactment to the contrary, where a magistrates' court is required by this section to sit in a petty-sessional or occasional court-house, it shall sit in open court.

(5) A magistrates' court composed of a single justice, or sitting in an occasional court-house, shall not impose imprisonment for a period exceeding 14 days or order a person to pay more than £1.

(6) Subject to the provisions of subsection (7) below, the justices composing the court before which any proceedings take place shall be present during the whole of the proceedings; but, if during the course of the proceedings any justice absents himself, he shall cease to act further therein and, if the remaining justices are enough to satisfy the requirements of the preceding provisions of this section, the proceedings may continue before a court composed of those justices.

(7) Where the trial of an information is adjourned after the accused has been convicted and before he is sentenced or otherwise dealt with, the court which sentences or deals with him need not be composed of the same justices as that which convicted him; but, where among the justices composing the court which sentences or deals with an offender there are any who were not sitting when he was convicted, the court which sentences or deals with the offender shall before doing so make such inquiry into the facts and circumstances of the case as will enable the justices who were not sitting when the offender was convicted to be fully acquainted with those facts and circumstances.

(8) This section shall have effect subject to the provisions of this Act relating to family proceedings.

122 Appearance by legal representative

(1) A party to any proceedings before a magistrates' court may be represented by a legal representative.

(2) Subject to subsection (3) below, an absent party so represented shall be deemed not to be absent.

(3) Appearance of a party by a legal representative shall not satisfy any provision of any enactment or any condition of a recognizance expressly requiring his presence.

144 Rule committee and rules of procedure

(1) The Lord Chancellor may appoint a rule committee for magistrates' courts, and may on the advice of or after consultation with the rule committee make rules for regulating and prescribing the procedure and practice to be followed in magistrates' courts and by justices' clerks.

(2) The rule committee shall consist of the Lord Chief Justice, the President of the Family Division of the High Court, the chief metropolitan stipendiary magistrate and such number of other persons appointed by the Lord Chancellor as he may determine.

(3) Among the members of the committee appointed by the Lord Chancellor there shall be at least

  (a) one justices' clerk;

  (b) one person who has a Supreme Court qualification (within the meaning of section 71 of the Courts and Legal Services Act 1990); and

  (c) one person who has been granted by an authorised body, under Part II of that Act, the right to conduct litigation in relation to all proceedings in the Supreme Court.

(4) The power to make rules conferred by this section shall be exercisable by statutory instrument which shall be subject to annulment by resolution of either House of Parliament.

(5) In this section the expression 'justices' clerk' means a clerk to the justices for a petty sessions area.

148 'Magistrates' court'

(1) In this Act the expression 'magistrates' court' means any justice or justices of the peace acting under any enactment or by virtue of his or their commission or under the common law.

(2) Except where the contrary is expressed, anything authorised or required by this Act to be done by, to or before the magistrates' court by, to or before which any other thing was done, or is to be done, may be done by, to or before any magistrates' court acting for the same petty sessions area as that court.

150 Interpretation of other terms

(1) In this Act, unless the context otherwise requires, the following expressions have the meaning hereby assigned to them, that is to say –

'bail in criminal proceedings' has the same meaning as in the Bail Act 1976;

'commit to custody' means commit to prison or, where any enactment authorises or requires committal to some other place of detention instead of committal to prison, to that other place;

'committal proceedings' means proceedings before a magistrates' court acting as examining justices; ...

'fine', except for the purposes of any enactment imposing a limit on the amount of any fine, includes any pecuniary penalty or pecuniary forfeiture or pecuniary compensation payable under a conviction;

'impose imprisonment' means pass a sentence of imprisonment or fix a term of imprisonment for failure to pay any sum of money, or for want of sufficient distress to satisfy any sum of money, or for failure to do or abstain from doing anything required to be done or left undone;

'legal representative' means an authorised advocate or authorised litigator, as defined by section 119(1) of the Courts and Legal Services Act 1990; ...

'petty-sessional court-house' means any of the following, that is to say –

(a) a court-house or place at which justices are accustomed to assemble for holding special or petty sessions or for the time being appointed as a substitute for such a court-house or place (including, where justices are accustomed to assemble for either special or petty sessions at more than one court-house or place in a petty sessional division, any such court-house or place);

(b) a court-house or place at which a stipendiary magistrate is authorised by law to do alone any act authorised to be done by more than one justice of the peace;

'petty sessions area' has the same meaning as in the Justices of the Peace Act 1979;

'prescribed' means prescribed by the rules;

'the register' means the register of proceedings before a magistrates' court required by the rules to be kept by the clerk of the court;

'the rules' means rules made under section 144 above;

'sentence' does not include a committal in default of payment of any sum of money, or for want of sufficient distress to satisfy any sum of money, or for failure to do or abstain from doing anything required to be done or left undone;

'sum enforceable as a civil debt' means –

(a) any sum recoverable summarily as a civil debt which is adjudged to be paid by the order of a magistrates' court;

(b) any other sum expressed by this or any other Act to be so enforceable; ...

(2) Except where the contrary is expressed or implied, anything required or authorised by this Act to be done by justices may, where two or more justices are present, be done by one of them on behalf of the others.

(3) Any reference in this Act to a sum adjudged to be paid by a conviction or order of a magistrates' court shall be construed as including a reference to any costs, damages or compensation adjudged to be paid by the conviction or order of which the amount is ascertained by the conviction or order; but this subsection does not prejudice the definition of 'sum adjudged to be paid by a conviction' contained in subsection (8) of section 81 above for the purposes of that section.

(4) Where the age of any person at any time is material for the purposes of any provision of this Act regulating the powers of a magistrates' court, his age at the material time shall be deemed to be or to have been that which appears to the court after considering any available evidence to be or to have been his age at that time ...

SCHEDULE 1

OFFENCES TRIABLE EITHER WAY BY VIRTUE OF SECTION 17

1. Offences at common law of public nuisance.

2. Offences under section 8 of the Disorderly Houses Act 1751 (appearing to be keeper of bawdy houses, etc) ...

5. Offences under the following provisions of the Offences against the Person Act 1861 –

(a) section 16 (threats to kill);

(b) section 20 (inflicting bodily injury, with or without a weapon);

(c) section 26 (not providing apprentices or servants with food, etc);

(d) section 27 (abandoning or exposing child);

(e) section 34 (doing or omitting to do anything so as to endanger railway passengers);

(f) section 36 (assaulting a clergyman at a place of worship, etc);

(g) section 38 (assault with intent to resist apprehension);

(h) section 47 (assault occasioning bodily harm);

(i) section 57 (bigamy);

(j) section 60 (concealing the birth of a child) ...

23 Offences under the following provisions of the Sexual Offences Act 1956 –

(a) section 6 (unlawful sexual intercourse with a girl under 16);

(b) section 13 (indecency between men) ;

(c) section 26 (permitting a girl under 16 to use premises for sexual intercourse) ...

26. The following offences under the Criminal Law Act 1967 –

(a) offences under section 4(1) (assisting offenders); and

(b) offences under section 5(1) (concealing arrestable offences and giving false information),

where the offence to which they relate is triable either way ...

28. All indictable offences under the Theft Act 1968 except: –

(a) robbery, aggravated burglary, blackmail and assault with intent to rob;

(b) burglary comprising the commission of, or an intention to commit, an offence which is triable only on indictment;

(c) burglary in a dwelling if any person in the dwelling was subjected to violence or the threat of violence ...

32 Committing an indecent assault upon a person whether male or female.

33. Aiding, abetting, counselling or procuring the commission of any offence listed in the preceding paragraphs of this Schedule except paragraph 26.

35. Any offence consisting in the incitement to commit an offence triable either way except an offence mentioned in paragraph 33.

SCHEDULE 2

OFFENCES FOR WHICH THE VALUE INVOLVED IS RELEVANT TO THE MODE OF TRIAL

Offence	*Value involved*	*How measured*

1. Offences under section 1 of the Criminal Damage Act 1971 (destroying or damaging property), excluding any offence committed by destroying or damaging property by fire.	As regards property alleged to have been destroyed, its value.
	
	As regards property alleged to have been damaged, the value of the alleged damaged.
		[For property destroyed] What the property would probably have cost to buy in the open market at the material time.
		
		(a) If immediately after the material time the damage was capable of repair –
		
		  (i) what would probably then have been the market price for the repair of the damage, or
		
		  (ii) what the property alleged to have been damaged would probably have cost to buy in the open market at the material time,
		
		whichever is the less; or
		
		(b) if immediately after the material time the damage was beyond repair, what the said property would probably have cost to buy in the open market at the material time.

2. The following offences, namely –

(a) aiding, abetting, counselling or procuring the commission of any offence mentioned in paragraph 1 above;

(b) attempting to commit any offence so mentioned; and

(c) inciting another to commit any offence so mentioned.

The value indicated in paragraph 1 above for the offence alleged to have been aided, abetted, counselled or procured, or attempted or incited.

As for the corresponding entry in paragraph 1 above.

3. Offences under section 12A of the Theft Act 1968 (aggravated vehicle-taking) where no allegation is made under subsection (1)(b) other than of damage, whether to the vehicle or other property or both.

The total value of the damage alleged to have been caused.

(1) In the case of damage to any property other than the vehicle involved in the offence, as for the corresponding entry in paragraph 1 above, substituting a reference to the time of the accident concerned for any reference to the material time.

(2) In the case of damage to the vehicle involved in the offence –

(a) if immediately after the vehicle was recovered the damage was capable of repair –

(i) what would probably then have been the market price for the repair of the damage, or

(ii) what the vehicle would probably have cost to buy in the open market immediately before it was unlawfully taken, which is the less; or

(b) if immediately after the vehicle was recovered the damage was beyond repair, what the vehicle would probably have cost to buy in the open market immediately before it was unlawfully taken.

As amended by the Criminal Justice Act 1982, ss59, 61, 66(2), 77, 78, 79, Schedule 9, para 1(c), Schedule 14, paras 47, 48, 49, 51, Schedule 16, Schedule 17, para 1; Police and Criminal Evidence Act 1984, s47(8)(a); Local Government Act 1985, s12(11); Prosecution of Offences Act 1985, s31(5), Schedule 1, Pt I, para 2; Family Law Reform Act 1987, s33(1), Schedule 2, para 80; Criminal Justice Act 1988, ss38, 61(1), (6), 123(6), 170(1), (2), Schedule 8, Pt I, para 2, Schedule 15, paras 65, 66, 67, Schedule 16; Children Act 1989, ss92(11), 108(7), Schedule 11, Pt II, para 8(c)-(g), Schedule 15; Football Spectators Act 1989, s23(3)(c); Courts and Legal Services Act 1990, s125(3), Schedule 18, para 25(1), (2), (3)(a), (b), 4 (a), (6), (7); Criminal Justice Act 1991, ss17(2)(a), (b), (c), (3)(a), (b), 68, 100, 101(2), Schedule 4, Pts I, II, Schedule 8, para 6(1)(a), (b), (c), 6(2), Schedule 11, paras 25, 26, Schedule 13; Aggravated Vehicle-Taking Act 1992, s2(1), (2), (3).

SUPREME COURT ACT 1981
(1981 c 54)

PART I

CONSTITUTION OF SUPREME COURT

1 The Supreme Court

(1) The Supreme Court of England and Wales shall consist of the Court of Appeal, the High Court of Justice and the Crown Court, each having such jurisdiction as is conferred on it by or under this or any other Act.

(2) The Lord Chancellor shall be president of the Supreme Court.

2 The Court of Appeal

(1) The Court of Appeal shall consist of ex-officio judges and not more than 29 ordinary judges.

(2) The following shall be ex-officio judges of the Court of Appeal –

    (a) the Lord Chancellor;

    (b) any person who has been Lord Chancellor;

    (c) any Lord of Appeal in Ordinary who at the date of his appointment was, or was qualified for appointment as, an ordinary judge of the Court of Appeal or held an office within paragraphs (d) to (g);

    (d) the Lord Chief Justice;

    (e) the Master of the Rolls;

    (f) the President of the Family Division; and

    (g) the Vice-Chancellor;

but a person within paragraph (b) or (c) shall not be required to sit and act as a judge of the Court of Appeal unless at the Lord Chancellor's request he consents to do so.

(3) The ordinary judges of the Court of Appeal (including the vice-president, if any, of either division) shall be styled 'Lords Justices of Appeal'.

(4) Her Majesty may by Order in Council from time to time amend subsection (1) so as to increase or further increase the maximum number of ordinary judges of the Court of Appeal.

(5) No recommendation shall be made to Her Majesty in Council to make an Order under subsection (4) unless a draft of the Order has been laid before Parliament and approved by resolution of each House of Parliament.

(6) The Court of Appeal shall be taken to be duly constituted notwithstanding any vacancy in the office of Lord Chancellor, Lord Chief Justice, Master of the Rolls, President of the Family Division or Vice-Chancellor.

3 Divisions of Court of Appeal

(1) There shall be two divisions of the Court of Appeal, namely the criminal division and the civil division.

(2) The Lord Chief Justice shall be president of the criminal division of the Court of Appeal, and the Master of the Rolls shall be president of the civil division of that court.

(3) The Lord Chancellor may appoint one of the ordinary judges of the Court of Appeal as vice-president of both divisions of that court, or one of those judges as vice-president of the criminal division and another of them as vice-president of the civil division.

(4) When sitting in a court of either division of the Court of Appeal in which no ex-officio judge of the Court of Appeal is sitting, the vice-president (if any) of that division shall preside.

(5) Any number of courts of either division of the Court of Appeal may sit at the same time.

4 The High Court

(1) The High Court shall consist of –

    (a) the Lord Chancellor;
    (b) the Lord Chief Justice;

(c) the President of the Family Division;

(d) the Vice-Chancellor;

(dd) the Senior Presiding Judge; and

(e) not more than 98 puisne judges of the court.

(2) The puisne judges of the High Court shall be styled 'Justices of the High Court'.

(3) All the judges of the High Court shall, except where this Act expressly provides otherwise, have in all respects equal power, authority and jurisdiction.

(4) Her Majesty may by Order in Council from time to time amend subsection (1) so as to increase or further increase the maximum number of puisne judges of the High Court.

(5) No recommendation shall be made to Her Majesty in Council to make an Order under subsection (4) unless a draft of the Order has been laid before Parliament and approved by resolution of each House of Parliament.

(6) The High Court shall be taken to be duly constituted notwithstanding any vacancy in the office of Lord Chancellor, Lord Chief Justice, President of the Family Division, Vice-Chancellor or Senior Presiding Judge.

5   Divisions of High Court

(1) There shall be three divisions of the High Court, namely –

(a) the Chancery Division, consisting of the Lord Chancellor, who shall be president thereof, the Vice-Chancellor, who shall be vice-president thereof, and such of the puisne judges as are for the time being attached thereto in accordance with this section;

(b) the Queen's Bench Division, consisting of the Lord Chief Justice, who shall be president thereof, and such of the puisne judges as are for the time being so attached thereto; and

(c) the Family Division, consisting of the President of the Family Division and such of the puisne judges as are for the time being so attached thereto.

(2) The puisne judges of the High Court shall be attached to the various Divisions by direction of the Lord Chancellor; and any such judge may with his consent be transferred from one Division to another by direction of the Lord Chancellor, but shall be so

transferred only with the concurrence of the senior judge of the Division from which it is proposed to transfer him.

(3) Any judge attached to any Division may act as an additional judge of any other Division at the request of the Lord Chief Justice made with the concurrence of the President of the Family Division or the Vice-Chancellor, or both, as appropriate.

(4) Nothing in this section shall be taken to prevent a judge of any Division (whether nominated under section 6(2) or not) from sitting, whenever required, in a divisional court of another Division or for any judge of another Division.

(5) Without prejudice to the provisions of this Act relating to the distribution of business in the High Court, all jurisdiction vested in the High Court under this Act shall belong to all the Divisions alike.

6   The Patents, Admiralty and Commercial Courts

(1) There shall be –

(a) as part of the Chancery Division, a Patents Court; and

(b) as parts of the Queen's Bench Division, an Admiralty Court and a Commercial Court.

(2) The judges of the Patents Court, of the Admiralty Court and of the Commercial Court shall be such of the puisne judges of the High Court as the Lord Chancellor may from time to time nominate to be judges of the Patents Court, Admiralty Judges and Commercial Judges respectively.

7   Power to alter Divisions or transfer certain courts to different Divisions

(1) Her Majesty may from time to time, on a recommendation of the judges mentioned in subsection (2), by Order in Council direct that –

(a) any increase or reduction in the number of Divisions of the High Court; or

(b) the transfer of any of the courts mentioned in section 6(1) to a different Division,

be carried into effect in pursuance of the recommendation.

(2) Those judges are the Lord Chancellor, the Lord Chief Justice, the Master of the Rolls, the President of the Family Division and the Vice-Chancellor.

(3) An Order in Council under this section may include such incidental, supplementary or consequential provisions as appear to Her Majesty necessary or expedient, including amendments of provisions referring to particular Divisions contained in this Act or any other statutory provision.

(4) Any Order in Council under this section shall be subject to annulment in pursuance of a resolution of either House of Parliament.

8   The Crown Court

(1) The jurisdiction of the Crown Court shall be exercisable by –

(a) any judge of the High Court; or

(b) any Circuit judge or Recorder; or

(c) subject to and in accordance with the provisions of sections 74 and 75(2), a judge of the High Court, Circuit judge or Recorder sitting with not more than four justices of the peace,

and any such persons when exercising the jurisdiction of the Crown Court shall be judges of the Crown Court.

(2) A justice of the peace shall not be disqualified from acting as a judge of the Crown Court for the reason that the proceedings are not at a place within the area for which he was appointed as a justice, or because the proceedings are not related to that area in any other way.

(3) When the Crown Court sits in the City of London it shall be known as the Central Criminal Court; and the Lord Mayor of the City and any Alderman of the City shall be entitled to sit as judges of the Central Criminal Court with any judge of the High Court or any Circuit judge or Recorder.

9   Assistance for transaction of judicial business of Supreme Court

(1) A person within any entry in column 1 of the following Table may at any time, at the request of the appropriate authority, act –

(a) as a judge of a relevant court specified in the request; or

(b) if the request relates to a particular division of a relevant court so specified, as a judge of that court in that division.

TABLE	
1	2
Judge or ex-judge	*Where competent to act on request*
1. A judge of the Court of Appeal.	The High Court and the Crown Court.
2. A person who has been a judge of the Court of Appeal.	The Court of Appeal, the High Court and the Crown Court.
3. A puisne judge of the High Court.	The Court of Appeal.
4. A person who has been a puisne judge of the High Court.	The Court of Appeal, the High Court and the Crown Court.
5. A Circuit judge.	The High Court.
6. A Recorder.	The High Court.

(2) In subsection (1) –

'the appropriate authority' –

(a) in the case of a request to a judge of the High Court to act in the criminal division of the Court of Appeal as a judge of that court, means the Lord Chief Justice or, at any time when the Lord Chief Justice is unable to make such a request himself or there is a vacancy in the office of Lord Chief Justice, the Master of the Rolls;

(b) in any other case means the Lord Chancellor;

'relevant court', in the case of a person within any entry in column 1 of the Table, means a court specified in relation to that entry in column 2 of the Table.

(3) In the case of –

(a) a request under subsection (1) to a Lord Justice of Appeal to act in the High Court; or

(b) any request under that subsection to a puisne judge of the High Court or a Circuit judge,

it shall be the duty of the person to whom the request is made to comply with it.

(4) Without prejudice to section 24 of the Courts Acts 1971 (temporary appointment of deputy Circuit judges and assistant Recorders), if it appears to the Lord Chancellor that it is expedient as a temporary measure to make an appointment under this subsection in order to facilitate the disposal of business in the High Court or the Crown Court, he may appoint a person qualified for appointment as a puisne judge of the High Court to be a deputy judge of the High Court during such period or on such occasions as the Lord Chancellor thinks fit; and during the period or on the occasions for which a person is appointed as a deputy judge under this subsection, he may act as a puisne judge of the High Court.

(5) Every person while acting under this section shall, subject to subsection (6), be treated for all purposes as, and accordingly may perform any of the functions of, a judge of the court in which he is acting.

(6) A person shall not by virtue of subsection (5) –

(a) be treated as a judge of the court in which he is acting for the purposes of section 98(2) or of any statutory provision relating to –

(i) the appointment, retirement, removal or disqualification of judges of that court;

(ii) the tenure of office and oaths to be taken by such judges; or

(iii) the remuneration, allowances or pensions of such judges; or

(b) subject to subsection (7), be treated as having been a judge of a court in which he has acted only under this section.

(7) Notwithstanding the expiry of any period for which a person is authorised by virtue of subsection (1) or (4) to act as a judge of a particular court –

(a) he may attend at that court for the purpose of continuing to deal with, giving judgment in, or dealing with any ancillary matter relating to, any case begun before him while acting as a judge of that court; and

(b) for that purpose, and for the purpose of any proceedings arising out of any such case or matter, he shall be treated as being or, as the case may be, having been a judge of that court.

(8) Such remuneration and allowances as the Lord Chancellor may, with the concurrence of the Minister for the Civil Service, determine may be paid out of money provided by Parliament –

(a) to any person who has been –

(i) a Lord of Appeal in Ordinary; or
(ii) a judge of the Court of Appeal; or
(iii) a judge of the High Court,

and is by virtue of subsection (1) acting as mentioned in that subsection;

(b) to any deputy judge of the High Court appointed under subsection (4).

10 Appointment of judges of Supreme Court

(1) Whenever the office of Lord Chief Justice, Master of the Rolls, President of the Family Division or Vice-Chancellor is vacant, Her Majesty may by letters patent appoint a qualified person to that office.

(2) Subject to the limits on numbers for the time being imposed by sections 2(1) and 4(1), Her Majesty may from time to time by letters patent appoint qualified persons as Lord Justices of Appeal or as puisne judges of the High Court.

(3) No person shall be qualified for appointment –

(a) as Lord Chief Justice, Master of the Rolls, President of the Family Division or Vice-Chancellor, unless he is qualified for appointment as a Lord Justice of Appeal or is a judge of the Court of Appeal;

(b) as a Lord Justice of Appeal, unless –

(i) he has a ten year High Court qualification within the meaning of section 71 of the Courts and Legal Services Act 1990; or
(ii) he is a judge of the High Court; or

(c) as a puisne judge of the High Court, unless –

(i) he has a ten year High Court qualification within the meaning of section 71 of the Courts and Legal Services Act 1990; or

(ii) he is a Circuit judge who has held that office for at least two years.

(4) Every person appointed to an office mentioned in subsection (1) or as a Lord Justice of Appeal or puisne judge of the High Court shall, as soon as may be after his acceptance of office, take the oath of allegiance and the judicial oath, as set out in the Promissory Oaths Act 1868, in the presence of the Lord Chancellor.

11   Tenure of office of judges of Supreme Court

(1) This section applies to the office of any judge of the Supreme Court except the Lord Chancellor.

(2) A person appointed to an office to which this section applies shall vacate it on the day on which he attains the age of 75 years unless by virtue of this section he has ceased to hold it before then.

(3) A person appointed to an office to which this section applies shall hold that office during good behaviour, subject to a power of removal by Her Majesty on an address presented to Her by both Houses of Parliament.

(4) A person holding an office within section 2(2)(d) to (g) shall vacate that office on becoming Lord Chancellor or a Lord of Appeal in Ordinary.

(5) A Lord Justice of Appeal shall vacate that office on becoming an ex-officio judge of the Court of Appeal.

(6) A puisne judge of the High Court shall vacate that office on becoming a judge of the Court of Appeal.

(7) A person who holds an office to which this section applies may at any time resign it by giving the Lord Chancellor notice in writing to that effect.

(8) The Lord Chancellor, if satisfied by means of a medical certificate that a person holding an office to which this section applies –

(a) is disabled by permanent infirmity from the performance of the duties of his office; and

(b) is for the time being incapacitated from resigning his office, may, subject to subsection (9), by instrument under his hand declare that person's office to have been vacated; and the instrument shall have the like effect for all purposes as if that person had on the date of the instrument resigned his office.

(9) A declaration under subsection (8) with respect to a person shall be of no effect unless it is made –

(a) in the case of any of the Lord Chief Justice, the Master of the Rolls, the President of the Family Division and the Vice-Chancellor, with the concurrence of two others of them;

(b) in the case of a Lord Justice of Appeal, with the concurrence of the Master of the Rolls;

(c) in the case of a puisne judge of any Division of the High Court, with the concurrence of the senior judge of that Division.

13   Precedence of judges of Supreme Court

(1) When sitting in the Court of Appeal –

(a) the Lord Chief Justice and the Master of the Rolls shall rank in that order; and

(b) Lords of Appeal in Ordinary and persons who have been Lord Chancellor shall rank next after the Master of the Rolls and, among themselves, according to the priority of the dates on which they respectively became Lords of Appeal in Ordinary or Lord Chancellor, as the case may be.

(2) Subject to subjection (1)(b), the President of the Family Division shall rank next after the Master of the Rolls.

(3) The Vice-Chancellor shall rank next after the President of the Family Division.

(4) The vice-president or vice-presidents of the divisions of the Court of Appeal shall rank next after the Vice-Chancellor; and if there are two vice-presidents of those divisions, they shall rank, among themselves, according to the priority of the dates on which they respectively became vice-presidents.

(5) The Lord Justices of Appeal (other than the vice-president or vice-presidents of the divisions of the Court of Appeal) shall rank after the ex-officio judges of the Court of Appeal and, among themselves, according to the priority of the dates on which they respectively became judges of that court.

(6) The puisne judges of the High Court shall rank next after the judges of the Court of Appeal and, among themselves, according to the priority of the dates on which they respectively became judges of the High Court.

14 Power of judges of Supreme or Crown Court to act in cases relating to rates and taxes

(1) A judge of the Supreme Court or of the Crown Court shall not be incapable of acting as such in any proceedings by reason of being, as one of a class of ratepayers, taxpayers, or persons of any other description, liable in common with others to pay, or contribute to, or benefit from, any rate or tax which may be increased, reduced or in any way affected by those proceedings.

(2) In this section 'rate or tax' means any rate, tax, duty or liability, whether public, general or local, and includes –

(a) any fund formed from the proceeds of any such rate, tax, duty or liability; and

(b) any fund applicable for purposes the same as, or similar to, those for which the proceeds of any such rate, tax, duty or liability are or might be applied.

PART II

JURISDICTION

THE COURT OF APPEAL

15 General jurisdiction of Court of Appeal

(1) The Court of Appeal shall be a superior court of record.

(2) Subject to the provisions of this Act, there shall be exercisable by the Court of Appeal –

(a) all such jurisdiction (whether civil or criminal) as is conferred on it by this or any other Act; and

(b) all such other jurisdiction (whether civil or criminal) as was exercisable by it immediately before the commencement of this Act.

(3) For all purposes of or incidental to –

(a) the hearing and determination of any appeal to the civil division of the Court of Appeal; and

(b) the amendment, execution and enforcement of any judgment or order made on such an appeal,

the Court of Appeal shall have all the authority and jurisdiction of the court or tribunal from which the appeal was brought.

(4) It is hereby declared that any provision in this or any other Act which authorises or requires the taking of any steps for the execution or enforcement of a judgment or order of the High Court applies in relation to a judgment or order of the civil division of the Court of Appeal as it applies in relation to a judgment or order of the High Court.

16 Appeals from High Court

(1) Subject as otherwise provided by this or any other Act (and in particular to the provision in section 13(2)(a) of the Administration of Justice Act 1969 excluding appeals to the Court of Appeal in cases where leave to appeal from the High Court directly to the House of Lords is granted under Part II of that Act), the Court of Appeal shall have jurisdiction to hear and determine appeals from any judgment or order of the High Court.

(2) An appeal from a judgment or order of the High Court when acting as a prize court shall not be to the Court of Appeal, but shall be to Her Majesty in Council in accordance with the Prize Acts 1864 to 1944.

17 Applications for new trial

(1) Where any cause or matter, or any issue in any cause or matter, has been tried in the High Court, any application for a new trial thereof, or to set aside a verdict, finding or judgment therein, shall be heard and determined by the Court of Appeal except where rules of court made in pursuance of subsection (2) provide otherwise.

(2) As regards cases where the trial was by a judge alone and no error of the court at the trial is alleged, or any prescribed class of such cases, rules of court may provide that any such application as is mentioned in subsection (1) shall be heard and determined by the High Court.

(3) Nothing in this section shall alter the practice in bankruptcy.

18   Restrictions on appeals to Court of Appeal

(1) No appeal shall lie to the Court of Appeal –

(a) except as provided by the Administration of Justice Act 1960, from any judgment of the High Court in any criminal cause or matter;

(b) from any order of the High Court or any other court or tribunal allowing an extension of time for appealing from a judgment or order;

(c) from any order, judgment or decision of the High Court or any other court or tribunal which, by virtue of any provision (however expressed) of this or any other Act, is final;

(d) from a decree absolute of divorce or nullity of marriage, by a party who, having had time and opportunity to appeal from the decree nisi on which that decree was founded, has not appealed from the decree nisi;

(g) except as provided by the Arbitration Act 1979, from any decision of the High Court –

(i) on an appeal under section 1 of that Act on a question of law arising out of an arbitration award; or

(ii) under section 2 of that Act on a question of law arising in the course of a reference.

(1A) In any such class of case as may be prescribed by Rules of the Supreme Court, an appeal shall lie to the Court of Appeal only with the leave of the Court of Appeal or such court or tribunal as may be specified by the rules in relation to that class.

(1B) Any enactment which authorises leave to appeal to the Court of Appeal being given by a single judge, or by a court consisting of two judges, shall have effect subject to any provision which –

(a) is made by Rules of the Supreme Court; and

(b) in such classes of case as may be prescribed by the rules, requires leave to be given by such greater number of judges (not exceeding three) as may be so specified.

THE HIGH COURT

19   General jurisdiction

(1) The High Court shall be a superior court of record.

(2) Subject to the provisions of this Act, there shall be exercisable by the High Court –

(a) all such jurisdiction (whether civil or criminal) as is conferred on it by this or any other Act; and

(b) all such other jurisdiction (whether civil or criminal) as was exercisable by it immediately before the commencement of this Act (including jurisdiction conferred on a judge of the High Court by any statutory provision).

(3) Any jurisdiction of the High Court shall be exercised only by a single judge of that court, except in so far as it is –

(a) by or by virtue of rules of court or any other statutory provision required to be exercised by a divisional court; or

(b) by rules of court made exercisable by a master, registrar or other officer of the court, or by any other person.

(4) The specific mention elsewhere in this Act of any jurisdiction covered by subsection (2) shall not derogate from the generality of that subsection.

20 Admiralty jurisdiction of High Court

(1) The Admiralty jurisdiction of the High Court shall be as follows, that is to say –

(a) jurisdiction to hear and determine any of the questions and claims mentioned in subsection (2);

(b) jurisdiction in relation to any of the proceedings mentioned in subsection (3);

(c) any other Admiralty jurisdiction which it had immediately before the commencement of this Act; and

(d) any jurisdiction connected with ships or aircraft which is vested in the High Court apart from this section and is for the time being by rules of court made or coming into force after the commencement of this Act assigned to the Queen's Bench Division and directed by the rules to be exercised by the Admiralty Court.

(2) The questions and claims referred to in subsection (1)(a) are –

(a) any claim to the possession or ownership of a ship or to the ownership of any share therein;

(b) any question arising between the co-owners of a ship as to possession, employment or earnings of that ship;

(c) any claim in respect of a mortgage of or charge on a ship or any share therein;

(d) any claim for damage received by a ship;

(e) any claim for damage done by a ship;

(f) any claim for loss of life or personal injury sustained in consequence of any defect in a ship or in her apparel or equipment, or in consequence of the wrongful act, neglect or default of –

(i) the owners, charterers or persons in possession or control of a ship; or

(ii) the master or crew of a ship, or any other person for whose wrongful acts, neglects or defaults the owners, charterers or persons in possession or control of a ship are responsible,

being an act, neglect or default in the navigation or management of the ship, in the loading, carriage or discharge of goods on, in or from the ship, or in the embarkation, carriage or disembarkation of persons on, in or from the ship; ...

(3) The proceedings referred to in subsection (1)(b) are –

(a) any application to the High Court under the Merchant Shipping Acts 1894 to 1979 other than an application under section 55 of the Merchant Shipping Act 1894 for the appointment of a person to act as a substitute for a person incapable of acting;

(b) any action to enforce a claim for damage, loss of life or personal injury arising out of –

(i) a collision between ships; or

(ii) the carrying out of or omission to carry out a manoeuvre in the case of one or more of two or more ships; or

(iii) non-compliance, on the part of one or more of two or more ships, with the collision regulations;

(c) any action by shipowners or other persons under the Merchant Shipping Acts 1894 to 1979 for the limitation of the amount of their liability in connection with a ship or other property.

(4) The jurisdiction of the High Court under subsection (2)(b) includes power to settle any account outstanding and unsettled

between the parties in relation to the ship, and to direct that the ship, or any share thereof, shall be sold, and to make such other order as the court thinks fit.

(5) Subsection (2)(e) extends to –

(a) any claim in respect of a liability incurred under the Merchant Shipping (Oil Pollution) Act 1971; and

(b) any claim in respect of a liability falling on the International Oil Pollution Compensation Fund, or on the International Oil Pollution Compensation Fund 1984, under Part I of the Merchant Shipping Act 1974 ...

25 Probate jurisdiction of High Court

(1) Subject to the provisions of Part V, the High Court shall, in accordance with section 19(2), have the following probate jurisdiction, that is to say all such jurisdiction in relation to probates and letters of administration as it had immediately before the commencement of this Act, and in particular all such contentious and non-contentious jurisdiction as it then had in relation to –

(a) testamentary causes or matters;

(b) the grant, amendment or revocation of probates and letters of administration; and

(c) the real and personal estate of deceased persons.

(2) Subject to the provisions of Part V, the High Court shall, in the exercise of its probate jurisdiction, perform all such duties with respect to the estates of deceased persons as fell to be performed by it immediately before the commencement of this Act.

26 Matrimonial jurisdiction of High Court

The High Court shall, in accordance with section 19(2), have all such jurisdiction in relation to matrimonial causes and matters as was immediately before the commencement of the Matrimonial Causes Act 1857 vested in or exercisable by any ecclesiastical court or person in England or Wales in respect of –

(a) divorce a mensa et thoro (renamed judicial separation by that Act);

(b) nullity of marriage; and

(c) any matrimonial cause or matter except marriage licences.

27 Prize jurisdiction of High Court

The High Court shall, in accordance with section 19(2), have as a prize court –

(a) all such jurisdiction as is conferred on it by the Prize Acts 1864 to 1944 (in which references to the High Court of Admiralty are by virtue of paragraph 1 of Schedule 4 to this Act to be construed as references to the High Court); and

(b) all such other jurisdiction on the high seas and elsewhere as it had as a prize court immediately before the commencement of this Act.

28 Appeals from Crown Court and inferior courts

(1) Subject to subsection (2), any order, judgment or other decision of the Crown Court may be questioned by any party to the proceedings, on the ground that it is wrong in law or is in excess of jurisdiction, by applying to the Crown Court to have a case stated by that court for the opinion of the High Court.

(2) Subsection (1) shall not apply to –

(a) a judgment or other decision of the Crown Court relating to trial on indictment; or

(b) any decision of that court under the Betting, Gaming and Lotteries Act 1963, the Licensing Act 1964, the Gaming Act 1968 or the Local Government (Miscellaneous Provisions) Act 1982 which, by any provision of any of those Acts, is to be final.

(3) Subject to the provisions of this Act and to rules of court, the High Court shall, in accordance with section 19(2), have jurisdiction to hear and determine –

(a) any application, or any appeal (whether by way of case stated or otherwise), which it has power to hear and determine under or by virtue of this or any other Act; and

(b) all such other appeals as it had jurisdiction to hear and determine immediately before the commencement of this Act.

29 Orders of mandamus, prohibition and certiorari

(1) The High Court shall have jurisdiction to make orders of mandamus, prohibition and certiorari in those classes of cases in

which it had power to do so immediately before the commencement of this Act.

(2) Every such order shall be final, subject to any right of appeal therefrom.

(3) In relation to the jurisdiction of the Crown Court, other than its jurisdiction in matters relating to trial on indictment, the High Court shall have all such jurisdiction to make orders of mandamus, prohibition or certiorari as the High Court possesses in relation to the jurisdiction of an inferior court.

(4) The power of the High Court under any enactment to require justices of the peace or a judge or officer of a county court to do any act relating to the duties of their respective offices, or to require a magistrates' court to state a case for the opinion of the High Court, in any case where the High Court formerly had by virtue of any enactment jurisdiction to make a rule absolute, or an order, for any of those purposes, shall be exercisable by order of mandamus ...

30 Injunctions to restrain persons from acting in offices in which they are not entitled to act

(1) Where a person not entitled to do so acts in an office to which this section applies, the High Court may –

(a) grant an injunction restraining him from so acting; and

(b) if the case so requires, declare the office to be vacant.

(2) This section applies to any substantive office of a public nature and permanent character which is held under the Crown or which has been created by any statutory provision or royal charter.

31 Application for judicial review

(1) An application to the High Court for one or more of the following forms of relief, namely –

(a) an order of mandamus, prohibition or certiorari;

(b) a declaration or injunction under subsection (2); or

(c) an injunction under section 30 restraining a person not entitled to do so from acting in an office to which that section applies, shall be made in accordance with rules of court by a procedure to be known as an application for judicial review.

(2) A declaration may be made or an injunction granted under this subsection in any case where an application for judicial review, seeking that relief, has been made and the High Court considers that, having regard to –

(a) the nature of the matters in respect of which relief may be granted by orders of mandamus, prohibition or certiorari;

(b) the nature of the persons and bodies against whom relief may be granted by such orders; and

(c) all the circumstances of the case,

it would be just and convenient for the declaration to be made or the injunction to be granted, as the case may be.

(3) No application for judicial review shall be made unless the leave of the High Court has been obtained in accordance with rules of court; and the court shall not grant leave to make such an application unless it considers that the applicant has a sufficient interest in the matter to which the application relates.

(4) On an application for judicial review the High Court may award damages to the applicant if –

(a) he has joined with his application a claim for damages arising from any matter to which the application relates; and

(b) the court is satisfied that, if the claim had been made in an action begun by the applicant at the time of making his application, he would have been awarded damages.

(5) If, on an application for judicial review seeking an order of certiorari, the High Court quashes the decision to which the application relates, the High Court may remit the matter to the court, tribunal or authority concerned, with a direction to reconsider it and reach a decision in accordance with the findings of the High Court.

(6) Where the High Court considers that there has been undue delay in making an application for judicial review, the court may refuse to grant –

(a) leave for the making of the application; or

(b) any relief sought on the application,

if it considers that the granting of the relief sought would be likely to cause substantial hardship to, or substantially prejudice the rights of, any person or would be detrimental to good administration.

(7) Subsection (6) is without prejudice to any enactment or rule of court which has the effect of limiting the time within which an application for judicial review may be made.

32   Orders for interim payment

(1) As regards proceedings pending in the High Court, provision may be made by rules of court for enabling the court, in such circumstances as may be prescribed, to make an order requiring a party to the proceedings to make an interim payment of such amount as may be specified in the order, with provision for the payment to be made to such other party to the proceedings as may be so specified or, if the order so provides, by paying it into court.

(2) Any rules of court which make provision in accordance with subsection (1) may include provision for enabling a party to any proceedings who, in pursuance of such an order, has made an interim payment to recover the whole or part of the amount of the payment in such circumstances, and from such other party to the proceedings, as may be determined in accordance with the rules ...

(5) In this section 'interim payment', in relation to a party to any proceedings, means a payment on account of any damages, debt or other sum (excluding any costs) which that party may be held liable to pay to or for the benefit of another party to the proceedings if a final judgment or order of the court in the proceedings is given or made in favour of that other party.

32A Orders for provisional damages for personal injuries

(1) This section applies to an action for damages for personal injuries in which there is proved or admitted to be a chance that at some definite or indefinite time in the future the injured person will, as a result of the act or omission which gave rise to the cause of action, develop some serious disease or suffer serious deterioration in his physical or mental condition.

(2) Subject to subsection (4) below, as regards any action for damages to which this section applies in which a judgment is given

in the High Court, provision may be made by rules of court for enabling the court, in such circumstances as may be prescribed, to award the injured person –

(a) damages assessed on the assumption that the injured person will not develop the disease or suffer the deterioration in his condition; and

(b) further damages at a future date if he develops the disease or suffers the deterioration.

(3) Any rules made by virtue of this section may include such incidental, supplementary and consequential provisions as the rule-making authority may consider necessary or expedient.

(4) Nothing in this section shall be construed –

(a) as affecting the exercise of any power relating to costs, including any power to make rules of court relating to costs; or

(b) as prejudicing any duty of the court under any enactment or rule of law to reduce or limit the total damages which would have been recoverable apart from any such duty.

35A Power of High Court to award interest on debts and damages

(1) Subject to rules of court, in proceedings (whenever instituted) before the High Court for the recovery of a debt or damages there may be included in any sum for which judgment is given simple interest, at such rate as the court thinks fit or as rules of court may provide, on all or any part of the debt or damages in respect of which judgment is given, or payment is made before judgment, for all or any part of the period between the date when the cause of action arose and –

(a) in the case of any sum paid before judgment, the date of the payment; and

(b) in the case of the sum for which judgment is given, the date of the judgment.

(2) In relation to a judgment given for damages for personal injuries or death which exceed £200 subsection (1) shall have effect –

(a) with the substitution of 'shall be included' for 'may be included'; and

(b) with the addition of 'unless the court is satisfied that there are special reasons to the contrary' after 'given', where first occurring.

(3) Subject to rules of court, where –

(a) there are proceedings (whenever instituted) before the High Court for the recovery of a debt; and

(b) the defendant pays the whole debt to the plaintiff (otherwise than in pursuance of a judgment in the proceedings),

the defendant shall be liable to pay the plaintiff simple interest at such rate as the court thinks fit or as rules of court may provide on all or any part of the debt for all or any part of the period between the date when the cause of action arose and the date of the payment.

(4) Interest in respect of a debt shall not be awarded under this section for a period during which, for whatever reason, interest on the debt already runs.

(5) Without prejudice to the generality of section 84, rules of court may provide for a rate of interest by reference to the rate specified in section 17 of the Judgments Act 1838 as that section has effect from time to time or by reference to a rate for which any other enactment provides.

(6) Interest under this section may be calculated at different rates in respect of different periods.

(7) In this section 'plaintiff' means the person seeking the debt or damages and 'defendant' means the person from whom the plaintiff seeks the debt or damages and 'personal injuries' includes any disease and any impairment of a person's physical or mental condition.

(8) Nothing in this section affects the damages recoverable for the dishonour of a bill of exchange.

37 Powers of High Court with respect to injunctions and receivers

(1) The High Court may by order (whether interlocutory or final) grant an injunction or appoint a receiver in all cases in which it appears to the court to be just and convenient to do so.

(2) Any such order may be made either unconditionally or on such terms and conditions as the court thinks just.

(3) The power of the High Court under subsection (1) to grant an interlocutory injunction restraining a party to any proceedings from removing from the jurisdiction of the High Court, or otherwise dealing with, assets located within that jurisdiction shall be exercisable in cases where that party is, as well as in cases where he is not, domiciled, resident or present within that jurisdiction.

(4) The power of the High Court to appoint a receiver by way of equitable execution shall operate in relation to all legal estates and interests in land; and that power –

(a) may be exercised in relation to an estate or interest in land whether or not a charge has been imposed on that land under section 1 of the Charging Orders Act 1979 for the purpose of enforcing the judgment, order or award in question; and

(b) shall be in addition to, and not in derogation of, any power of any court to appoint a receiver in proceedings for enforcing such a charge.

(5) Where an order under the said section 1 imposing a charge for the purpose of enforcing a judgment, order or award has been, or has effect as if, registered under section 6 of the Land Charges Act 1972, subsection (4) of the said section 6 (effect of non-registration of writs and orders registrable under that section) shall not apply to an order appointing a receiver made either –

(a) in proceedings for enforcing the charge; or

(b) by way of equitable execution of the judgment, order or award or, as the case may be, of so much of it as requires payment of moneys secured by the charge.

42   Restriction of vexatious legal proceedings

(1) If, on an application made by the Attorney General under this section, the High Court is satisfied that any person has habitually and persistently and without any reasonable ground –

(a) instituted vexatious civil proceedings, whether in the High Court or any inferior court, and whether against the same person or against different persons; or

(b) made vexatious applications in any civil proceedings, whether in the High Court or any inferior court, and whether instituted by him or another; or

(c) instituted vexatious prosecutions (whether against the same person or different persons),

the court may, after hearing that person or giving him an opportunity of being heard, make a civil proceedings order, a criminal proceedings order or an all proceedings order.

(1A) In this section –

'civil proceedings order' means an order that –

(a) no civil proceedings shall without the leave of the High Court be instituted in any court by the person against whom the order is made;

(b) any civil proceedings instituted by him in any court before the making of the order shall not be continued by him without the leave of the High Court; and

(c) no application (other than one for leave under this section) shall be made by him, in any civil proceedings instituted in any court by any person, without the leave of the High Court;

'criminal proceedings order' means that an order that –

(a) no information shall be laid before a justice of the peace by the person against whom the order is made without the leave of the High Court; and

(b) no application for leave to prefer a bill of indictment shall be made by him without the leave of the High Court; and

'all proceedings order' means an order which has the combined effect of the two other orders.

(2) An order under subsection (1) may provide that it is to cease to have effect at the end of a specified period, but shall otherwise remain in force indefinitely.

(3) Leave for the institution or continuance of, or for the making of an application in, any civil proceedings by a person who is the subject of an order for the time being in force under subsection (1) shall not be given unless the High Court is satisfied that the proceedings or application are not an abuse of the process of the court in question and that there are reasonable grounds for the proceedings or application.

(3A) Leave for the laying of an information or for an application for leave to prefer a bill of indictment by a person who is the subject of an order for the time being in force under subsection (1) shall not be given unless the High Court is satisfied that the institution of the prosecution is not an abuse of the criminal process and that there are reasonable grounds for the institution of the prosecution by the applicant.

(4) No appeal shall lie from a decision of the High Court refusing leave required by virtue of this section.

(5) A copy of any order made under subsection (1) shall be published in the London Gazette.

THE CROWN COURT

45 General jurisdiction of Crown Court

(1) The Crown Court shall be a superior court of record.

(2) Subject to the provisions of this Act, there shall be exercisable by the Crown Court –

(a) all such appellate and other jurisdiction as is conferred on it by or under this or any other Act; and

(b) all such other jurisdiction as was exercisable by it immediately before the commencement of this Act.

(3) Without prejudice to subsection (2), the jurisdiction of the Crown Court shall include all such powers and duties as were exercisable or fell to be performed by it immediately before the commencement of this Act.

(4) Subject to section 8 of the Criminal Procedure (Attendance of Witnesses) Act 1965 (substitution in criminal cases of procedure in that Act for procedure by way of subpoena) and to any provision contained in or having effect under this Act, the Crown Court shall, in relation to the attendance and examination of witnesses, any contempt of court, the enforcement of its orders and all other matters incidental to its jurisdiction, have the like powers, rights, privileges and authority as the High Court.

(5) The specific mention elsewhere in this Act of any jurisdiction covered by subsections (2) and (3) shall not derogate from the generality of those subsections.

46 Exclusive jurisdiction of Crown Court in trial on indictment

(1) All proceedings on indictment shall be brought before the Crown Court.

(2) The jurisdiction of the Crown Court with respect to proceedings on indictment shall include jurisdiction in proceedings on indictment for offences wherever committed, and in particular proceedings on indictment for offences within the jurisdiction of the Admiralty of England.

48 Appeals to Crown Court

(1) The Crown Court may, in the course of hearing any appeal, correct any error or mistake in the order or judgment incorporating the decision which is the subject of the appeal.

(2) On the termination of the hearing of an appeal the Crown Court –

(a) may confirm, reverse or vary any part of the decision appealed against, including a determination not to impose a separate penalty in respect of an offence; or

(b) may remit the matter with its opinion thereon to the authority whose decision is appealed against; or

(c) may make such other order in the matter as the court thinks just, and by such order exercise any power which the said authority might have exercised.

(3) Subsection (2) has effect subject to any enactment relating to any such appeal which expressly limits or restricts the powers of the court on the appeal.

(4) If the appeal is against a conviction or a sentence, the preceding provisions of this section shall be construed as including power to award any punishment, whether more or less severe than that awarded by the magistrates' court whose decision is appealed against, if that is a punishment which that magistrates' court might have awarded.

(5) This section applies whether or not the appeal is against the whole of the decision.

(6) In this section 'sentence' includes any order made by a court when dealing with an offender, including –

(a) a hospital order under Part III of the Mental Health Act 1983, with or without a restriction order, and an interim hospital order under that Act; and

(b) a recommendation for deportation made when dealing with an offender ...

GENERAL PROVISIONS

49   Concurrent administration of law and equity

(1) Subject to the provisions of this or any other Act, every court exercising jurisdiction in England or Wales in any civil cause or matter shall continue to administer law and equity on the basis that, wherever there is any conflict or variance between the rules of equity and the rules of common law with reference to the same matter, the rules of equity shall prevail.

(2) Every such court shall give the same effect as hitherto –

(a) to all equitable estates, titles, rights, reliefs, defences and counterclaims, and to all equitable duties and liabilities; and

(b) subject thereto, to all legal claims and demands and all estates, titles, rights, duties, obligations and liabilities existing by the common law or by any custom or created by any statute,

and, subject to the provisions of this or any other Act, shall so exercise its jurisdiction in every cause or matter before it as to secure that, as far as possible, all matters in dispute between the parties are completely and finally determined, and all multiplicity of legal proceedings with respect to any of those matters is avoided.

(3) Nothing in this Act shall affect the power of the Court of Appeal or the High Court to stay any proceedings before it, where it thinks fit to do so, either of its own motion or on the application of any person, whether or not a party to the proceedings.

50   Power to award damages as well as, or in substitution for, injunction or specific performance

Where the Court of Appeal or the High Court has jurisdiction to entertain an application for an injunction or specific performance, it may award damages in addition to, or in substitution for, an injunction or specific performance.

51 Costs in civil division of Court of Appeal, High Court and county courts

(1) Subject to the provisions of this or any other enactment and to rules of court, the costs of and incidental to all proceedings in –

(a) the civil division of the Court of Appeal;

(b) the High Court; and

(c) any county court,

shall be in the discretion of the court.

(2) Without prejudice to any general power to make rules of court, such rules may make provision for regulating matters relating to the costs of those proceedings including, in particular, prescribing scales of costs to be paid to legal or other representatives.

(3) The court shall have full power to determine by whom and to what extent the costs are to be paid.

(4) In subsections (1) and (2) 'proceedings' includes the administration of estates and trusts.

(5) Nothing in subsection (1) shall alter the practice in any criminal cause, or in bankruptcy.

(6) In any proceedings mentioned in subsection (1), the court may disallow, or (as the case may be) order the legal or other representative concerned to meet, the whole of any wasted costs or such part of them as may be determined in accordance with rules of court.

(7) In subsection (6), 'wasted costs' means any costs incurred by a party –

(a) as a result of any improper, unreasonable or negligent act or omission on the part of any legal or other representative or any employee of such a representative; or

(b) which, in the light of any such act or omission occurring after they were incurred, the court considers it is unreasonable to expect that party to pay.

(8) Where –

(a) a person has commenced proceedings in the High Court; but

(b) those proceedings should, in the opinion of the court, have been commenced in a county court in accordance with any provision made under section 1 of the Courts and Legal Services Act 1990 or by or under any other enactment,

the person responsible for determining the amount which is to be awarded to that person by way of costs shall have regard to those circumstances.

(9) Where, in complying with subsection (8), the responsible person reduces the amount which would otherwise be awarded to the person in question –

(a) the amount of that reduction shall not exceed 25 per cent; and

(b) on any taxation of the costs payable by that person to his legal representative, regard shall be had to the amount of the reduction.

(10) The Lord Chancellor may by order amend subsection (9)(a) by substituting, for the percentage for the time being mentioned there, a different percentage.

(11) Any such order shall be made by statutory instrument and may make such transitional or incidental provision as the Lord Chancellor considers expedient.

(12) No such statutory instrument shall be made unless a draft of the instrument has been approved by both Houses of Parliament.

(13) In this section 'legal or other representative', in relation to a party to proceedings, means any person exercising a right of audience or right to conduct litigation on his behalf.

PART III

PRACTICE AND PROCEDURE

THE COURT OF APPEAL

53 Distribution of business between civil and criminal divisions

(1) Rules of court may provide for the distribution of business in the Court of Appeal between the civil and criminal divisions, but subject to any such rules business shall be distributed in accordance with the following provisions of this section.

(2) The criminal division of the Court of Appeal shall exercise –

(a) all jurisdiction of the Court of Appeal under Parts I and II of the Criminal Appeal Act 1968;

(b) the jurisdiction of the Court of Appeal under section 13 of the Administration of Justice Act 1960 (appeals in cases of contempt of court) in relation to appeals from orders and decisions of the Crown Court;

(c) all other jurisdiction expressly conferred on that division by this or any other Act; and

(d) the jurisdiction to order the issue of writs of venire de novo.

(3) The civil division of the Court of Appeal shall exercise the whole of the jurisdiction of that court not exercisable by the criminal division.

(4) Where any class of proceedings in the Court of Appeal is by any statutory provision assigned to the criminal division of that court, rules of court may provide for any enactment relating to –

(a) appeals to the Court of Appeal under Part I of the Criminal Appeal Act 1968; or

(b) any matter connected with or arising out of such appeals,

to apply in relation to proceedings of that class or, as the case may be, to any corresponding matter connected with or arising out of such proceedings, as it applies in relation to such appeals or, as the case may be, to the relevant matter within paragraph (b), with or without prescribed modifications in either case.

54   Court of civil division

(1) This section relates to the civil division of the Court of Appeal; and in this section 'court', except where the context otherwise requires, means a court of that division.

(2) A court shall be duly constituted for the purpose of exercising any of its jurisdiction if it consists of an uneven number of judges not less than three.

(3) Where –

(a) part of any proceedings before a court has been heard by an uneven number of judges greater than three; and

(b) one or more members of the court are unable to continue,

the court shall remain duly constituted for the purpose of those proceedings so long as the number of members (whether even or uneven) is not reduced to less than three.

(4) A court shall, if it consists of two judges, be duly constituted for the purpose of –

(a) hearing and determining any appeal against an interlocutory order or interlocutory judgment;

(aa) hearing and determining any application for leave to appeal;

(b) hearing and determining any appeal against a decision of a single judge acting by virtue of section 58(1);

(c) hearing and determining any appeal where all the parties have before the hearing filed a consent to the appeal being heard and determined by two judges;

(d) hearing the remainder of, and determining, any appeal where part of it has been heard by three or more judges of whom one or more are unable to continue and all the parties have consented to the remainder of the appeal being heard, and the appeal being determined, by two remaining judges; or

(e) hearing and determining an appeal of any such description or in any such circumstances not covered by paragraphs (a) to (d) as may be prescribed for the purposes of this subsection by an order made by the Lord Chancellor with the concurrence of the Master of the Rolls.

(5) Where –

(a) an appeal has been heard by a court consisting of an even number of judges; and

(b) the members of the court are equally divided,

the case shall, on the application of any party to the appeal, be re-argued before and determined by an uneven number of judges not less than three, before any appeal to the House of Lords.

(6) An application to the civil division of the Court of Appeal for leave to appeal to that court may be determined by a single judge of that court, and no appeal shall lie from a decision of a single judge acting under this subsection.

(7) In any cause or matter pending before the civil division of the Court of Appeal a single judge of that court may at any time during

vacation make an interim order to prevent prejudice to the claims of any parties pending an appeal ...

55 Court of criminal division

(1) This section relates to the criminal division of the Court of Appeal; and in this section 'court' means a court of that division.

(2) A court shall be duly constituted for the purpose of exercising any of its jurisdiction if it consists of an uneven number of judges not less than three.

(3) Where –

(a) part of any proceedings before a court has been heard by an uneven number of judges greater than three; and

(b) one or more members of the court are unable to continue,

the court shall remain duly constituted for the purpose of those proceedings so long as the number of members (whether even or uneven) is not reduced to less than three.

(4) A court shall, if it consists of two judges, be duly constituted for every purpose except –

(a) determining an appeal against –

(i) conviction; or

(ii) a verdict of not guilty by reason of insanity; or

(iii) a finding of a jury under section 4 of the Criminal Procedure (Insanity) Act 1964 (unfitness to plead) that a person is under a disability;

(aa) reviewing sentencing under Part IV of the Criminal Justice Act 1988;

(b) determining an application for leave to appeal to the House of Lords; and

(c) refusing an application for leave to appeal to the criminal division against conviction or any such verdict or finding as is mentioned in paragraph (a)(ii) or (iii), other than an application which has been refused by a single judge.

(5) Where an appeal has been heard by a court consisting of an even number of judges and the members of the court are equally divided, the case shall be re-argued before and determined by an uneven number of judges not less than three.

56 Judges not to sit on appeal from their own judgments, etc

(1) No judge shall sit as a member of the civil division of the Court of Appeal on the hearing of, or shall determine any application in proceedings incidental or preliminary to, an appeal from a judgment or order made in any case by himself or by any court of which he was a member.

(2) No judge shall sit as a member of the criminal division of the Court of Appeal on the hearing of, or shall determine any application in proceedings incidental or preliminary to, an appeal against –

(a) a conviction before himself or a court of which he was a member; or

(b) a sentence passed by himself or such a court.

THE HIGH COURT

61 Distribution of business among Divisions

(1) Subject to any provision made by or under this or any other Act (and in particular to any rules of court made in pursuance of subsection (2) and any order under subsection (3)), business in the High Court of any description mentioned in Schedule 1, as for the time being in force, shall be distributed among the Divisions in accordance with that Schedule.

(2) Rules of court may provide for the distribution of business in the High Court among the Divisions; but any rules made in pursuance of this subsection shall have effect subject to any orders for the time being in force under subsection (3).

(3) Subject to subsection (5), the Lord Chancellor may by order –

(a) direct that any business in the High Court which is not for the time being assigned by or under this or any other Act to any Division be assigned to such Division as may be specified in the order;

(b) if at any time it appears to him desirable to do so with a view to the more convenient administration of justice, direct that any business for the time being assigned by or under this or any other Act to any Division be assigned to such other Division as may be specified in the order; and

(c) amend Schedule 1 so far as may be necessary in consequence of provision made by order under paragraph (a) or (b).

(4) The powers conferred by subsection (2) and subsection (3) include power to assign business of any description to two or more Divisions concurrently.

(5) No order under subsection (3)(b) relating to any business shall be made without the concurrence of the senior judge of –

(a) the Division or each of the Divisions to which the business is for the time being assigned; and

(b) the Division or each of the Divisions to which the business is to be assigned by the order.

(6) Subject to rules of court, the fact that a cause or matter commenced in the High Court falls within a class of business assigned by or under this Act to a particular Division does not make it obligatory for it to be allocated or transferred to that Division.

(7) Without prejudice to subsections (1) to (5) and section 63, rules of court may provide for the distribution of the business (other than business required to be heard by a divisional court) in any Division of the High Court among the judges of that Division.

(8) Any order under subsection (3) shall be made by statutory instrument, which shall be laid before Parliament after being made.

62   Business of Patents, Admiralty and Commercial Courts

(1) The Patents Court shall take such proceedings relating to patents as are within the jurisdiction conferred on it by the Patents Act 1977, and such other proceedings relating to patents or other matters as may be prescribed.

(2) The Admiralty Court shall take Admiralty business, that is to say causes and matters assigned to the Queen's Bench Division and involving the exercise of the High Court's Admiralty jurisdiction or its jurisdiction as a prize court.

(3) The Commercial Court shall take such causes and matters as may in accordance with rules of court be entered in the commercial list.

64 Choice of Division by plaintiff

(1) Without prejudice to the power of transfer under section 65, the person by whom any cause or matter is commenced in the High Court shall in the prescribed manner allocate it to whichever Division he thinks fit.

(2) Where a cause or matter is commenced in the High Court, all subsequent interlocutory or other steps or proceedings in the High Court in that cause or matter shall be taken in the Division to which the cause or matter is for the time being allocated (whether under subsection (1) or in consequence of its transfer under section 65).

65 Power of transfer

(1) Any cause or matter may at any time and at any stage thereof, and either with or without application from any of the parties, be transferred, by such authority and in such manner as rules of court may direct, from one Division or judge of the High Court to another Division or judge thereof.

(2) The transfer of a cause or matter under subsection (1) to a different Division or judge of the High Court shall not affect the validity of any steps or proceedings taken or order made in that cause or matter before the transfer.

66 Divisional courts of High Court

(1) Divisional courts may be held for the transaction of any business in the High Court which is, by or by virtue of rules of court or any other statutory provision, required to be heard by a divisional court.

(2) Any number of divisional courts may sit at the same time.

(3) A divisional court shall be constituted of not less than two judges.

(4) Every judge of the High Court shall be qualified to sit in any divisional court.

(5) The judge who is, according to the order of precedence under this Act, the senior of the judges constituting a divisional court shall be the president of the court.

69   Trial by jury

(1) Where, on the application of any party to an action to be tried in the Queen's Bench Division, the court is satisfied that there is in issue –

(a) a charge of fraud against that party; or

(b) a claim in respect of libel, slander, malicious prosecution or false imprisonment; or

(c) any question or issue of a kind prescribed for the purposes of this paragraph,

the action shall be tried with a jury, unless the court is of opinion that the trial requires any prolonged examination of documents or accounts or any scientific or local investigation which cannot conveniently be made with a jury.

(2) An application under subsection (1) must be made not later than such time before the trial as may be prescribed.

(3) An action to be tried in the Queen's Bench Division which does not by virtue of subsection (1) fall to be tried with a jury shall be tried without a jury unless the court in its discretion orders it to be tried with a jury.

(4) Nothing in subsections (1) to (3) shall affect the power of the court to order, in accordance with rules of court, that different questions of fact arising in any action be tried by different modes of trial; and where any such order is made, subsection (1) shall have effect only as respects questions relating to any such charge, claim, question or issue as is mentioned in that subsection.

(5) Where for the purpose of disposing of any action or other matter which is being tried in the High Court by a judge with a jury it is necessary to ascertain the law of any other country which is applicable to the facts of the case, any question as to the effect of the evidence given with respect to that law shall, instead of being submitted to the jury, be decided by the judge alone.

THE CROWN COURT

73   General provisions

(1) Subject to the provisions of section 8(1)(c), 74 and 75(2) as respects courts comprising justices of the peace, all proceedings in

the Crown Court shall be heard and disposed of before a single judge of that court.

(2) Crown Court Rules may authorise or require a judge of the High Court, Circuit judge or Recorder, in such circumstances as are specified by the rules, at any stage to continue with any proceedings with a court from which any one or more of the justices initially constituting the court has withdrawn, or is absent for any reason.

(3) Where a judge of the High Court, Circuit judge or Recorder sits with justices of the peace he shall preside, and –

(a) the decision of the Crown Court may be a majority decision; and

(b) if the members of the court are equally divided, the judge of the High Court, Circuit judge or Recorder shall have a second and casting vote.

74   Appeals and committals for sentence

(1) On any hearing by the Crown Court –

(a) of any appeal; or

(b) of proceedings on committal to the Crown Court for sentence,

the Crown Court shall consist of a judge of the High Court or a Circuit judge or a Recorder who, subject to the following provisions of this section, shall sit with not less than two nor more than four justices of the peace.

(2) Crown Court Rules may, with respect to hearings falling within subsection (1) –

(a) prescribe the number of justices of the peace constituting the court (within the limits mentioned in that subsection); and

(b) prescribe the qualifications to be possessed by any such justices of the peace;

and the rules may make different provision for different descriptions of cases, different places of sitting or other different circumstances.

(3) Crown Court Rules may authorise or require a judge of the High Court, Circuit judge or Recorder, in such circumstances as are specified by the rules, to enter on, or at any stage to continue with,

any proceedings with a court not comprising the justices required by subsections (1) and (2).

(4) The Lord Chancellor may from time to time, having regard to the number of justices, or the number of justices with any prescribed qualifications, available for service in the Crown Court, give directions providing that, in such descriptions of proceedings as may be specified by the Lord Chancellor, the provisions of subsections (1) and (2) shall not apply.

(5) Directions under subsection (4) may frame descriptions of proceedings by reference to the place of trial, or by reference to the time of trial, or in any other way.

(6) No decision of the Crown Court shall be questioned on the ground that the court was not constituted as required by or under subsections (1) and (2) unless objection was taken by or on behalf of a party to the proceedings not later than the time when the proceedings were entered on, or when the alleged irregularity began ...

75   Allocation of cases according to composition of court, etc

(1) The cases or classes of cases in the Crown Court suitable for allocation respectively to a judge of the High Court and to a Circuit judge or Recorder, and all other matters relating to the distribution of Crown Court business, shall be determined in accordance with directions given by or on behalf of the Lord Chief Justice with the concurrence of the Lord Chancellor.

(2) Subject to section 74(1), the cases or classes of cases in the Crown Court suitable for allocation to a court comprising justices of the peace (including those by way of trial on indictment which are suitable for allocation to such a court) shall be determined in accordance with directions given by or on behalf of the Lord Chief Justice with the concurrence of the Lord Chancellor.

81   Bail

(1) The Crown Court may grant bail to any person –

(a) who has been committed in custody for appearance before the Crown Court or in relation to whose case a notice of transfer has been given under section 4 of the Criminal Justice Act 1987; or

(b) who is in custody pursuant to a sentence imposed by a magistrates' court, and who has appealed to the Crown Court against his conviction or sentence; or

(c) who is in the custody of the Crown Court pending the disposal of his case by that court; or

(d) who, after the decision of his case by the Crown Court, has applied to that court for the statement of a case for the High Court on that decision; or

(e) who has applied to the High Court for an order of certiorari to remove proceedings in the Crown Court in his case into the High Court, or has applied to the High Court for leave to make such an application; or

(f) to whom the Crown Court has granted a certificate under section 1(2) or 11(1A) of the Criminal Appeal Act 1968 or under subsection (1B) below; or

(g) who has been remanded in custody by a magistrates' court on adjourning a case under –

(i) section 5 (adjournment of inquiry into offence);

(ii) section 10 (adjournment of trial);

(iii) section 18 (initial procedure on information against adult for offence triable either way); or

(iv) section 30 (remand for medical examination),

of the Magistrates' Courts Act 1980;

and the time during which a person is released on bail under any provision of this subsection shall not count as part of any term of imprisonment or detention under his sentence.

(1A) The power of conferred by subsection (1)(f) does not extend to a case to which section 12 or 15 of the Criminal Appeal Act 1968 (appeal against verdict of not guilty by reason of insanity or against findings that the accused is under a disability and that he did the act or made the omission charged against him) applies.

(1B) A certificate under this subsection is a certificate that a case is fit for appeal on a ground which involves a question of law alone.

(1C) The power conferred by subsection (1)(f) is to be exercised –

(a) where the appeal is under section 1 or 9 of the Criminal Appeal Act 1968, by the judge who tried the case; and

(b) where it is under section 10 of that Act, by the judge who passed the sentence.

(1D) The power may only be exercised within 28 days from the date of the conviction appealed against, or in the case of appeal against sentence, from the date on which sentence was passed or, in the case of an order made or treated as made on conviction, from the date of the making of the order.

(1E) The power may not be exercised if the appellant has made an application to the Court of Appeal for bail in respect of the offence or offences to which the appeal relates.

(1F) It shall be a condition of bail granted in the exercise of the power that, unless a notice of appeal has previously been lodged in accordance with subsection (1) of section 18 of the Criminal Appeal Act 1968 –

(a) such a notice shall be so lodged within the period specified in subsection (2) of that section; and

(b) not later than 14 days from the end of that period, the appellant shall lodge with the Crown Court a certificate from the registrar of criminal appeals that a notice of appeal was given within that period.

(1G) If the Crown Court grants bail to a person in the exercise of the power, it may direct him to appear –

(a) if a notice of appeal is lodged within the period specified in section 18(2) of the Criminal Appeal Act 1968, at such time and place as the Court of Appeal may require, and

(b) if no such notice is lodged within that period, at such time and place as the Crown Court may require.

(1H) Where the Crown Court grants a person bail under subsection (1)(g) it may direct him to appear at a time and place which the magistrates' court could have directed and the recognizance of any surety shall be conditioned accordingly.

(1J) The Crown Court may only grant bail to a person under subsection (1)(g) if the magistrates' court which remanded him in custody has certified under section 5(6A) of the Bail Act 1976 that it heard full argument on his application for bail before it refused the application.

(2) Provision may be made by Crown Court Rules as respects the powers of the Crown Court relating to bail, including any provision –

(a) except in the case of bail in criminal proceedings (within the meaning of the Bail Act 1976), allowing the court instead of requiring a person to enter into a recognizance, to consent to his giving other security;

(b) allowing the court to direct that a recognizance shall be entered into or other security given before a magistrates' court or a justice of the peace, or, if the rules so provide, a person of such other description as is specified in the rules;

(c) prescribing the manner in which a recognizance is to be entered into or other security given, and the persons by whom and the manner in which the recognizance or security may be enforced;

(d) authorising the recommittal, in such cases and by such courts or justices as may be prescribed by the rules, of persons released from custody in pursuance of the powers;

(e) making provision corresponding to sections 118 and 119 of the Magistrates' Courts Act 1980 (varying or dispensing with requirements as to sureties, and postponement of taking recognizances).

(3) Any reference in any enactment to a recognizance shall include, unless the context otherwise requires, a reference to any other description of security given instead of a recognizance, whether in pursuance of subsection (2)(a) or otherwise.

(4) The Crown Court, on issuing a warrant for the arrest of any person, may endorse the warrant for bail, and in any such case –

(a) the person arrested under the warrant shall, unless the Crown Court otherwise directs, be taken to a police station; and

(b) the officer in charge of the station shall release him from custody if he, and any sureties required by the endorsement and approved by the officer, enter into recognizances of such amount as may be fixed by the endorsement:

Provided that in the case of bail in criminal proceedings (within the meaning of the Bail Act 1976) the person arrested shall not be required to enter into a recognizance.

(5) A person in custody in pursuance of a warrant issued by the Crown Court with a view to his appearance before that court shall be brought forthwith before either the Crown Court or a magistrates' court.

(6) A magistrates' court shall have jurisdiction, and a justice of the peace may act, under or in pursuance of rules under subsection (2) whether or not the offence was committed, or the arrest was made, within the court's area, or the area for which he was appointed.

83 Right of audience for solicitors in certain Crown Court centres

(1) The Lord Chancellor may at any time direct, as respects one or more specified places where the Crown Court sits, that solicitors, or such category of solicitors as may be specified in the direction, may have rights of audience in the Crown Court.

(2) Any such direction may be limited to apply only in relation to proceedings of a description specified in the direction.

(3) In considering whether to exercise his powers under this section the Lord Chancellor shall have regard, in particular, to the need to secure the availability of persons with rights of audience in the court or proceedings in question.

(4) Any direction under this section may be revoked by direction of the Lord Chancellor.

(5) Any direction under this section may be subject to such conditions and restrictions as appear to the Lord Chancellor to be necessary or expedient.

(6) Any exercise by the Lord Chancellor of his power to give a direction under this section shall be with the concurrence of the Lord Chief Justice, the Master of the Rolls, the President of the Family Division and the Vice-Chancellor.

84 Power to make rules of court

(1) Rules of court may be made for the purpose of regulating and prescribing the practice and procedure to be followed in the Supreme Court ...

85 The Supreme Court Rule Committee

(1) The power to make rules of court under section 84 in relation to the High Court and the civil division of the Court of Appeal shall

be exercisable by the Lord Chancellor together with any four or more of the following persons, namely –

(a) the Lord Chief Justice,

(b) the Master of the Rolls,

(c) the President of the Family Division,

(d) the Vice-Chancellor,

(e) three other judges of the Supreme Court,

(f) two persons who have a Supreme Court qualification (within the meaning of section 71 of the Courts and Legal Services Act 1990); and

(g) two persons who have been granted by an authorised body, under Part II of that Act, the right to conduct litigation in relation to all proceedings in the Supreme Court.

(2) The persons mentioned in subsection (1), acting in pursuance of that subsection, shall be known as 'the Supreme Court Rule Committee'.

(3) The persons to act in pursuance of subsection (1) with the Lord Chancellor, other than those eligible to act by virtue of their office, shall be appointed by the Lord Chancellor for such time as he may think fit.

(4) Before appointing a person under paragraph (f) or (g) of subsection (1), the Lord Chancellor shall consult any authorised body with members who are eligible for appointment under that paragraph.

86   The Crown Court Rule Committee

(1) The power to make rules of court under section 84 in relation to the Crown Court and the criminal division of the Court of Appeal shall be exercisable by the Lord Chancellor together with any four or more of the following persons, namely –

(a) the Lord Chief Justice,

(b) two other judges of the Supreme Court,

(c) two Circuit judges,

(d) the registrar of criminal appeals,

(e) a justice of the peace,

(f) two persons who have a Supreme Court qualification (within the meaning of section 71 of the Courts and Legal Services Act 1990); and

(g) two persons who have been granted by an authorised body, under Part II of that Act, the right to conduct litigation in relation to all proceedings in the Supreme Court.

(2) The persons mentioned in subsection (1), acting in pursuance of that subsection, shall be known as 'the Crown Court Rule Committee'.

(3) The persons to act in pursuance of subsection (1) with the Lord Chancellor, other than those eligible to act by virtue of their office, shall be appointed by the Lord Chancellor for such time as he may think fit.

(4) Before appointing a person under paragraph (f) or (g) of subsection (1), the Lord Chancellor shall consult any authorised body with members who are eligible for appointment under that paragraph.

PART V

PROBATE CAUSES AND MATTERS

127 Probate rules

(1) The President of the Family Division may, with the concurrence of the Lord Chancellor, make rules of court (in this Part referred to as 'probate rules') for regulating and prescribing the practice and procedure of the High Court with respect to non-contentious or common form probate business.

(2) Without prejudice to the generality of subsection (1), probate rules may make provision for regulating the classes of persons entitled to grants of probate or administration in particular circumstances and the relative priorities of their claims thereto.

(3) Probate rules shall be made by statutory instrument subject to annulment in pursuance of a resolution of either House of Parliament; and the Statutory Instruments Act 1946 shall apply to a statutory instrument containing probate rules in like manner as if they had been made by a Minister of the Crown.

128 Interpretation of Part V and other probate provisions

In this Part, and in the other provisions of this Act relating to probate causes and matters, unless the context otherwise requires –

'administration' includes all letters of administration of the effects of deceased persons, whether with or without a will annexed, and whether granted for general, special or limited purposes;

'estate' means real and personal estate, and 'real estate' includes –

(a) chattels real and land in possession, remainder or reversion and every interest in or over land to which the deceased person was entitled at the time of his death, and

(b) real estate held on trust or by way of mortgage or security, but not money to arise under a trust for sale of land, nor money secured or charged on land;

'grant' means a grant of probate or administration;

'non-contentious or common form probate business' means the business of obtaining probate and administration where there is no contention as to the right thereto, including –

(a) the passing of probates and administrations through the High Court in contentious cases where the contest has been terminated,

(b) all business of a non-contentious nature in matters of testacy and intestacy not being proceedings in any action, and

(c) the business of lodging caveats against the grant of probate or administration;

'Principal Registry' means the Principal Registry of the Family Division;

'probate rules' means rules of court made under section 127;

'trust corporation' means the Public Trustee or a corporation either appointed by the court in any particular case to be a trustee or authorised by rules made under section 4(3) of the Public Trustee Act 1906 to act as a custodian trustee;

'will' includes a nuncupative will and any testamentary document of which probate may be granted.

PART VI

MISCELLANEOUS AND SUPPLEMENTARY

138 Effect of writs of execution against goods

(1) Subject to subsection (2), a writ of fieri facias or other writ of execution against goods issued from the High Court shall bind the property in the goods of the execution debtor as from the time when the writ is delivered to the sheriff to be executed.

(2) Such a writ shall not prejudice the title to any goods of the execution debtor acquired by a person in good faith and for valuable consideration unless he had, at the time when he acquired his title –

(a) notice that that writ or any other such writ by virtue of which the goods of the execution debtor might be seized or attached had been delivered to and remained unexecuted in the hands of the sheriff; or

(b) notice that an application for the issue of a warrant of execution against the goods of the execution debtor had been made to the registrar of a county court and that the warrant issued on the application either –

(i) remained unexecuted in the hands of the registrar of the court from which it was issued; or

(ii) had been sent for execution to, and received by, the registrar of another county court, and remained unexecuted in the hands of the registrar of that court.

(3) For the better manifestation of the time mentioned in subsection (1), it shall be the duty of the sheriff (without fee) on receipt of any such writ as is there mentioned to endorse on its back the hour, day, month and year when he received it.

(3A) Every sheriff or officer executing any writ of execution issued from the High Court against the goods of any person may by virtue of it seize –

(a) any of that person's goods except –

(i) such tools, books, vehicles and other items of equipment as are necessary to that person for use personally by him in his employment, business or vocation;

(ii) such clothing, bedding, furniture, household equipment and provisions as are necessary for satisfying the basic domestic needs of that person and his family; and

(b) any money, banknotes, bills of exchange, promissory notes, bonds, specialties or securities for money belonging to that person.

(4) For the purposes of this section –

(a) 'property' means the general property in goods, and not merely a special property;

(b) 'sheriff' includes any officer charged with the enforcement of a writ of execution;

(c) any reference to the goods of the execution debtor includes a reference to anything else of his that may lawfully be seized in execution; and

(d) a thing shall be treated as done in good faith if it is in fact done honestly, whether it is done negligently or not.

138A   Sales under executions

(1) Where any goods seized under a writ of execution issued from the High Court are to be sold for a sum exceeding £20 (including legal incidental expenses), the sale shall, unless the court otherwise orders, be made by public auction, and not by bill of sale or private contract, and shall be publicly advertised by the sheriff on, and during three days preceding, the day of sale.

(2) Where any goods are seized under a writ of execution issued from the High Court and the sheriff has notice of another execution or other executions, the court shall not consider an application for leave to sell privately until the prescribed notice has been given to the other execution creditor or creditors, who may appear before the court and be heard on the application.

138B   Protection of officer selling goods under execution

(1) Where any goods in the possession of an execution debtor at the time of seizure by a sheriff or other officer charged with the enforcement of a writ of execution issued from the High Court are sold by the sheriff or other officer without any claims having been made to them –

(a) the purchaser of the goods so sold shall acquire a good title to those goods; and

(b) no person shall be entitled to recover against the sheriff or other officer, or anyone lawfully acting under his authority, for any sale of the goods or for paying over the proceeds prior to the receipt of a claim to the goods,

unless it is proved that the person from whom recovery is sought had notice, or might by making reasonable enquiry have ascertained, that the goods were not the property of the execution debtor.

(2) Nothing in this section shall affect the right of any lawful claimant (that it to say, any person who proves that at the time of sale he had a title to any goods so seized and sold) to any remedy to which he may be entitled against any person other than the sheriff or other officer.

(3) The provisions of this section have effect subject to those of sections 183, 184 and 346 of the Insolvency Act 1986.

151 Interpretation of this Act, and rules of construction for other Acts and documents

(1) In this Act, unless the context otherwise requires –

'action' means any civil proceedings commenced by writ or in any other manner prescribed by rules of court;

'appeal', in the context of appeals to the civil division of the Court of Appeal, includes –

(a) an application for a new trial, and

(b) an application to set aside a verdict, finding or judgment in any cause or matter in the High Court which has been tried, or in which any issue has been tried, by a jury;

'arbitration agreement' has the same meaning as it has in the Arbitration Act 1950 by virtue of section 32 of that Act;

'cause' means any action or any criminal proceedings;

'Division', where it appears with a capital letter, means a division of the High Court;

'judgment' includes a decree;

'jurisdiction' includes powers;

'matter' means any proceedings in court not in a cause;

'party', in relation to any proceedings, includes any person who pursuant to or by virtue of rules of court or any other statutory provision has been served with notice of, or has intervened in, those proceedings;

'prescribed' means –

(a) except in relation to fees, prescribed by rules of court; and

(b) in relation to fees, prescribed by an order under section 130;

'senior judge', where the reference is to the senior judge of a Division, means –

(a) in the case of the Chancery Division, the Vice-Chancellor;

(b) in the other case, the president of the Division in question;

'solicitor' means a solicitor of the Supreme Court;

'statutory provision' means any enactment, whenever passed, or any provision contained in subordinate legislation (as defined in section 21(1) of the Interpretation Act 1978), whenever made;

'this or any other Act' includes an Act passed after this Act.

(2) Section 128 contains definitions of expressions used in Part V and in the other provisions of this Act relating to probate causes and matters.

(3) Any reference in this Act to rules of court under section 84 includes a reference to rules of court under any provision of this or any other Act which confers on the Supreme Court Rule Committee or the Crown Court Rule Committee power to make rules of court.

(4) Except where the context otherwise requires, in this or any other Act –

'Criminal Appeal Rules' means rules of court made by the Crown Court Rule Committee in relation to the criminal division of the Court of Appeal;

'Crown Court Rules' means rules of court made by the Crown Court Rule Committee in relation to the Crown Court;

'divisional court' (with or without capital letters) means a divisional court constituted under section 66;

'judge of the Supreme Court' means –

(a) a judge of the Court of Appeal other than an ex-officio judge within paragraph (b) or (c) of section 2(2), or

(b) a judge of the High Court,

and accordingly does not include, as such, a judge of the Crown Court;

'official referees' business' has the meaning given by section 68(6);

'Rules of the Supreme Court' means rules of court made by the Supreme Court Rule Committee.

(5) The provisions of Schedule 4 (construction of references to superseded courts and officers) shall have effect.

SCHEDULE 1

DISTRIBUTION OF BUSINESS IN HIGH COURT

1. To the Chancery Division are assigned all causes and matters relating to –

(a) the sale, exchange or partition of land, or the raising of charges on land;

(b) the redemption or foreclosure of mortgages;

(c) the execution of trusts;

(d) the administration of the estates of deceased persons;

(e) bankruptcy;

(f) the dissolution of partnerships or the taking of partnership or other accounts;

(g) the rectification, setting aside or cancellation of deeds or other instruments in writing;

(h) probate business, other than non-contentious or common form business;

(i) patents, trade marks, registered designs, copyright or design right;

(j) the appointment of a guardian of a minor's estate,

and all causes and matters involving the exercise of the High Court's jurisdiction under the enactments relating to companies.

2. To the Queen's Bench Division are assigned –

(a) applications for writs of habeas corpus, except applications made by a parent or guardian of a minor for such a writ concerning the custody of the minor;

(b) applications for judicial review;

(c) all causes and matters involving the exercise of the High Court's Admiralty jurisdiction or its jurisdiction as a prize court; and

(d) all causes and matters entered in the commercial list.

3. To the Family Division are assigned –

(a) all matrimonial causes and matters (whether at first instance or on appeal);

(b) all causes and matters (whether at first instance or on appeal) relating to –

(i) legitimacy;

(ii) the exercise of the inherent jurisdiction of the High Court with respect to minors, the maintenance of minors and any proceedings under the Children Act 1989, except proceedings solely for the appointment of a guardian of a minor's estate;

(iii) adoption;

(iv) non-contentious or common form probate business;

(c) applications for consent to the marriage of a minor or for a declaration under section 27B(5) of the Marriage Act 1949;

(d) proceedings on appeal under section 13 of the Administration of Justice Act 1960 from an order or decision made under section 63(3) of the Magistrates' Courts Act 1980 to enforce an order of a magistrates' court made in matrimonial proceedings or with respect to the guardianship of a minor;

(e) applications under Part III of the Family Law Act 1986;

(e) proceedings under the Children Act 1989;

(f) all proceedings under –

(i) the Domestic Violence and Matrimonial Proceedings Act 1976;

(ii) the Child Abduction and Custody Act 1985;

(iii) the Family Law Act 1986;

(iv) section 30 of the Human Fertilisation and Embryology Act 1990; and

(g) all proceedings for the purpose of enforcing an order made in any proceedings of a type described in this paragraph.

(h) all proceedings under the Child Support Act 1991.

As amended by the Local Government (Miscellaneous Provisions) Act 1982, s2, Schedule 3, para 27(6); Administration of Justice Act 1982, ss6(1), 15(1), 29(1), 58, 60(1); Mental Health (Amendment) Act 1982, s65(1); Mental Health Act 1983, s148, Schedule 4, para 58; Prosecution of Offences Act 1985, s24(1)-(6); Family Law Act 1986, s68(1), (2), Schedule 1, paras 25, 26, Schedule 2; Maximum Number of Judges Order 1987; Merchant Shipping Act 1988, s57(4), Schedule 6; Criminal Justice Act 1988, ss15, 156, Schedule 2, para 12; Children Act 1989, s108(5), Schedule 13, para 45(1), (3); Statute Law (Repeals) Act 1989, s1(2), Schedule 2, Pt I, para 4; Courts and Legal Services Act 1990, ss4(1), 7, 15(1), 67, 71(1), 72(6), s125(2), (3), (7), Schedule 17, para 12, Schedule 18, paras 36, 41, Schedule 20; Criminal Procedure (Insanity and Unfitness to Plead) Act 1991, s7, Schedule 3, para 6; High Court (Distribution of Business) Order 1991; Maximum Number of Judges Order 1993; High Court (Distribution of Business) Order 1993; Maximum Number of Judges (No 2) Order 1993.

CRIMINAL JUSTICE ACT 1982
(1982 c 48)

37   The standard scale of fines for summary offences

(1) There shall be a standard scale of fines for summary offences, which shall be known as 'the standard scale'.

(2) The standard scale is shown below –

Level on the scale	Amount of fine
1	£200
2	£500
3	£1,000
4	£2,500
5	£5,000

(3) Where any enactment (whether contained in an Act passed before or after this Act) provides –

(a) that a person convicted of a summary offence shall be liable on conviction to a fine or a maximum fine by reference to a specified level on the standard scale; or

(b) confers power by subordinate instrument to make a person liable on conviction of a summary offence (whether or not created by the instrument) to a fine or maximum fine by reference to a specified level on the standard scale,

it is to be construed as referring to the standard scale for which this section provides as that standard scale has effect from time to time by virtue either of this section or of an order under section 143 of the Magistrates' Courts Act 1980.

As amended by the Criminal Justice Act 1991, ss17(1), 101(1), Schedule 12, para 6.

COUNTY COURTS ACT 1984
(1984 c 28)

PART I

CONSTITUTION AND ADMINISTRATION

1   County courts to be held for districts

(1) For the purposes of this Act, England and Wales shall be divided into districts, and a court shall be held under this Act for each district at one or more places in it; and throughout the whole of each district the court so held for the district shall have such jurisdiction and powers as are conferred by this Act and any other enactment for the time being in force.

(2) Every court so held shall be called a county court and shall be a court of record and shall have a seal.

(3) Nothing in this section affects the operation of section 42 of the Courts Act 1971 (City of London).

5   Judges of county courts

(1) Every Circuit judge shall, by virtue of his office, be capable of sitting as a judge for any county court district in England and Wales, and the Lord Chancellor shall assign one or more Circuit judges to each district and may from time to time vary the assignment of Circuit judges among the districts.

(2) Subject to any directions given by or on behalf of the Lord Chancellor, in any case where more than one Circuit judge is assigned to a district under subsection (1), any function conferred by or under this Act on the judge for a district may be exercised by any of the Circuit judges for the time being assigned to that district.

(3) The following, that is –

every judge of the Court of Appeal,

every judge of the High Court,

every Recorder,

shall, by virtue of his office, be capable of sitting as a judge for any county court district in England and Wales and, if he consents to do so, shall sit as such a judge at such times and on such occasions as the Lord Chancellor considers desirable.

(4) Notwithstanding that he is not for the time being assigned to a particular district, a Circuit judge –

(a) shall sit as a judge of that district at such times and on such occasions as the Lord Chancellor may direct; and

(b) may sit as a judge of that district in any case where it appears to him that the judge of that district is not, or none of the judges of that district is, available to deal with the case.

6   District judges

(1) Subject to the provisions of this section, there shall be a district judge for each district, who shall be appointed by the Lord Chancellor and paid such salary as the Lord Chancellor may, with the concurrence of the Treasury, direct.

(2) The Lord Chancellor may, if he thinks fit, appoint a person to be district judge for two or more districts.

(3) The Lord Chancellor may, if he thinks fit, appoint two or more persons to execute jointly the office of district judge for a district and may, in any case where joint district judges are appointed, give directions with respect to the division between them of the duties of the office.

(4) The Lord Chancellor may, as he thinks fit, on the death, resignation or removal of a joint district judge, either appoint another person to be joint district judge in his place or give directions that the continuing district judge shall act as sole district judge or, as the case may be, that the continuing district judges shall execute jointly the office of district judge.

(5) The district judge for any district shall be capable of acting in any other district for the district judge of that other district.

7   Assistant district judges

(1) The Lord Chancellor may, with the concurrence of the Treasury as to numbers and salaries, appoint in connection with any court such assistant district judges as he considers necessary for carrying out the work of the court.

(2) An assistant district judge shall be capable of discharging any of the functions of the district judge, and in so doing shall have the same powers and be subject to the same liabilities as if he were the district judge.

8   Deputy district judges

(1) If it appears to the Lord Chancellor that it is expedient as a temporary measure to make an appointment under this subsection in order to facilitate the disposal of business in county courts, he may appoint a person to be deputy district judge for any county court district during such period or on such occasions as the Lord Chancellor thinks fit; and a deputy district judge, while acting under his appointment, shall have the same powers and be subject to the same liabilities as if he were the district judge.

(2) Notwithstanding the expiry of any period for which a person is appointed under this section to be deputy district judge, he may act as such for the purpose of continuing to deal with, giving judgment in, or dealing with any ancillary matters relating to, any case with which he may have been concerned during the period of his appointment, and for that purpose shall be treated as acting under that appointment.

(3) The Lord Chancellor may pay to any person appointed under this section as deputy district judge such remuneration and allowances as he may, with the approval of the Treasury, determine.

9   Qualifications

No person shall be appointed a district judge, assistant district judge or deputy district judge unless he has a seven year general qualification, within the meaning of the Courts and Legal Services Act 1990.

11 Tenure of office

(1) This subsection applies –

(a) to the office of district judge or assistant district judge; and

(b) to the office of part-time district judge or part-time assistant district judge.

(2) Subject to the following provisions of this section, a person who holds an office to which subsection (1) applies shall vacate his office at the end of the completed year of service in which he attains the age of 72 years.

(3) Where the Lord Chancellor considers it desirable in the public interest to retain in office a person who holds an office to which subsection (1) applies after the time when he would otherwise retire in accordance with subsection (2), the Lord Chancellor may from time to time authorise the continuance in office of that person until such date, not being later than the date on which that person attains the age of 75 years, as he thinks fit.

(4) A person appointed to an office to which subsection (1) applies shall hold that office during good behaviour.

(5) The power to remove such a person from his office on account of misbehaviour shall be exercisable by the Lord Chancellor.

(6) The Lord Chancellor may also remove such a person from his office on account of inability to perform the duties of his office.

PART II

JURISDICTION AND TRANSFER OF PROCEEDINGS

15 General jurisdiction in actions of contract and tort

(1) Subject to subsection (2), a county court shall have jurisdiction to hear and determine any action founded on contract or tort.

(2) A county court shall not, except as in this Act provided, have jurisdiction to hear and determine –

(b) any action in which the title to any toll, fair, market or franchise is in question; or

(c) any action for libel or slander.

16 Money recoverable by statute

A county court shall have jurisdiction to hear and determine an action for the recovery of a sum recoverable by virtue of any enactment for the time being in force, if –

(a) it is not provided by that or any other enactment that such sums shall only be recoverable in the High Court or shall only be recoverable summarily.

17 Abandonment of part of claim to give court jurisdiction

(1) Where a plaintiff has a cause of action for more than the county court limit in which, if it were not for more than the county court limit a county court would have jurisdiction, the plaintiff may abandon the excess, and thereupon a county court shall have jurisdiction to hear and determine the action, but the plaintiff shall not recover in the action an amount exceeding the county court limit.

(2) Where the court has jurisdiction to hear and determine an action by virtue of this section, the judgment of the court in the action shall be in full discharge of all demands in respect of the cause of action, and entry of the judgment shall be made accordingly.

18 Jurisdiction by agreement in certain actions

If the parties to any action, other than an action which, if commenced in the High Court, would have been assigned to the Chancery Division or to the Family Division or have involved the exercise of the High Court's Admiralty jurisdiction, agree, by a memorandum signed by them or by their respective legal representatives, that a county court specified in the memorandum shall have jurisdiction in the action, that court shall have jurisdiction to hear and determine the action accordingly.

21 Actions for recovery of land and actions where title is in question

(1) A county court shall have jurisdiction to hear and determine any action for the recovery of land.

(2) A county court shall have jurisdiction to hear and determine any action in which the title to any hereditament comes in question.

(3) Where a mortgage of land consists of or includes a dwelling-house and no part of the land is situated in Greater London then, subject to subsection (4), if a county court has jurisdiction by virtue of this section to hear and determine an action in which the mortgagee under that mortgage claims possession of the mortgaged property, no court other than a county court shall have jurisdiction to hear and determine that action.

(4) Subsection (3) shall not apply to an action for foreclosure or sale in which a claim for possession of the mortgaged property is also made.

(7) In this section –

'dwelling-house' includes any building or part of a building which is used as a dwelling;

'mortgage' includes a charge and 'mortgagor' and 'mortgagee' shall be construed accordingly;

'mortgagor' and 'mortgagee' include any person deriving title under the original mortgagor or mortgagee.

(8) The fact that part of the premises comprised in a dwelling-house is used as a shop or office or for business, trade or professional purposes shall not prevent the dwelling-house from being a dwelling-house for the purposes of this section.

(9) This section does not apply to a mortgage securing an agreement which is a regulated agreement within the meaning of the Consumer Credit Act 1974.

23   Equity jurisdiction

A county court shall have all the jurisdiction of the High Court to hear and determine –

(a) proceedings for the administration of the estate of a deceased person, where the estate does not exceed in amount or value the county court limit;

(b) proceedings –

(i) for the execution of any trust, or

(ii) for a declaration that a trust subsists, or

(iii) under section 1 of the Variation of Trusts Act 1958,

where the estate or fund subject, or alleged to be subject, to the trust does not exceed in amount or value the county court limit;

(c) proceedings for foreclosure or redemption of any mortgage or for enforcing any charge or lien, where the amount owing in respect of the mortgage, charge or lien does not exceed the county court limit;

(d) proceedings for the specific performance, or for the rectification, delivery up or cancellation, of any agreement for the sale, purchase or lease of any property, where, in the case of a sale or purchase, the purchase money, or in the case of a lease, the value of the property, does not exceed the county court limit;

(e) proceedings relating to the maintenance or advancement of a minor, where the property of the minor does not exceed in amount or value the county court limit;

(f) proceedings for the dissolution or winding-up of any partnership (whether or not the existence of the partnership is in dispute), where the whole assets of the partnership do not exceed in amount or value the county court limit;

(g) proceedings for relief against fraud or mistake, where the damage sustained or the estate or fund in respect of which relief is sought does not exceed in amount or value the county court limit.

24 Jurisdiction by agreement in certain equity proceedings

(1) If, as respects any proceedings to which this section applies, the parties agree, by a memorandum signed by them or by their respective legal representatives or agents, that a county court specified in the memorandum shall have jurisdiction in the proceedings, that court shall, notwithstanding anything in any enactment, have jurisdiction to hear and determine the proceedings accordingly.

(2) Subject to subsection (3), this section applies to any proceedings in which a county court would have jurisdiction by virtue of –

(a) section 113(3) of the Settled Land Act 1925,

(b) section 63A of the Trustee Act 1925,

(c) sections 3(7), 49(4), 66(4), 89(7), 90(3), 91(8), 92(2), 136(3), 181(2), 188(2) of, and paragraph 3A of Part III and paragraph 1(3A) and (4A) of Part IV of Schedule 1 to, the Law of Property Act 1925,

(d) sections 17(2), 38(4), 41(1A) and 43(4) of the Administration of Estates Act 1925,

(e) section 6(1) of the Leasehold Property (Repairs) Act 1938,

(f) sections 1(6A) and 5(11) of the Land Charges Act 1972, and

(g) sections 23 and 25 of this Act,

but for the limits of the jurisdiction of the court provided by those enactments.

(3) This section does not apply to proceedings under section 1 of the Variation of Trusts Act 1958.

25 Jurisdiction under Inheritance (Provision for Family and Dependants) Act 1975

A county court shall have jurisdiction to hear and determine any application for an order under section 2 of the Inheritance (Provision for Family and Dependants) Act 1975 (including any application for permission to apply for such an order and any application made, in the proceedings on an application for such an order, for an order under any other provision of that Act).

26 Districts for Admiralty purposes

(1) If at any time it appears expedient to the Lord Chancellor that any county court should have Admiralty jurisdiction, it shall be lawful for him, by order –

(a) to appoint that court to have, as from such date as may be specified in the order, such Admiralty jurisdiction as is provided in this Act; and

(b) to assign to that court as its district for Admiralty purposes any part or parts of any county court district or of two or more county court districts.

(2) Where a district has been so assigned to a court as its district for Admiralty purposes, the parts of the sea (if any) adjacent to that district to a distance of three miles from the shore thereof shall be deemed to be included in that district, and the judge and all officers of the court shall have jurisdiction and authority for those purposes throughout that district as if it were the district for the court for all purposes.

(3) Where an order is made under this section for the discontinuance of the Admiralty jurisdiction of any county court, whether wholly or within a part of the district assigned to it for Admiralty purposes,

provision may be made in the order with respect to any Admiralty proceedings commenced in that court before the order comes into operation.

(4) The power to make orders under this section shall be exercisable by statutory instrument.

27 Admiralty jurisdiction

(1) Subject to the limitations of amount specified in subsection (2), an Admiralty county court shall have the following Admiralty jurisdiction, that is to say, jurisdiction to hear and determine –

(a) any claim for damage received by a ship;

(b) any claim for damage done by a ship;

(c) any claim for loss of life or personal injury sustained in consequence of any defect in a ship or in her apparel or equipment, or in consequence of the wrongful act, neglect or default of –

(i) the owners, charterers or persons in possession or control of a ship; or

(ii) the master or crew of a ship, or any other person for whose wrongful acts, neglects or defaults the owners, charterers or persons in possession or control of a ship are responsible,

being an act, neglect or default in the navigation or management of the ship, in the loading, carriage or discharge of goods on, in or from the ship, or in the embarkation, carriage or disembarkation of persons on, in or from the ship; ...

(2) The limitations of amount referred to in subsection (1) are that the court shall not have jurisdiction to hear and determine –

(a) a claim in the nature of salvage where the value of the property salved exceeds £15,000; or

(b) any other claim mentioned in that subsection for an amount exceeding £5,000 ...

(6) If, as regards any proceedings as to any such claim as is mentioned in subsection (1), the parties agree, by a memorandum signed by them or by their respective legal representatives or agents, that a particular county court specified in the memorandum shall have jurisdiction in the proceedings, that court shall, notwithstanding anything in subsection (2) or in county court rules

for prescribing the courts in which proceedings shall be brought, have jurisdiction to hear and determine the proceedings accordingly.

(7) Nothing in this section shall be taken to affect the jurisdiction of any county court to hear and determine any proceedings in which it has jurisdiction by virtue of section 15 or 17.

(8) Nothing in this section, or in section 26 or in any order made under that section, shall be taken to confer on a county court the jurisdiction of a prize court within the meaning of the Naval Prize Acts 1864 to 1916 ...

32 Contentious probate jurisdiction

(1) Where –

(a) an application for the grant or revocation of probate or administration has been made through the principal registry of the Family Division or district probate registry under section 105 of the Supreme Court Act 1981; and

(b) it is shown to the satisfaction of a county court that the value at the date of the death of the deceased of his net estate does not exceed the county court limit,

the county court shall have the jurisdiction of the High Court in respect of any contentious matter arising with the grant or revocation.

(2) In subsection (1) 'net estate', in relation to a deceased person, means the estate of that person exclusive of any property he was possessed of or entitled to as a trustee and not beneficially, and after making allowances for funeral expenses and for debts and liabilities.

35 Division of causes of action

It shall not be lawful for any plaintiff to divide any cause of action for the purpose of bringing two or more actions in one or more of the county courts.

36 No action on judgment of High Court

No action shall be brought in a county court on any judgment of the High Court.

37   Persons who may exercise jurisdiction of court

(1) Any jurisdiction and powers conferred by this or any other Act –

(a) on a county court; or
(b) on the judge of a county court,

may be exercised by any judge of the court.

(2) Subsection (1) applies to jurisdiction and power conferred on all county courts or judges of county courts or on any particular county court or the judge of any particular county court.

38   Remedies available in county courts

(1) Subject to what follows, in any proceedings in a county court the court may make any order which could be made by the High Court if the proceedings were in the High Court.

(2) Any order made by a county court may be –

(a) absolute or conditional;
(b) final or interlocutory.

(3) A county court shall not have power –

(a) to order mandamus, certiorari or prohibition; or
(b) to make any order of a prescribed kind.

(4) Regulations under subsection (3) –

(a) may provide for any of their provisions not to apply in such circumstances or descriptions of case as may be specified in the regulations;
(b) may provide for the transfer of the proceedings to the High Court for the purpose of enabling an order of a kind prescribed under subsection (3) to be made;
(c) may make such provision with respect to matters of procedure as the Lord Chancellor considers expedient; and
(d) may make provision amending or repealing any provision made by or under any enactment, so far as may be necessary or expedient in consequence of the regulations.

(5) In this section 'prescribed' means prescribed by regulations made by the Lord Chancellor under this section.

(6) The power to make regulations under this section shall be exercised by statutory instrument.

(7) No such statutory instrument shall be made unless a draft of the instrument has been approved by both Houses of Parliament.

40 Transfer of proceedings to county court

(1) Where the High Court is satisfied that any proceedings before it are required by any provision of a kind mentioned in subsection (8) to be in a county court it shall –

   (a) order the transfer of the proceedings to a county court; or

   (b) if the court is satisfied that the person bringing the proceedings knew, or ought to have known, of that requirement, order that they be struck out.

(2) Subject to any such provision, the High Court may order the transfer of any proceedings before it to a county court.

(3) An order under this section may be made either on the motion of the High Court itself or on the application of any party to the proceedings.

(4) Proceedings transferred under this section shall be transferred to such county court as the High Court considers appropriate, having taken into account the convenience of the parties and that of any other persons likely to be affected and the state of business in the courts concerned.

(5) The transfer of any proceedings under this section shall not affect any right of appeal from the order directing the transfer.

(6) Where proceedings for the enforcement of any judgment or order of the High Court are transferred under this section –

   (a) the judgment or order may be enforced as if it were a judgment or order of a county court; and

   (b) subject to subsection (7), it shall be treated as a judgment or order of that court for all purposes.

(7) Where proceedings for the enforcement of any judgment or order of the High Court are transferred under this section –

   (a) the powers of any court to set aside, correct, vary or quash a judgment or order of the High Court, and the enactments relating to appeals from such a judgment or order, shall continue to apply; and

(b) the powers of any court to set aside, correct, vary or quash a judgment or order of a county court, and the enactments relating to appeals from such a judgment or order, shall not apply.

(8) The provisions referred to in subsection (1) are any made –

(a) under section 1 of the Courts and Legal Services Act 1990; or

(b) by or under any other enactment.

(9) This section does not apply to family proceedings within the meaning of Part V of the Matrimonial and Family Proceedings Act 1984.

41   Transfer to High Court by order of High Court

(1) If at any stage in proceedings commenced in a county court or transferred to a county court under section 40, the High Court thinks it desirable that the proceedings, or any part of them, should be heard and determined in the High Court, it may order the transfer to the High Court of the proceedings or, as the case may be, of that part of them.

(2) The power conferred by subsection (1) is without prejudice to section 29 of the Supreme Court Act 1981 (power of High Court to issue prerogative orders) but shall be exercised in relation to family proceedings (within the meaning of Part V of the Matrimonial and Family Proceedings Act 1984) in accordance with any directions given under section 37 of that Act (directions as to distribution and transfer of family business and proceedings).

(3) The power conferred by subsection (1) shall be exercised subject to any provision made –

(a) under section 1 of the Courts and Legal Services Act 1990; or

(b) by or under any other enactment.

42   Transfer to High Court by order of a county court

(1) Where a county court is satisfied that any proceedings before it are required by any provision of a kind mentioned in subsection (7) to be in the High Court, it shall –

(a) order the transfer of the proceedings to the High Court; or

(b) if the court is satisfied that the person bringing the proceedings knew, or ought to have known, of that requirement, order that they be struck out.

(2) Subject to any such provision, a county court may order the transfer of any proceedings before it to the High Court.

(3) An order under this section may be made either on the motion of the court itself or on the application of any party to the proceedings.

(4) The transfer of any proceedings under this section shall not affect any right of appeal from the order directing the transfer.

(5) Where proceedings for the enforcement of any judgment or order of a county court are transferred under this section –

(a) the judgment or order may be enforced as if it were a judgment or order of the High Court; and

(b) subject to subsection (6), it shall be treated as a judgment or order of that court for all purposes.

(6) Where proceedings for the enforcement of any judgment or order of a county court are transferred under this section –

(a) the powers of any court to set aside, correct, vary or quash a judgment or order of a county court, and the enactments relating to appeals from such a judgment or order, shall continue to apply; and

(b) the powers of any court to set aside, correct, vary or quash a judgment or order of the High Court, and the enactments relating to appeals from such a judgment or order, shall not apply.

(7) The provisions referred to in subsection (1) are any made –

(a) under section 1 of the Courts and Legal Services Act 1990; or

(b) by or under any other enactment.

(8) This section does not apply to family proceedings within the meaning of Part V of the Matrimonial and Family Proceedings Act 1984.

PART III

PROCEDURE

47 Minors

A minor may prosecute any action in a county court for any sum of money not exceeding the county court limit which may be due to him for wages or piece work, or for work as a servant, in the same manner as if he were of full age.

58 Persons who may take affidavits for use in county courts

(1) An affidavit to be used in a county court may be sworn before –

(a) the judge or registrar of any court; or

(b) any justice of the peace; or

(c) an officer of any court appointed by the judge of that court for the purpose,

as well as before a commissioner for oaths or any other person authorised to take affidavits under the Commissioner for Oaths Acts 1889 and 1891.

(2) An affidavit sworn before a judge or registrar or before any such officer may be sworn without the payment of any fee.

60 Right of audience

(2) Where an action is brought in a county court by a local authority for either or both of the following –

(a) the recovery of possession of a house belonging to the authority;

(b) the recovery of any rent, mesne profits, damages or other sum claimed by the authority in respect of the occupation by any person of such a house,

then, in so far as the proceedings in the action are heard by the district judge, any officer of the authority authorised by the authority in that behalf, may address the district judge.

(3) In this section –

'local authority' means a county council, a district council, the Broads Authority, a London borough council, a joint authority established by Part IV of the Local Government Act 1985 or the Common Council of the City of London; and

'house' includes a part of a house, a flat or any other dwelling and also includes any yard, garden, outhouse or appurtenance occupied with a house or part of a house or with a flat or other dwelling,

and any reference to the occupation of a house by a person includes a reference to anything done by that person, or caused or permitted by him to be done, in relation to the house as occupier of the house, whether under a tenancy or licence or otherwise.

61 Right of audience by direction of Lord Chancellor

(1) The Lord Chancellor may at any time direct that such categories of persons in relevant legal employment as may be specified in the direction may address the court in any proceedings in a county court, or in proceedings in a county court of such description as may be so specified.

(2) In subsection (1), 'relevant legal employment' means employment which consists of or includes giving assistance in the conduct of litigation to a legal representative whether in private practice or not.

(3) A direction under this section may be given subject to such conditions and restrictions as appear to the Lord Chancellor to be necessary or expedient, and may be expressed to have effect as respects every county court or as respects a specified county court or as respects one or more specified places where a county court sits.

(4) The power to give directions conferred by this section includes a power to vary or rescind any direction given under this section.

64 Reference to arbitration

(1) County court rules –

(a) may prescribe cases in which proceedings are (without any order of the court) to be referred to arbitration, and

(b) may prescribe the manner in which and the terms on which cases are to be so referred, and

(c) may, where cases are so referred, require other matters within the jurisdiction of the court in dispute between the parties also to be referred to arbitration.

(2) County court rules –

(a) may prescribe cases in which proceedings may be referred to arbitration by order of the court, and

(b) may authorise the court also to order other matters in dispute between the parties and within the jurisdiction of the court to be so referred.

(2A) County court rules may prescribe the procedures and rules of evidence to be followed on any reference under subsection (1) or (2).

(2B) Rules made under subsection (2A) may, in particular, make provision with respect to the manner of taking and questioning evidence.

(3) On a reference under subsection (1) or (2) the award of the arbitrator, arbitrators or umpire shall be entered as the judgment in the proceedings and shall be as binding and effectual to all intents, subject to subsection (4), as if it had been given by the judge.

(4) The judge may, if he thinks fit, on application made to him within such time as may be prescribed, set aside the award, or may, with the consent of the parties, revoke the reference or order another reference to be made in the manner specified in this section.

(5) In this section 'award' includes an interim award.

66   Trial by jury

(1) In the following proceedings in a county court the trial shall be without a jury –

(a) Admiralty proceedings;

(b) proceedings arising –

(i) under Part I, II or III of the Rent (Agriculture) Act 1976; or

(ii) under any provision of the Rent Act 1977 other than a provision contained in Part V, sections 103 to 106 or Part IX; or

(iii) under Part I of the Protection from Eviction Act 1977; or

(iv) under Part I of the Housing Act 1988;

(c) any appeal to the county court under the Housing Act 1985.

(2) In all other proceedings in a county court the trial shall be without a jury unless the court otherwise orders on an application made in that behalf by any party to the proceedings in such manner and within such time before the trial as may be prescribed.

(3) Where, on any such application, the court is satisfied that there is in issue –

(a) a charge of fraud against the party making the application; or

(b) a claim in respect of libel, slander, malicious prosecution or false imprisonment; or

(c) any question or issue of a kind prescribed for the purposes of this paragraph,

the action shall be tried with a jury, unless the court is of opinion that the trial requires any prolonged examination of documents or accounts or any scientific or local investigation which cannot conveniently be made with a jury.

(4) There shall be payable, in respect of the trial with a jury of proceedings in a county court, such fees as may be prescribed by the fees order.

67   Impanelling and swearing of jury

At any county court where proceedings are to be tried with a jury, eight jurymen shall be impanelled and sworn as occasion requires to give their verdicts in the proceedings brought before them, and being once sworn need not be re-sworn in each trial.

69   Power to award interest on debts and damages

(1) Subject to county court rules, in proceedings (whenever instituted) before a county court for the recovery of a debt or damages there may be included in any sum for which judgment is given simple interest, at such rate as the court thinks fit or as may be prescribed, on all or any part of the debt or damages in respect of which judgment is given, or payment is made before judgment, for all or any part of the period between the date when the cause of action arose and –

(a) in the case of any sum paid before judgment, the date of the payment; and

(b) in the case of the sum for which judgment is given, the date of the judgment.

(2) In relation to a judgment given for damages for personal injuries or death which exceed £200 subsection (1) shall have effect –

(a) with the substitution of 'shall be included' for 'may be included'; and

(b) with the addition of 'unless the court is satisfied that there are special reasons to the contrary' after 'given', where first occurring.

(3) Subject to county court rules, where –

(a) there are proceedings (whenever instituted) before a county court for the recovery of a debt; and

(b) the defendant pays the whole debt to the plaintiff (otherwise than in pursuance of a judgment in the proceedings),

the defendant shall be liable to pay the plaintiff simple interest, at such rate as the court thinks fit or as may be prescribed, on all or any part of the debt for all or any part of the period between the date when the cause of action arose and the date of the payment.

(4) Interest in respect of a debt shall not be awarded under this section for a period during which, for whatever reason, interest on the debt already runs.

(5) Interest under this section may be calculated at different rates in respect of different periods.

(6) In this section 'plaintiff' means the person seeking the debt or damages and 'defendant' means the person from whom the plaintiff seeks the debt or damages and 'personal injuries' includes any disease and any impairment of a person's physical or mental condition.

(7) Nothing in this section affects the damages recoverable for the dishonour of a bill of exchange.

(8) In determining whether the amount of any debt or damages exceeds that prescribed by or under any enactment, no account shall be taken of any interest payable by virtue of this section except where express provision to the contrary is made by or under that or any other enactment.

75   County court rules

(1) The rule committee may make county court rules regulating the practice of the courts and forms of proceedings in them and prescribing scales of costs to be paid to counsel and solicitors.

(2) The power to make county court rules shall extend to all matters of procedure or practice, or matters relating to or concerning the effect or operation in law of any procedure or practice, in any case within the cognisance of county courts as to which rules of the Supreme Court have been or might lawfully be made for cases within the cognisance of the High Court ...

(7) The rule committee shall consist of the following persons appointed by the Lord Chancellor –

> (a) five judges of county courts;
>
> (b) two district judges;
>
> (c) two persons who have a Supreme Court qualification (within the meaning of section 71 of the Courts and Legal Services Act 1990); and
>
> (d) two persons who have been granted by an authorised body, under Part II of that Act, the right to conduct litigation in relation to all proceedings in the Supreme Court ...

(9) Any rules made by the rule committee shall be certified under the hands of the members of the committee, or any three or more of them, and submitted to the Lord Chancellor, who may allow or disallow or alter them.

(10) Any rules so made, as allowed or altered by the Lord Chancellor, shall –

> (a) come into operation on such day as the Lord Chancellor may direct;
>
> (b) be embodied in a statutory instrument to which the Statutory Instruments Act 1946 shall apply as if it embodied rules made by a Minister of the Crown.

76   Application of practice of High Court

In any case not expressly provided for by or in pursuance of this Act, the general principles of practice in the High Court may be adopted and applied to proceedings in a county court.

PART IV

APPEALS, ETC

77 Appeals: general provisions

(1) Subject to the provisions of this section and the following provisions of this Part of this Act, if any party to any proceedings in a county court is dissatisfied with the determination of the judge or jury, he may appeal from it to the Court of Appeal in such manner and subject to such conditions as may be provided by the rules of the Supreme Court.

(1A) Without prejudice to the generality of the power to make county court rules under section 75, such rules may make provision for any appeal from the exercise by a district judge, assistant district judge or deputy district judge of any power given to him by virtue of any enactment to be to a judge of a county court.

(2) The Lord Chancellor may by order prescribe classes of proceedings in which there is to be no right of appeal under this section without the leave either of the judge of the county court or of the Court of Appeal ...

(6) In proceedings in which either the plaintiff or the defendant is claiming possession of any premises this section shall not confer any right of appeal on any question of fact if by virtue of –

(a) section 13(4) of the Landlord and Tenant Act 1954; or

(b) Cases III to IX in Schedule 4 to the Rent (Agriculture) Act 1976; or

(c) section 98 of the Rent Act 1977, as it applies to Cases 1 to 6 and 8 and 9 in Schedule 15 to that Act, or that section as extended or applied by any other enactment; or

(d) section 99 of the Rent Act 1977, as it applies to Cases 1 to 6 and 9 in Schedule 15 to that Act; or

(e) section 84(2)(a) of the Housing Act 1985; or

(ee) section 7 of the Housing Act 1988, as it applies to the grounds in Part II of Schedule 2 to that Act; or

(f) any other enactment,

the court can only grant possession on being satisfied that it is reasonable to do so ...

79 Agreement not to appeal

(1) No appeal shall lie from any judgment, direction, decision or order of a judge of county courts if, before the judgment, direction, decision or order is given or made, the parties agree, in writing signed by themselves or their legal representatives or agents, that it shall be final.

80 Judge's note on appeal

(1) At the hearing of any proceedings in a county court in which there is a right of appeal or from which an appeal may be brought with leave, the judge shall, at the request of any party, make a note –

(a) of any question of law raised at the hearing; and

(b) of the facts in evidence in relation to any such question; and

(c) of his decision on any such question and of his determination of the proceedings.

(2) Where such a note has been taken, the judge shall (whether notice of appeal has been served or not), on the application of any party to the proceedings, and on payment by that party of such fee as may be prescribed by the fees orders, furnish him with a copy of the note, and shall sign the copy, and the copy so signed shall be used at the hearing of the appeal.

81 Powers of Court of Appeal on appeal from county court

(1) On the hearing of an appeal, the Court of Appeal may draw any inference of fact and either –

(a) order a new trial on such terms as the court thinks just; or

(b) order judgment to be entered for any party; or

(c) make a final or other order on such terms as the court thinks proper to ensure the determination on the merits of the real question in controversy between the parties.

(2) Subject to any rules of the Supreme Court, on any appeal from a county court the Court of Appeal may reverse or vary, in favour of a party seeking to support the judgment or order of the county court in whole or in part, any determination made in the county court on questions of fact, notwithstanding that the appeal is an

appeal on a point of law only, or any such determinations on points of law, notwithstanding that the appeal is an appeal on a question of fact only.

(3) Subsection (2) shall not enable the Court of Appeal to reverse or vary any determination, unless the party dissatisfied with the determination would have been entitled to appeal in respect of it if aggrieved by the judgment or order.

82 Decision of Court of Appeal on probate appeals to be final

No appeal shall lie from the decision of the Court of Appeal on any appeal from a county court in any probate proceedings.

PART V

ENFORCEMENT OF JUDGMENTS AND ORDERS

85 Execution of judgments or orders for payment of money

(1) Subject to article 8 of the High Court and County Courts Jurisdiction Order 1991, any sum of money payable under a judgment or order of a county court may be recovered, in case of default or failure of payment, forthwith or at the time or times and in the manner thereby directed, by execution against the goods of the party against whom the judgment or order was obtained.

(2) The district judge, on the application of the party prosecuting any such judgment or order, shall issue a warrant of execution in the nature of a writ of fieri facias whereby the district judge shall be empowered to levy or cause to be levied by distress and sale of the goods, wherever they may be found within the district of the court, the money payable under the judgment or order and the costs of the execution.

(3) The precise time of the making of the application to the district judge to issue such a warrant shall be entered by him in the record prescribed for the purpose under section 12 and on the warrant.

(4) It shall be the duty of every constable within his jurisdiction to assist in the execution of every such warrant.

89   Goods which may be seized

(1) Every bailiff or officer executing any warrant of execution issued from a county court against the goods of any person may by virtue of it seize –

> (a) any of that person's goods except –
>
> > (i) such tools, books, vehicles and other items of equipment as are necessary to that person for use personally by him in his employment, business or vocation;
> > (ii) such clothing, bedding, furniture, household equipment and provisions as are necessary for satisfying the basic domestic needs of that person and his family;
>
> (b) any money, banknotes, bills of exchange, promissory notes, bonds, specialties or securities for money belonging to that person.

(2) Any reference to the goods of an execution debtor in this Part of this Act includes a reference to anything else of his that may lawfully be seized in execution.

93   Period to elapse before sale

No goods seized in execution under process of a county court shall be sold for the purpose of satisfying the warrant of execution until the expiration of a period of at least five days next following the day on which the goods have been so seized unless –

> (a) the goods are of a perishable nature; or
> (b) the person whose goods have been seized so requests in writing.

94   Goods not to be sold except by brokers or appraisers

No goods seized in execution under process of a county court shall be sold for the purpose of satisfying the warrant of execution except by one of the brokers or appraisers appointed under this Part of this Act.

95   Appointment of brokers, appraisers, etc

(1) The district judge may from time to time as he thinks fit appoint such number of persons for keeping possession, and such number

of brokers and appraisers for the purpose of selling or valuing any goods seized in execution under process of the court, as appears to him to be necessary.

(2) The district judge may direct security to be taken from any broker, appraiser or other person so appointed for such sum and in such manner as he thinks fit for the faithful performance of his duties without injury or oppression.

(3) The judge or district judge may dismiss any broker, appraiser or other person so appointed.

(4) There shall be payable to brokers and appraisers so appointed in respect of their duties, out of the produce of goods distrained or sold, such fees as may be prescribed by the fees orders.

97 Sales under executions to be published unless otherwise ordered

(1) Where any goods are to be sold under execution for a sum exceeding £20 (including legal incidental expenses), the sale shall, unless the court from which the warrant of execution issued otherwise orders, be made by public auction and not by bill of sale or private contract, and shall be publicly advertised by the district judge on, and during three days next preceding, the day of sale.

(2) Where any goods are seized in execution and the district judge has notice of another execution or other executions, the court shall not consider an application for leave to sell privately until the prescribed notice has been given to the other execution creditor or creditors, who may appear before the court and be heard upon the application.

107 Receivers

(1) The power of the county court to appoint a receiver by way of equitable execution shall operate in relation to all legal estates and interests in land.

(2) The said power may be exercised in relation to an estate or interest in land whether or not a charge has been imposed on that land under section 1 of the Charging Orders Act 1979 for the purpose of enforcing the judgment, decree, order or award in question, and the said power shall be in addition to and not in derogation of any power of any court to appoint a receiver in proceedings for enforcing such a charge.

(3) Where an order under section 1 of the Charging Orders Act 1979 imposing a charge for the purpose of enforcing a judgment, decree, order or award has been registered under section 6 of the Land Charges Act 1972, subsection (4) of that section (which provides that, amongst other things, an order appointing a receiver and any proceedings pursuant to the order or in obedience to it, shall be void against a purchaser unless the order is for the time being registered under that section) shall not apply to an order appointing a receiver made either in proceedings for enforcing the charge or by way of equitable execution of the judgment, decree, order or award or, as the case may be, of so much of it as requires payment of moneys secured by the charge.

108 Attachment of debts

(1) Subject to any order for the time being in force under subsection (4), this section applies to the following accounts, namely –

(a) any deposit account with a bank or other deposit-taking institution; and

(b) any withdrawable share account with any deposit-taking institution.

(2) In determining whether, for the purposes of the jurisdiction of the county court to attach debts for the purpose of satisfying judgments or orders for the payment of money, a sum standing to the credit of a person in an account to which this section applies is a sum due or accruing to that person and, as such, attachable in accordance with county court rules, any condition mentioned in subsection (3) which applies to the account shall be disregarded.

(3) Those conditions are –

(a) any condition that notice is required before any money or share is withdrawn;

(b) any condition that a personal application must be made before any money or share is withdrawn;

(c) any condition that a deposit book or share-account book must be produced before any money or share is withdrawn; or

(d) any other prescribed condition.

(4) The Lord Chancellor may by order make such provision as he thinks fit, by way of amendment of this section or otherwise, for all or any of the following purposes, namely –

(a) including in, or excluding from, the accounts to which this section applies accounts of any description specified in the order;

(b) excluding from the accounts to which this section applies all accounts with any particular deposit-taking institution so specified or with any deposit-taking institution of a description so specified.

(5) An order under subsection (4) shall be made by statutory instrument subject to annulment in pursuance of a resolution of either House of Parliament.

PART VI

ADMINISTRATION ORDERS

112 Power to make administration order

(1) Where a debtor –

(a) is unable to pay forthwith the amount of a judgment obtained against him; and

(b) alleges that his whole indebtedness amounts to a sum not exceeding the county court limit, inclusive of the debt for which the judgment was obtained;

a county court may make an order providing for the administration of his estate.

(2) In this Part of this Act –

'administration order' means an order under this section; and

'the appropriate court', in relation to an administration order, means the court which has the power to make the order.

(3) Before an administration order is made, the appropriate court shall, in accordance with county court rules, send to every person whose name the debtor has notified to the appropriate court as being a creditor of him, a notice that that person's name has been so notified.

(4) So long as an administration order is in force, a creditor whose name is included in the schedule to the order shall not, without the leave of the appropriate court, be entitled to present, or join in, a bankruptcy petition against the debtor unless –

(a) his name was so notified; and

(b) the debt by virtue of which he presents, or joins in, the petition, exceeds £1,500; and

(c) the notice given under subsection (3) was received by the creditor within 28 days immediately preceding the day on which the petition is presented.

(5) An administration order shall not be invalid by reason only that the total amount of the debts is found at any time to exceed the county court limit, but in that case the court may, if it thinks fit, set aside the order.

(6) An administration order may provide for the payment of the debts of the debtor by instalments or otherwise, and either in full or to such extent as appears practicable to the court under the circumstances of the case, and subject to any conditions as to his future earnings or income which the court may think just.

(7) The Secretary of State may by regulations increase or reduce the sum for the time being specified in subsection (4)(b); but no such increase in the sum so specified shall affect any case in which the bankruptcy petition was presented before the coming into force of the increase.

(8) The power to make regulations under subsection (7) shall be exercisable by statutory instrument; and no such regulations shall be made unless a draft of them has been approved by resolution of each House of Parliament.

114 Effect of administration order

(1) Subject to sections 115 and 116, when an administration order is made, no creditor shall have any remedy against the person or property of the debtor in respect of any debt –

(a) of which the debtor notified the appropriate court before the administration order was made; or

(b) which has been scheduled to the order,

except with the leave of the appropriate court, and on such terms as that court may impose.

(2) Subject to subsection (3), any county court in which proceedings are pending against the debtor in respect of any debt so notified or scheduled shall, on receiving notice of the administration order, stay

the proceedings, but may allow costs already incurred by the creditor, and such costs may, on application, be added to the debt.

(3) The requirement to stay proceedings shall not operate as a requirement that a county court in which proceedings in bankruptcy against the debtor are pending shall stay those proceedings.

PART VII

COMMITTALS

118 Power to commit for contempt

(1) If any person –

(a) wilfully insults the judge of a county court, or any juror or witness, or any officer of the court during his sitting or attendance in court, or in going to or returning from the court; or

(b) wilfully interrupts the proceedings of a county court or otherwise misbehaves in court;

any officer of the court, with or without the assistance of any other person, may, by order of the judge, take the offender into custody and detain him until the rising of the court, and the judge may, if he thinks fit –

(i) make an order committing the offender for a specified period not exceeding one month to prison; or

(ii) impose upon the offender, for every offence, a fine of an amount not exceeding £2,500, or may both make such an order and impose such a fine.

(2) The judge may at any time revoke an order committing a person to prison under this section and, if he is already in custody, order his discharge.

(3) A district judge, assistant district judge or deputy district judge shall have the same powers under this section in relation to proceedings before him as a judge.

147 Interpretation

(1) In this Act, unless the context otherwise requires –

'action' means any proceedings in a county court which may be commenced as prescribed by plaint;

'Admiralty county court' means a county court appointed to have Admiralty jurisdiction by order under this Act;

'Admiralty proceedings' means proceedings in which the claim would not be within the jurisdiction of a county court but for sections 26 and 27;

'bailiff' includes a district judge;

'the county court limit' means –

(a) in relation to any enactment contained in this Act for which a limit is for the time being specified by an Order under section 145, that limit,

(c) in relation to any enactment contained in this Act and not within paragraph (a), the county court limit for the time being specified by any other Order in Council or order defining the limit of county court jurisdiction for the purposes of that enactment;

'county court rules' means rules made under section 75;

'court' and 'county court' mean a court held for a district under this Act; ...

'district' and 'county district' mean a district for which a court is to be held under section 2; ...

'hearing' includes trial, and 'hear' and 'heard' shall be construed accordingly; ...

'judge', in relation to a county court, means a judge assigned to the district of that court under subsection (1) of section 5 and any person sitting as a judge for that district under subsection (3) or (4) of that section;

'judgment summons' means a summons issued on the application of a person entitled to enforce a judgment or order under section 5 of the Debtors Act 1869 requiring a person, or, where two or more persons are liable under the judgment or order, requiring any one or more of them, to appear and be examined on oath as to his or their means; ...

'legal representative' means an authorised advocate or authorised litigator, as defined by section 119(1) of the Courts and Legal Services Act 1990;

'matter' means every proceeding in a county court which may be commenced as prescribed otherwise than by plaint;

'officer', in relation to a court, means any district judge, deputy district judge or assistant district judge of that court, and any clerk, bailiff, usher or messenger in the service of that court; ...

'party' includes every person served with notice of, or attending, any proceeding, whether named as a party to that proceeding or not;

'prescribed' means prescribed by county court rules;

'probate proceedings' means proceedings brought in a county court by virtue of section 32 or transferred to that court under section 40;

'proceedings' includes both actions and matters; ...

'return day' means the day appointed in any summons or proceeding for the appearance of the defendant or any other day fixed for the hearing of any proceedings;

'the rule committee' means the committee constituted under section 75;

'ship' includes any description of vessel used in navigation;

'solicitor' means solicitor of the Supreme Court; 'standard scale' has the meaning given by section 75 of the Criminal Justice Act 1982; and

'statutory maximum' has the meaning given by section 74 of that Act.

Note. For an addition to s58(1) above in the case of family proceedings, see the Family Proceedings Rules 1991, r10.13.

As amended by the Matrimonial and Family Proceedings Act 1984, s46(1), Schedule 1, para 30; Insolvency Act 1985, s220(2); Housing (Consequential Provisions) Act 1985, s4, Schedule 2, para 57(2), (3); Administration of Justice Act 1985, s67(1), (2), Schedule 7, para 8, Schedule 8, Pt II; Statute Law (Repeals) Act 1986; Housing Act 1988, s140(1), Schedule 17, Pt I, para 35(1), (2); Courts and Legal Services Act 1990, ss2(1), (2), 3, 6, 16, 71(2), 74(6), 125(2), (3), (7), Schedule 10, para 57, Schedule 17, para 15, Schedule 18, paras 42, 46, 47, 49(2), (3), Schedule 20; High Court and County Courts Jurisdiction Order 1991; Criminal Justice Act 1991, s17(3)(a), Schedule 4, Pt I.

POLICE AND CRIMINAL EVIDENCE ACT 1984
(1984 c 60)

PART I

POWERS TO STOP AND SEARCH

1 Power of constable to stop and search persons, vehicles, etc

(1) A constable may exercise any power conferred by this section –

(a) in any place to which at the time when he proposes to exercise the power the public or any section of the public has access, on payment or otherwise, as of right or by virtue of express or implied permission; or

(b) in any other place to which people have ready access at the time when he proposes to exercise the power but which is not a dwelling.

(2) Subject to subsections (3) to (5) below, a constable –

(a) may search –

(i) any person or vehicle;
(ii) anything which is in or on a vehicle,

for stolen or prohibited articles or any article to which subsection (8A) below applies; and

(b) may detain a person or vehicle for the purpose of such a search.

(3) This section does not give a constable power to search a person or vehicle or anything in or on a vehicle unless he has reasonable grounds for suspecting that he will find stolen or prohibited articles or any article to which subsection (8A) below applies.

(4) If a person is in a garden or yard occupied with and used for the

purposes of a dwelling or on other land so occupied and used, a constable may not search him in the exercise of the power conferred by this section unless the constable has reasonable grounds for believing –

(a) that he does not reside in the dwelling; and

(b) that he is not in the place in question with the express or implied permission of a person who resides in the dwelling.

(5) If a vehicle is in a garden or yard occupied with and used for the purposes of a dwelling or on other land so occupied and used, a constable may not search the vehicle or anything in or on it in the exercise of the power conferred by this section unless he has reasonable grounds for believing –

(a) that the person in charge of the vehicle does not reside in the dwelling; and

(b) that the vehicle is not in the place in question with the express or implied permission of a person who resides in the dwelling.

(6) If in the course of such a search a constable discovers an article which he has reasonable grounds for suspecting to be a stolen or prohibited article or an article to which subsection (8A) below applies, he may seize it.

(7) An article is prohibited for the purposes of this Part of this Act if it is –

(a) an offensive weapon; or

(b) an article –

(i) made or adapted for use in the course of or in connection with an offence to which this sub-paragraph applies; or

(ii) intended by the person having it with him for such use by him or by some other person.

(8) The offences to which subsection (7)(b)(i) above applies are –

(a) burglary;

(b) theft;

(c) offences under section 12 of the Theft Act 1968 (taking motor vehicle or other conveyance without authority); and

(d) offences under section 15 of that Act (obtaining property by deception).

(8A) This subsection applies to any article in relation to which a person has committed, or is committing or is going to commit an offence under section 139 of the Criminal Justice Act 1988.

(9) In this Part of this Act 'offensive weapon' means any article –

(a) made or adapted for use for causing injury to persons; or

(b) intended by the person having it with him for such use by him or by some other person.

2 Provisions relating to search under section 1 and other powers

(1) A constable who detains a person or vehicle in the exercise –

(a) of the power conferred by section 1 above; or

(b) of any other power –

(i) to search a person without first arresting him; or

(ii) to search a vehicle without making an arrest,

need not conduct a search if it appears to him subsequently –

(i) that no search is required; or

(ii) that a search is impracticable.

(2) If a constable contemplates a search, other than a search of an unattended vehicle, in the exercise –

(a) of the power conferred by section 1 above; or

(b) of any other power, except the power conferred by section 6 below and the power conferred by section 27(2) of the Aviation Security Act 1982 –

(i) to search a person without first arresting him; or

(ii) to search a vehicle without making an arrest,

it shall be his duty, subject to subsection (4) below, to take reasonable steps before he commences the search to bring to the attention of the appropriate person –

(i) if the constable is not in uniform, documentary evidence that he is a constable; and

(ii) whether he is in uniform or not, the matters specified in subsection (3) below;

and the constable shall not commence the search until he has performed that duty.

(3) The matters referred to in subsection (2)(ii) above are –

(a) the constable's name and the name of the police station to which he is attached;

(b)the object of the proposed search;

(c) the constable's grounds for proposing to make it; and

(d) the effect of section 3(7) or (8) below, as may be appropriate.

(4) A constable need not bring the effect of section 3(7) or (8) below to the attention of the appropriate person if it appears to the constable that it will not be practicable to make the record in section 3(1) below.

(5) In this section 'the appropriate person' means –

(a) if the constable proposes to search a person, that person; and

(b) if he proposes to search a vehicle, or anything in or on a vehicle, the person in charge of the vehicle.

(6) On completing a search of an unattended vehicle or anything in or on such a vehicle in the exercise of any such power as is mentioned in subsection (2) above a constable shall leave a notice –

(a) stating that he has searched it;

(b) giving the name of the police station to which he is attached;

(c) stating that an application for compensation for any damage caused by the search may be made to that police station; and

(d) stating the effect of section 3(8) below.

(7) The constable shall leave the notice inside the vehicle unless it is not reasonably practicable to do so without damaging the vehicle.

(8) The time for which a person or vehicle may be detained for the purposes of such a search is such time as is reasonably required to permit a search to be carried out either at the place where the person or vehicle was first detained or nearby.

(9) Neither the power conferred by section 1 above nor any other power to detain and search a person without first arresting him or to detain and search a vehicle without making an arrest is to be construed –

(a) as authorising a constable to require a person to remove any of his clothing in public other than an outer coat, jacket or gloves; or

(b) as authorising a constable not in uniform to stop a vehicle.

(10) This section and section 1 above apply to vessels, aircraft and hovercraft as they apply to vehicles.

3 Duty to make records concerning searches

(1) Where a constable has carried out a search in the exercise of any such power as is mentioned in section 2(1) above, other than a search –

(a) under section 6 below; or

(b) under section 27(2) of the Aviation Security Act 1982,

he shall make a record of it in writing unless it is not practicable to do so.

(2) If –

(a) a constable is required by subsection (1) above to make a record of a search; but

(b) it is not practicable to make the record on the spot,

he shall make it as soon as practicable after the completion of the search.

(3) The record of a search of a person shall include a note of his name, if the constable knows it, but a constable may not detain a person to find out his name.

(4) If a constable does not know the name of a person whom he has searched, the record of the search shall include a note otherwise describing that person.

(5) The record of a search of a vehicle shall include a note describing the vehicle.

(6) The record of a search of a person or a vehicle –

(a) shall state –

(i) the object of the search;

(ii) the grounds for making it;

(iii) the date and time when it was made;

(iv) the place where it was made;

(v) whether anything, and if so what, was found;

(vi) whether any, and if so what, injury to a person or damage to property appears to the constable to have resulted from the search; and

(b) shall identify the constable making it.

(7) If a constable who conducted a search of a person made a record of it, the person who was searched shall be entitled to a copy of the record if he asks for one before the end of the period specified in subsection (9) below.

(8) If –

(a) the owner of a vehicle which has been searched or the person who was in charge of the vehicle at the time when it was searched asks for a copy of the record of the search before the end of the period specified in sub-section (9) below; and

(b) the constable who conducted the search made a record of it,

the person who made the request shall be entitled to a copy.

(9) The period mentioned in subsections (7) and (8) above is the period of 12 months beginning with the date on which the search was made.

(10) The requirements imposed by this section with regard to records of searches of vehicles shall apply also to records of searches of vessels, aircraft and hovercraft.

4   Road checks

(1) This section shall have effect in relation to the conduct of road checks by police officers for the purpose of ascertaining whether a vehicle is carrying –

(a) a person who has committed an offence other than a road traffic offence or a vehicles excise offence;

(b) a person who is a witness to such an offence;

(c) a person intending to commit such an offence; or

(d) a person who is unlawfully at large.

(2) For the purposes of this section a road check consists of the exercise in a locality of the power conferred by section 163 of the

Road Traffic Act 1988 in such a way as to stop during the period for which its exercise in that way in that locality continues all vehicles or vehicles selected by any criterion.

(3) Subject to subsection (5) below, there may only be such a road check if a police officer of the rank of superintendent or above authorises it in writing.

(4) An officer may only authorise a road check under subsection (3) above –

(a) for the purpose specified in subsection (1)(a) above, if he has reasonable grounds –

(i) for believing that the offence is a serious arrestable offence; and

(ii) for suspecting that the person is, or is about to be, in the locality in which vehicles would be stopped if the road check were authorised;

(b) for the purpose specified in subsection (1)(b) above, if he has reasonable grounds for believing that the offence is a serious arrestable offence;

(c) for the purpose specified in subsection (1)(c) above, if he has reasonable grounds –

(i) for believing that the offence would be a serious arrestable offence; and

(ii) for suspecting that the person is, or is about to be, in the locality in which vehicles would be stopped if the road check were authorised;

(d) for the purpose specified in subsection (1)(d) above, if he has reasonable grounds for suspecting that the person is, or is about to be, in that locality.

(5) An officer below the rank of superintendent may authorise such a road check if it appears to him that it is required as a matter of urgency for one of the purposes specified in subsection (1) above.

(6) If an authorisation is given under subsection (5) above, it shall be the duty of the officer who gives it –

(a) to make a written record of the time at which he gives it; and

(b) to cause an officer of the rank of superintendent or above to be informed that it has been given.

(7) The duties imposed by subsection (6) above shall be performed as soon as it is practicable to do so.

(8) An officer to whom a report is made under subsection (6) above may, in writing, authorise the road check to continue.

(9) If such an officer considers that the road check should not continue, he shall record in writing –

(a) the fact that it took place; and
(b) the purpose for which it took place.

(10) An officer giving an authorisation under this section shall specify the locality in which vehicles are to be stopped.

(11) An officer giving an authorisation under this section, other than an authorisation under subsection (5) above –

(a) shall specify a period, not exceeding seven days, during which the road check may continue; and
(b) may direct that the road check –

(i) shall be continuous; or
(ii) shall be conducted at specified times,

during that period.

(12) If it appears to an officer of the rank of superintendent or above that a road check ought to continue beyond the period for which it has been authorised he may, from time to time, in writing specify a further period, not exceeding seven days, during which it may continue.

(13) Every written authorisation shall specify –

(a) the name of the officer giving it;
(b) the purpose of the road check; and
(c) the locality in which vehicles are to be stopped.

(14) The duties to specify the purposes of a road check imposed by subsections (9) and (13) above include duties to specify any relevant serious arrestable offence.

(15) Where a vehicle is stopped in a road check, the person in charge of the vehicle at the time when it is stopped shall be entitled to obtain a written statement of the purpose of the road check if he applies for such a statement not later than the end of the period of 12 months from the day on which the vehicle was stopped.

(16) Nothing in this section affects the exercise by police officers of any power to stop vehicles for purposes other than those specified in subsection (1) above.

6   Statutory undertakers, etc

(1) A constable employed by statutory undertakers may stop, detain and search any vehicle before it leaves a goods area included in the premises of the statutory undertakers.

(2) In this section 'goods area' means any area used wholly or mainly for the storage or handling of goods.

(3) For the purposes of section 6 of the Public Stores Act 1875, any person appointed under the Special Constables Act 1923 to be a special constable within any premises which are in the possession or under the control of British Nuclear Fuels Limited shall be deemed to be a constable deputed by a public department and any goods and chattels belonging to or in the possession of British Nuclear Fuels Limited shall be deemed to be Her Majesty's Stores ...

7   Part I – supplementary

(3) In this Part of this Act 'statutory undertakers' means persons authorised by any enactment to carry on any railway, light railway, road transport, water transport, canal, inland navigation, dock or harbour undertaking.

PART II

POWERS OF ENTRY, SEARCH AND SEIZURE

8   Power of justice of the peace to authorise entry and search of premises

(1) If on an application made by a constable a justice of the peace is satisfied that there are reasonable grounds for believing –

(a) that a serious arrestable offence has been committed; and

(b) that there is material on premises specified in the application which is likely to be of substantial value (whether by itself or together with other material) to the investigation of the offence; and

(c) that the material is likely to be relevant evidence; and

(d) that it does not consist of or include items subject to legal privilege, excluded material or special procedure material; and

(e) that any of the conditions specified in subsection (3) below applies,

he may issue a warrant authorising a constable to enter and search the premises.

(2) A constable may seize and retain anything for which a search has been authorised under subsection (1) above.

(3) The conditions mentioned in subsection (1)(e) above are –

(a) that it is not practicable to communicate with any person entitled to grant entry to the premises;

(b) that it is practicable to communicate with a person entitled to grant entry to the premises but it is not practicable to communicate with any person entitled to grant access to the evidence;

(c) that entry to the premises will not be granted unless a warrant is produced;

(d) that the purpose of a search may be frustrated or seriously prejudiced unless a constable arriving at the premises can secure immediate entry to them.

(4) In this Act 'relevant evidence', in relation to an offence, means anything that would be admissible in evidence at a trial for the offence.

(5) The power to issue a warrant conferred by this section is in addition to any such power otherwise conferred.

9   Special provisions as to access

(1) A constable may obtain access to excluded material or special procedure material for the purposes of a criminal investigation by making an application under Schedule 1 below and in accordance with that Schedule.

(2) Any Act (including a local Act) passed before this Act under which a search of premises for the purposes of a criminal investigation could be authorised by the issue of a warrant to a

constable shall cease to have effect so far as it relates to the authorisation of searches –

(a) for items subject to legal privilege; or

(b) for excluded material; or

(c) for special procedure material consisting of documents or records other than documents.

10   Meaning of 'items subject to legal privilege'

(1) Subject to subsection (2) below, in this Act 'items subject to legal privilege' means –

(a) communications between a professional legal adviser and his client or any person representing his client made in connection with the giving of legal advice to the client;

(b) communications between a professional legal adviser and his client or any person representing his client or between such an adviser or his client or any such representative and any other person made in connection with or in contemplation of legal proceedings and for the purposes of such proceedings; and

(c) items enclosed with or referred to in such communications and made –

(i) in connection with the giving of legal advice; or

(ii) in connection with or in contemplation of legal proceedings and for the purposes of such proceedings,

when they are in the possession of a person who is entitled to possession of them.

(2) Items held with the intention of furthering a criminal purpose are not items subject to legal privilege.

11   Meaning of 'excluded material'

(1) Subject to the following provisions of this section, in this Act 'excluded material' means –

(a) personal records which a person has acquired or created in the course of any trade, business, profession or other occupation or for the purposes of any paid or unpaid office and which he holds in confidence;

(b) human tissue or tissue fluid which has been taken for the purposes of diagnosis or medical treatment and which a person holds in confidence;

(c) journalistic material which a person holds in confidence and which consists –

(i) of documents; or

(ii) of records other than documents.

(2) A person holds material other than journalistic material in confidence for the purposes of this section if he holds it subject –

(a) to an express or implied undertaking to hold it in confidence; or

(b) to a restriction on disclosure or an obligation of secrecy contained in any enactment, including an enactment contained in an Act passed after this Act.

(3) A person holds journalistic material in confidence for the purposes of this section if –

(a) he holds it subject to such an undertaking, restriction or obligation; and

(b) it has been continuously held (by one or more persons) subject to such an undertaking, restriction or obligation since it was first acquired or created for the purposes of journalism.

12 Meaning of 'personal records'

In this Part of this Act 'personal records' means documentary and other records concerning an individual (whether living or dead) who can be identified from them and relating –

(a) to his physical or mental health;

(b) to spiritual counselling or assistance given or to be given to him; or

(c) to counselling or assistance given or to be given to him, for the purposes of his personal welfare, by any voluntary organisations or by any individual who –

(i) by reason of his office or occupation has responsibilities for his personal welfare; or

(ii) by reason of an order of a court has responsibilities for his supervision.

13   Meaning of 'journalistic material'

(1) Subject to subsection (2) below, in this Act 'journalistic material' means material acquired or created for the purposes of journalism.

(2) Material is only journalistic material for the purposes of this Act if it is in the possession of a person who acquired or created it for the purposes of journalism.

(3) A person who receives material from someone who intends that the recipient shall use it for the purposes of journalism is to be taken to have acquired it for those purposes.

14   Meaning of 'special procedure material'

(1) In this Act 'special procedure material' means –

    (a) material to which subsection (2) below applies; and
    (b) journalistic material, other than excluded material.

(2) Subject to the following provisions of this section, this subsection applies to material, other than items subject to legal privilege and excluded material, in the possession of a person who –

    (a) acquired or created it in the course of any trade, business, profession or other occupation or for the purpose of any paid or unpaid office; and
    (b) holds it subject –

        (i) to an express or implied undertaking to hold it in confidence; or
        (ii) to a restriction or obligation such as is mentioned in section 11(2)(b) above.

(3) Where material is acquired –

    (a) by an employee from his employer and in the course of his employment; or
    (b) by a company from an associated company,

it is only special procedure material if it was special procedure material immediately before the acquisition.

(4) Where material is created by an employee in the course of his employment, it is only special procedure material if it would have been special procedure material had his employer created it.

(5) Where material is created by a company on behalf of an associated company, it is only special procedure material if it would have been special procedure material had the associated company created it.

(6) A company is to be treated as another's associated company for the purposes of this section if it would be so treated under section 302 of the Income and Corporation Taxes Act 1970.

15   Search warrants – safeguards

(1) This section and section 16 below have effect in relation to the issue to constables under any enactment, including an enactment contained in an Act passed after this Act, of warrants to enter and search premises; and an entry on or search of premises under a warrant is unlawful unless it complies with this section and section 16 below.

(2) Where a constable applies for any such warrant, it shall be his duty –

(a) to state –

(i) the ground on which he makes the application; and

(ii) the enactment under which the warrant would be issued;

(b) to specify the premises which it is desired to enter and search; and

(c) to identify, so far as is practicable, the articles or persons to be sought.

(3) An application for such a warrant shall be made ex parte and supported by an information in writing.

(4) The constable shall answer on oath any question that the justice of the peace or judge hearing the application asks him.

(5) A warrant shall authorise an entry on one occasion only.

(6) A warrant –

(a) shall specify –

(i) the name of the person who applies for it;

(ii) the date on which it is issued;

(iii) the enactment under which it is issued; and

(iv) the premises to be searched; and

(b) shall identify, so far as is practicable, the articles or persons to be sought.

(7) Two copies shall be made of a warrant.

(8) The copies shall be clearly certified as copies.

16   Execution of warrants

(1) A warrant to enter and search premises may be executed by any constable.

(2) Such a warrant may authorise persons to accompany any constable who is executing it.

(3) Entry and search under a warrant must be within one month from the date of its issue.

(4) Entry and search under a warrant must be at a reasonable hour unless it appears to the constable executing it that the purpose of a search may be frustrated on an entry at a reasonable hour.

(5) Where the occupier of premises which are to be entered and searched is present at the time when a constable seeks to execute a warrant to enter and search them, the constable –

(a) shall identify himself to the occupier and, if not in uniform, shall produce to him documentary evidence that he is a constable;
(b) shall produce the warrant to him; and
(c) shall supply him with a copy of it.

(6) Where –

(a) the occupier of such premises is not present at the time when a constable seeks to execute such a warrant; but
(b) some other person who appears to the constable to be in charge of the premises is present,

subsection (5) above shall have effect as if any reference to the occupier were a reference to that other person.

(7) If there is no person present who appears to the constable to be in charge of the premises, he shall leave a copy of the warrant in a prominent place on the premises.

(8) A search under a warrant may only be a search to the extent required for the purpose for which the warrant was issued.

(9) A constable executing a warrant shall make an endorsement on it stating –

(a) whether the articles or persons sought were found; and

(b) whether any articles were seized, other than articles which were sought.

(10) A warrant which –

(a) has been executed; or

(b) has not been executed within the time authorised for its execution,

shall be returned –

(i) if it was issued by a justice of the peace, to the clerk to the justices for the petty sessions area for which he acts; and

(ii) if it was issued by a judge, to the appropriate officer of the court from which he issued it.

(11) A warrant which is returned under subsection (10) above shall be retained for 12 months from its return –

(a) by the clerk to the justices, if it was returned under paragraph (i) of that subsection; and

(b) by the appropriate officer, if it was returned under paragraph (ii).

(12) If during the period for which a warrant is to be retained the occupier of the premises to which it relates asks to inspect it, he shall be allowed to do so.

17   Entry for purpose of arrest, etc

(1) Subject to the following provisions of this section, and without prejudice to any other enactment, a constable may enter and search any premises for the purpose –

(a) of executing –

(i) a warrant of arrest issued in connection with or arising out of criminal proceedings; or

(ii) a warrant of commitment issued under section 76 of the Magistrates' Courts Act 1980;

(b) of arresting a person for an arrestable offence;

(c) of arresting a person for an offence under –

(i) section 1 (prohibition of uniforms in connection with political objects) of the Public Order Act 1936;

(ii) any enactment contained in sections 6 to 8 or 10 of the Criminal Law Act 1977 (offences relating to entering and remaining on property);

(iii) section 4 of the Public Order Act 1986 (fear or provocation of violence);

(d) of recapturing a person who is unlawfully at large and whom he is pursuing; or

(e) of saving life or limb or preventing serious damage to property.

(2) Except for the purpose specified in paragraph (e) of subsection (1) above, the powers of entry and search conferred by this section –

(a) are only exercisable if the constable has reasonable grounds for believing that the person whom he is seeking is on the premises; and

(b) are limited, in relation to premises consisting of two or more separate dwellings, to powers to enter and search –

(i) any parts of the premises which the occupiers of any dwelling comprised in the premises use in common with the occupiers of any other such dwelling; and

(ii) any such dwelling in which the constable has reasonable grounds for believing that the person whom he is seeking may be.

(3) The powers of entry and search conferred by this section are only exercisable for the purposes specified in subsection (1)(c)(ii) above by a constable in uniform.

(4) The power of search conferred by this section is only a power to search to the extent that is reasonably required for the purpose for which the power of entry is exercised.

(5) Subject to subsection (6) below, all the rules of common law under which a constable has power to enter premises without a warrant are hereby abolished.

(6) Nothing in subsection (5) above affects any power of entry to deal with or prevent a breach of the peace.

18   Entry and search after arrest

(1) Subject to the following provisions of this section, a constable may enter and search any premises occupied or controlled by a person who is under arrest for an arrestable offence, if he has reasonable grounds for suspecting that there is on the premises evidence, other than items subject to legal privilege, that relates –

(a) to that offence; or

(b) to some other arrestable offence which is connected with or similar to that offence.

(2) A constable may seize and retain anything for which he may search under subsection (1) above.

(3) The power to search conferred by subsection (1) above is only a power to search to the extent that is reasonably required for the purpose of discovering such evidence.

(4) Subject to subsection (5) below, the powers conferred by this section may not be exercised unless an officer of the rank of inspector or above has authorised them in writing.

(5) A constable may conduct a search under subsection (1) above –

(a) before taking the person to a police station; and

(b) without obtaining an authorisation under subsection (4) above,

if the presence of that person at a place other than a police station is necessary for the effective investigation of the offence.

(6) If a constable conducts a search by virtue of subsection (5) above, he shall inform an officer of the rank of inspector or above that he has made the search as soon as practicable after he has made it.

(7) An officer who –

(a) authorises a search; or

(b) is informed of a search under subsection (6) above, shall make a record in writing –

(i) of the grounds for the search; and

(ii) of the nature of the evidence that was sought.

(8) If the person who was in occupation or control of the premises at the time of the search is in police detention at the time the record is to be made, the officer shall make the record as part of his custody record.

19   General power of seizure, etc

(1) The powers conferred by subsections (2), (3) and (4) below are exercisable by a constable who is lawfully on any premises.

(2) The constable may seize anything which is on the premises if he has reasonable grounds for believing –

   (a) that it has been obtained in consequence of the commission of an offence; and

   (b) that it is necessary to seize it in order to prevent it being concealed, lost, damaged, altered or destroyed.

(3) The constable may seize anything which is on the premises if he has reasonable grounds for believing –

   (a) that it is evidence in relation to an offence which he is investigating or any other offence; and

   (b) that it is necessary to seize it in order to prevent the evidence being concealed, lost, altered or destroyed.

(4) The constable may require any information which is contained in a computer and is accessible from the premises to be produced in a form in which it can be taken away and in which it is visible and legible if he has reasonable grounds for believing –

   (a) that –

      (i) it is evidence in relation to an offence which he is investigating or any other offence; or

      (ii) it has been obtained in consequence of the commission of an offence; and

   (b) that it is necessary to do so in order to prevent it being concealed, lost, tampered with or destroyed.

(5) The powers conferred by this section are in addition to any power otherwise conferred.

(6) No power of seizure conferred on a constable under any enactment (including an enactment contained in an Act passed after this Act) is to be taken to authorise the seizure of an item which the constable exercising the power has reasonable grounds for believing to be subject to legal privilege.

20 Extension of powers of seizure to computerised information

(1) Every power of seizure which is conferred by an enactment to which this section applies on a constable who has entered premises in the exercise of a power conferred by an enactment shall be construed as including a power to require any information contained in a computer and accessible from the premises to be produced in a form in which it can be taken away and in which it is visible and legible.

(2) This section applies –

(a) to any enactment contained in an Act passed before this Act;

(b) to sections 8 and 18 above;

(c) to paragraph 13 of Schedule 1 to this Act; and

(d) to any enactment contained in an Act passed after this Act.

21 Access and copying

(1) A constable who seizes anything in the exercise of a power conferred by any enactment, including an enactment contained in an Act passed after this Act, shall, if so requested by a person showing himself –

(a) to be the occupier of premises on which it was seized; or

(b) to have had custody or control of it immediately before the seizure,

provide that person with a record of what he seized.

(2) The officer shall provide the record within a reasonable time from the making of the request for it.

(3) Subject to subsection (8) below, if a request for permission to be granted access to anything which –

(a) has been seized by a constable; and

(b) is retained by the police for the purpose of investigating an offence,

is made to the officer in charge of the investigation by a person who had custody or control of the thing immediately before it was so seized or by someone acting on behalf of such a person, the officer shall allow the person who made the request access to it under the supervision of a constable.

(4) Subject to subsection (8) below, if a request for a photograph or copy of any such thing is made to the officer in charge of the investigation by a person who had custody or control of the thing immediately before it was so seized, or by someone acting on behalf of such a person, the officer shall –

(a) allow the person who made the request access to it under the supervision of a constable for the purpose of photographing or copying it; or

(b) photograph or copy it, or cause it to be photographed or copied.

(5) A constable may also photograph or copy, or have photographed or copied, anything which he has power to seize, without a request being made under subsection (4) above.

(6) Where anything is photographed or copied under subsection (4)(b) above, the photograph or copy shall be supplied to the person who made the request.

(7) The photograph or copy shall be so supplied within a reasonable time from the making of the request.

(8) There is no duty under this section to grant access to, or to supply a photograph or copy of, anything if the officer in charge of the investigation for the purposes of which it was seized has reasonable grounds for believing that to do so would prejudice –

(a) that investigation;

(b) the investigation of an offence other than the offence for the purposes of investigating which the thing was seized; or

(c) any criminal proceedings which may be brought as a result of –

(i) the investigation of which he is in charge; or

(ii) any such investigation as is mentioned in paragraph (b) above.

22 Retention

(1) Subject to subsection (4) below, anything which has been seized by a constable or taken away by a constable following a requirement made by virtue of section 19 or 20 above may be retained so long as is necessary in all the circumstances.

(2) Without prejudice to the generality of subsection (1) above –

(a) anything seized for the purposes of a criminal investigation may be retained, except as provided by subsection (4) below –

(i) for use as evidence at a trial for an offence; or

(ii) for forensic examination or for investigation in connection with an offence; and

(b) anything may be retained in order to establish its lawful owner, where there are reasonable grounds for believing that it has been obtained in consequence of the commission of an offence.

(3) Nothing seized on the ground that it may be used –

(a) to cause physical injury to any person;

(b) to damage property;

(c) to interfere with evidence; or

(d) to assist in escape from police detention or lawful custody,

may be retained when the person from whom it was seized is no longer in police detention or the custody of a court or is in the custody of a court but has been released on bail.

(4) Nothing may be retained for either of the purposes mentioned in subsection (2)(a) above if a photograph or copy would be sufficient for that purpose.

(5) Nothing in this section affects any power of a court to make an order under section 1 of the Police (Property) Act 1897.

23   Meaning of 'premises', etc

In this Act –

'premises' includes any place and, in particular, includes –

(a) any vehicle, vessel, aircraft or hovercraft;

(b) any offshore installation; and

(c) any tent or movable structure; and

'offshore installation' has the meaning given to it by section 1 of the Mineral Workings (Offshore Installations) Act 1971.

PART III

ARREST

24 Arrest without warrant for arrestable offences

(1) The powers of summary arrest conferred by the following subsections shall apply –

(a) to offences for which the sentence is fixed by law;

(b) to offences for which a person of 21 years of age or over (not previously convicted) may be sentenced to imprisonment for a term of five years (or might be so sentenced but for the restrictions imposed by section 33 of the Magistrates' Courts Act 1980); and

(c) to the offences to which subsection (2) below applies,

and in this Act 'arrestable offence' means any such offence.

(2) The offences to which this subsection applies are –

(a) offences for which a person may be arrested under the customs and excise Acts, as defined in section 1(1) of the Customs and Excise Management Act 1979;

(b) offences under the Official Secrets Act 1920 that are not arrestable offences by virtue of the term of imprisonment for which a person may be sentenced in respect of them;

(bb) offences under any provision of the Official Secrets Act 1989 except section 8(1), (4) or (5);

(c) offences under section 22 (causing prostitution of women) or 23 (procuration of girl under 21) of the Sexual Offences Act 1956;

(d) offences under section 12(1) (taking motor vehicle or other conveyance without authority, etc) or 25(1) (going equipped for stealing, etc) of the Theft Act 1968; and

(e) any offence under the Football (Offences) Act 1991.

(3) Without prejudice to section 2 of the Criminal Attempts Act 1981, the powers of summary arrest conferred by the following subsections shall also apply to the offences of –

(a) conspiring to commit any of the offences mentioned in subsection (2) above;

(b) attempting to commit any such offence other than an offence under s12(1) of the Theft Act 1968;

(c) inciting, aiding, abetting, counselling or procuring the commission of any such offence;

and such offences are also arrestable offences for the purposes of this Act.

(4) Any person may arrest without a warrant –

(a) anyone who is in the act of committing an arrestable offence;

(b) anyone whom he has reasonable grounds for suspecting to be committing such an offence.

(5) Where an arrestable offence has been committed, any person may arrest without a warrant –

(a) anyone who is guilty of the offence;

(b) anyone whom he has reasonable grounds for suspecting to be guilty of it.

(6) Where a constable has reasonable grounds for suspecting that an arrestable offence has been committed, he may arrest without a warrant anyone whom he has reasonable grounds for suspecting to be guilty of the offence.

(7) A constable may arrest without a warrant –

(a) anyone who is about to commit an arrestable offence;

(b) anyone whom he has reasonable grounds for suspecting to be about to commit an arrestable offence.

25   General arrest conditions

(1) Where a constable has reasonable grounds for suspecting that any offence which is not an arrestable offence has been committed or attempted, or is being committed or attempted, he may arrest the relevant person if it appears to him that service of a summons is impracticable or inappropriate because any of the general arrest conditions is satisfied.

(2) In this section 'the relevant person' means any person whom the constable has reasonable grounds to suspect of having committed or having attempted to commit the offence or of being in the course of committing or attempting to commit it.

(3) The general arrest conditions are –

(a) that the name of the relevant person is unknown to, and cannot be readily ascertained by, the constable;

(b) that the constable has reasonable grounds for doubting whether a name furnished by the relevant person as his name is his real name;

(c) that –

(i) the relevant person has failed to furnish a satisfactory address for service; or

(ii) the constable has reasonable grounds for doubting whether an address furnished by the relevant person is a satisfactory address for service;

(d) that the constable has reasonable grounds for believing that arrest is necessary to prevent the relevant person –

(i) causing physical injury to himself or any other person;

(ii) suffering physical injury;

(iii) causing loss of or damage to property;

(iv) committing an offence against public decency; or

(v) causing an unlawful obstruction of the highway;

(e) that the constable has reasonable grounds for believing that arrest is necessary to protect a child or other vulnerable person from the relevant person.

(4) For the purposes of subsection (3) above an address is a satisfactory address for service if it appears to the constable –

(a) that the relevant person will be at it for a sufficiently long period for it to be possible to serve him with a summons; or

(b) that some other person specified by the relevant person will accept service of a summons for the relevant person at it.

(5) Nothing in subsection (3)(d) above authorises the arrest of a person under sub-paragraph (iv) of that paragraph except where members of the public going about their normal business cannot reasonably be expected to avoid the person to be arrested.

(6) This section shall not prejudice any power of arrest conferred apart from this section.

27 Fingerprinting of certain offenders

(1) If a person –

(a) has been convicted of a recordable offence;

(b) has not at any time been in police detention for the offence; and

(c) has not had his fingerprints taken –

(i) in the course of the investigation of the offence by the police; or

(ii) since the conviction,

any constable may at any time not later than one month after the date of the conviction require him to attend a police station in order that his fingerprints may be taken.

(2) A requirement under subsection (1) above –

(a) shall give the person a period of at least seven days within which he must so attend; and

(b) may direct him to so attend at a specified time of day or between specified times of day.

(3) Any constable may arrest without warrant a person who has failed to comply with a requirement under subsection (1) above.

(4) The Secretary of State may by regulations make provision for recording in national police records convictions for such offences as are specified in the regulations.

(5) Regulations under this section shall be made by statutory instrument and shall be subject to annulment in pursuance of a resolution of either House of Parliament.

28 Information to be given on arrest

(1) Subject to subsection (5) below, where a person is arrested, otherwise than by being informed that he is under arrest, the arrest is not lawful unless the person arrested is informed that he is under arrest as soon as is practicable after his arrest.

(2) Where a person is arrested by a constable, subsection (1) above applies regardless of whether the fact of the arrest is obvious.

(3) Subject to subsection (5) below, no arrest is lawful unless the

person arrested is informed of the ground for the arrest at the time of, or as soon as is practicable after, the arrest.

(4) Where a person is arrested by a constable, subsection (3) above applies regardless of whether the ground for the arrest is obvious.

(5) Nothing in this section is to be taken to require a person to be informed –

(a) that he is under arrest; or

(b) of the ground for the arrest,

if it was not reasonably practicable for him to be so informed by reason of his having escaped from arrest before the information could be given.

29 Voluntary attendance at police station, etc

Where for the purpose of assisting with an investigation a person attends voluntarily at a police station or at any other place where a constable is present or accompanies a constable to a police station or any such other place without having been arrested –

(a) he shall be entitled to leave at will unless he is placed under arrest;

(b) he shall be informed at once that he is under arrest if a decision is taken by a constable to prevent him from leaving at will.

30 Arrest elsewhere than at police station

(1) Subject to the following provisions of this section, where a person –

(a) is arrested by a constable for an offence; or

(b) is taken into custody by a constable after being arrested for an offence by a person other than a constable,

at any place other than a police station, he shall be taken to a police station by a constable as soon as practicable after the arrest.

(2) Subject to subsections (3) and (5) below, the police station to which an arrested person is taken under subsection (1) above shall be a designated police station.

(3) A constable to whom this subsection applies may take an arrested person to any police station unless it appears to the

constable that it may be necessary to keep the arrested person in police detention for more than six hours.

(4) Subsection (3) above applies –

(a) to a constable who is working in a locality covered by a police station which is not a designated police station; and

(b) to a constable belonging to a body of constables maintained by an authority other than a police authority.

(5) Any constable may take an arrested person to any police station if –

(a) either of the following conditions is satisfied –

(i) the constable has arrested him without the assistance of any other constable and no other constable is available to assist him;

(ii) the constable has taken him into custody from a person other than a constable without the assistance of any other constable and no other constable is available to assist him; and

(b) it appears to the constable that he will be unable to take the arrested person to a designated police station without the arrested person injuring himself, the constable or some other person.

(6) If the first police station to which an arrested person is taken after his arrest is not a designated police station, he shall be taken to a designated police station not more than six hours after his arrival at the first police station unless he is released previously.

(7) A person arrested by a constable at a place other than a police station shall be released if a constable is satisfied, before the person arrested reaches a police station, that there are no grounds for keeping him under arrest.

(8) A constable who releases a person under subsection (7) above shall record the fact that he has done so.

(9) The constable shall make the record as soon as is practicable after the release.

(10) Nothing in subsection (1) above shall prevent a constable delaying taking a person who has been arrested to a police station if the presence of that person elsewhere is necessary in order to carry out such investigations as it is reasonable to carry out immediately.

(11) Where there is delay in taking a person who has been arrested to a police station after his arrest, the reasons for the delay shall be recorded when he first arrives at a police station.

(12) Nothing in subsection (1) above shall be taken to affect –

(a) paragraphs 16(3) or 18(1) of Schedule 2 to the Immigration Act 1971;

(b) section 34(1) of the Criminal Justice Act 1972; or

(c) section 15(6) and (9) of the Prevention of Terrorism (Temporary Provisions) Act 1989 and paragraphs 7(4) and 8(4) and (5) of Schedule 2 and paragraphs 6(6) and 7(4) and (5) of Schedule 5 to that Act.

(13) Nothing in subsection (10) above shall be taken to affect paragraph 18(3) of Schedule 2 to the Immigration Act 1971.

31   Arrest for further offence

Where –

(a) a person –

(i) has been arrested for an offence; and

(ii) is at a police station in consequence of that arrest; and

(b) it appears to a constable that, if he were released from that arrest, he would be liable to arrest for some other offence,

he shall be arrested for that other offence.

32   Search upon arrest

(1) A constable may search an arrested person, in any case where the person to be searched has been arrested at a place other than a police station, if the constable has reasonable grounds for believing that the arrested person may present a danger to himself or others.

(2) Subject to subsections (3) to (5) below, a constable shall also have power in any such case –

(a) to search the arrested person for anything –

(i) which he might use to assist him to escape from lawful custody; or

(ii) which might be evidence relating to an offence; and

(b) to enter and search any premises in which he was when arrested or immediately before he was arrested for evidence relating to the offence for which he has been arrested.

(3) The power to search conferred by subsection (2) above is only a power to search to the extent that is reasonably required for the purpose of discovering any such thing or any such evidence.

(4) The powers conferred by this section to search a person are not to be construed as authorising a constable to require a person to remove any of his clothing in public other than an outer coat, jacket or gloves.

(5) A constable may not search a person in the exercise of the power conferred by subsection (2)(a) above unless he has reasonable grounds for believing that the person to be searched may have concealed on him anything for which a search is permitted under that paragraph.

(6) A constable may not search premises in the exercise of the power conferred by subsection (2)(b) above unless he has reasonable grounds for believing that there is evidence for which a search is permitted under that paragraph on the premises.

(7) In so far as the power of search conferred by subsection (2)(b) above relates to premises consisting of two or more separate dwellings, it is limited to a power to search –

(a) any dwelling in which the arrest took place or in which the person arrested was immediately before his arrest; and

(b) any parts of the premises which the occupier of any such dwelling uses in common with the occupiers of any other dwellings comprised in the premises.

(8) A constable searching a person in the exercise of the power conferred by subsection (1) above may seize and retain anything he finds, if he has reasonable grounds for believing that the person searched might use it to cause physical injury to himself or to any other person.

(9) A constable searching a person in the exercise of the power conferred by subsection (2)(a) above may seize and retain anything he finds, other than an item subject to legal privilege, if he has reasonable grounds for believing –

(a) that he might use it to assist him to escape from lawful custody; or

(b) that it is evidence of an offence or has been obtained in consequence of the commission of an offence.

(10) Nothing in this section shall be taken to affect the power conferred by section 15(3), (4) and (5) of the Prevention of Terrorism (Temporary Provisions) Act 1989.

PART IV

DETENTION

34 Limitations on police detention

(1) A person arrested for an offence shall not be kept in police detention except in accordance with the provisions of this Part of this Act.

(2) Subject to subsection (3) below, if at any time a custody officer –

(a) becomes aware, in relation to any person in police detention, that the grounds for the detention of that person have ceased to apply; and

(b) is not aware of any other grounds on which the continued detention of that person could be justified under the provisions of this Part of this Act,

it shall be the duty of the custody officer, subject to subsection (4) below, to order his immediate release from custody.

(3) No person in police detention shall be released except on the authority of a custody officer at the police station where his detention was authorised or, if it was authorised at more than one station, a custody officer at the station where it was last authorised.

(4) A person who appears to the custody officer to have been unlawfully at large when he was arrested is not to be released under subsection (2) above.

(5) A person whose release is ordered under subsection (2) above shall be released without bail unless it appears to the custody officer –

(a) that there is need for further investigation of any matter in connection with which he was detained at any time during the period of his detention; or

(b) that proceedings may be taken against him in respect of any such matter,

and, if it so appears, he shall be released on bail.

(6) For the purposes of this Part of this Act a person arrested under section 6(5) of the Road Traffic Act 1988 is arrested for an offence.

35   Designated police stations

(1) The chief officer of police for each police area shall designate the police stations in his area which, subject to section 30(3) and (5) above, are to be the stations in that area to be used for the purpose of detaining arrested persons.

(2) A chief officer's duty under subsection (1) above is to designate police stations appearing to him to provide enough accommodation for that purpose.

(3) Without prejudice to section 12 of the Interpretation Act 1978 (continuity of duties) a chief officer –

(a) may designate a station which was not previously designated; and

(b) may direct that a designation of a station previously made shall cease to operate.

(4) In this Act 'designated police station' means a police station for the time being designated under this section.

36   Custody officers at police stations

(1) One or more custody officers shall be appointed for each designated police station.

(2) A custody officer for a designated police station shall be appointed –

(a) by the chief officer of police for the area in which the designated police station is situated; or

(b) by such other police officer as the chief officer of police for that area may direct.

(3) No officer may be appointed a custody officer unless he is of at least the rank of sergeant.

(4) An officer of any rank may perform the functions of a custody officer at a designated police station if a custody officer is not readily available to perform them.

(5) Subject to the following provisions of this section and to section 39(2) below, none of the functions of a custody officer in relation to a person shall be performed by an officer who at the time when the function falls to be performed is involved in the investigation of an offence for which that person is in police detention at that time.

(6) Nothing in subsection (5) above is to be taken to prevent a custody officer –

   (a) performing any function assigned to custody officers –

   (i) by this Act; or
   (ii) by a code of practice issued under this Act;

   (b) carrying out the duty imposed on custody officers by section 39 below;

   (c) doing anything in connection with the identification of a suspect; or

   (d) doing anything under sections 7 and 8 of the Road Traffic Act 1988.

(7) Where an arrested person is taken to a police station which is not a designated police station, the functions in relation to him which at a designated police station would be the functions of a custody officer shall be performed –

   (a) by an officer who is not involved in the investigation of an offence for which he is in police detention, if such an officer is readily available; and

   (b) if no such officer is readily available, by the officer who took him to the station or any other officer.

(8) References to a custody officer in the following provisions of this Act include references to an officer other than a custody officer who is performing the functions of a custody officer by virtue of subsection (4) or (7) above.

(9) Where by virtue of subsection (7) above an officer of a force maintained by a police authority who took an arrested person to a police station is to perform the functions of a custody officer in relation to him, the officer shall inform an officer who –

(a) is attached to a designated police station; and

(b) is of at least the rank of inspector,

that he is to do so.

(10) The duty imposed by subsection (9) above shall be performed as soon as it is practicable to perform it.

37   Duties of custody officer before charge

(1) Where –

(a) a person is arrested for an offence –

(i) without a warrant; or
(ii) under a warrant not endorsed for bail, or

(b) a person returns to a police station to answer to bail,

the custody officer at each police station where he is detained after his arrest shall determine whether he has before him sufficient evidence to charge that person with the offence for which he was arrested and may detain him at the police station for such period as is necessary to enable him to do so.

(2) If the custody officer determines that he does not have such evidence before him, the person arrested shall be released either on bail or without bail, unless the custody officer has reasonable grounds for believing that his detention without being charged is necessary to secure or preserve evidence relating to an offence for which he is under arrest or to obtain such evidence by questioning him.

(3) If the custody officer has reasonable grounds for so believing, he may authorise the person arrested to be kept in police detention.

(4) Where a custody officer authorises a person who has not been charged to be kept in police detention, he shall, as soon as is practicable, make a written record of the grounds for the detention.

(5) Subject to subsection (6) below, the written record shall be made in the presence of the person arrested who shall at that time be informed by the custody officer of the grounds for his detention.

(6) Subsection (5) above shall not apply where the person arrested is, at the time when the written record is made –

(a) incapable of understanding what is said to him;

(b) violent or likely to become violent; or

(c) in urgent need of medical attention.

(7) Subject to section 41(7) below, if the custody officer determines that he has before him sufficient evidence to charge the person arrested with the offence for which he was arrested, the person arrested –

(a) shall be charged; or

(b) shall be released without charge, either on bail or without bail.

(8) Where –

(a) a person is released under subsection (7)(b) above; and

(b) at the time of his release a decision whether he should be prosecuted for the offence for which he was arrested has not been taken,

it shall be the duty of the custody officer so to inform him.

(9) If the person arrested is not in a fit state to be dealt with under subsection (7) above, he may be kept in police detention until he is.

(10) The duty imposed on the custody officer under subsection (1) above shall be carried out by him as soon as practicable after the person arrested arrives at the police station or, in the case of a person arrested at the police station, as soon as practicable after the arrest.

(15) In this Part of this Act –

'arrested juvenile' means a person arrested with or without a warrant who appears to be under the age of 17;

'endorsed for bail' means endorsed with a direction for bail in accordance with section 117(2) of the Magistrates' Courts Act 1980.

38   Duties of custody officer after charge

(1) Where a person arrested for an offence otherwise than under a warrant endorsed for bail is charged with an offence, the custody officer shall order his release from police detention, either on bail or without bail, unless –

(a) if the person arrested is not an arrested juvenile –

(i) his name or address cannot be ascertained or the custody officer has reasonable grounds for doubting whether a name or address furnished by him as his name or address is his real name or address;

(ii) the custody officer has reasonable grounds for believing that the detention of the person arrested is necessary for his own protection or to prevent him from causing physical injury to any other person or from causing loss of or damage to property; or

(iii) the custody officer has reasonable grounds for believing that the person arrested will fail to appear in court to answer to bail or that his detention is necessary to prevent him from interfering with the administration of justice or with the investigation of offences or of a particular offence;

(b) if he is an arrested juvenile –

(i) any of the requirements of paragraph (a) above is satisfied; or

(ii) the custody officer has reasonable grounds for believing that he ought to be detained in his own interests.

(2) If the release of a person arrested is not required by subsection (1) above, the custody officer may authorise him to be kept in police detention.

(3) Where a custody officer authorises a person who has been charged to be kept in police detention, he shall, as soon as practicable, make a written record of the grounds for the detention.

(4) Subject to subsection (5) below, the written record shall be made in the presence of the person charged who shall at that time be informed by the custody officer of the grounds for his detention.

(5) Subsection (4) above shall not apply where the person charged is, at the time when the written record is made –

(a) incapable of understanding what is said to him;

(b) violent or likely to become violent; or

(c) in urgent need of medical attention.

(6) Where a custody officer authorises an arrested juvenile to be kept in police detention under subsection (1) above, the custody officer shall, unless he certifies –

(a) that, by reason of such circumstances as are specified in the certificate, it is impracticable for him to do so; or

(b) in the case of an arrested juvenile who has attained the age of

15 years, that no secure accommodation is available and that keeping him in other local authority accommodation would not be adequate to protect the public from serious harm from him,

secure that the arrested juvenile is moved to local authority accommodation.

(6A) In this section –

'local authority accommodation' means accommodation provided by or on behalf of a local authority (within the meaning of the Children Act 1989);

'secure accommodation' means accommodation provided for the purposes of restricting liberty;

'sexual offence' and 'violent offence' have the same meanings as in Part I of the Criminal Justice Act 1991;

and any reference, in relation to an arrested juvenile charged with a violent or sexual offence, to protecting the public from serious harm from him shall be construed as a reference to protecting members of the public from death or serious personal injury, whether physical or psychological, occasioned by further such offences committed by him.

(6B) Where an arrested juvenile is moved to local authority accommodation under subsection (6) above, it shall be lawful for any person acting on behalf of the authority to detain him.

(7) A certificate made under subsection (6) above in respect of an arrested juvenile shall be produced to the court before which he is first brought thereafter.

(8) In this Part of this Act 'local authority' has the same meaning as in the Children Act 1989.

39 Responsibilities in relation to persons detained

(1) Subject to subsections (2) and (4) below, it shall be the duty of the custody officer at a police station to ensure –

(a) that all persons in police detention at that station are treated in accordance with this Act and any code of practice issued under it and relating to the treatment of persons in police detention; and

(b) that all matters relating to such persons which are required by this Act or by such codes of practice to be recorded are recorded in the custody records relating to such persons.

(2) If the custody officer, in accordance with any code of practice issued under this Act, transfers or permits the transfer of a person in police detention –

(a) to the custody of a police officer investigating an offence for which that person is in police detention; or

(b) to the custody of an officer who has charge of that person outside the police station,

the custody officer shall cease in relation to that person to be subject to the duty imposed on him by subsection (1)(a) above; and it shall be the duty of the officer to whom the transfer is made to ensure that he is treated in accordance with the provisions of this Act and of any such codes of practice as are mentioned in subsection (1) above.

(3) If the person detained in subsequently returned to the custody of the custody officer, it shall be the duty of the officer investigating the offence to report to the custody officer as to the manner in which this section and the codes of practice have been complied with while that person was in his custody.

(4) If an arrested juvenile is moved to local authority accommodation in pursuance of arrangements made under section 38(6) above, the custody officer shall cease in relation to that person to be subject to the duty imposed on him by subsection (1) above.

40   Review of police detention

(1) Reviews of the detention of each person in police detention in connection with the investigation of an offence shall be carried out periodically in accordance with the following provisions of this section –

(a) in the case of a person who has been arrested and charged, by the custody officer; and

(b) in the case of a person who has been arrested but not charged, by an officer of at least the rank of inspector who has not been directly involved in the investigation.

(2) The officer to whom it falls to carry out a review is referred to in this section as a 'review officer'.

(3) Subject to subsection (4) below –

(a) the first review shall be not later than six hours after the detention was first authorised;

(b) the second review shall be not later than nine hours after the first;

(c) subsequent reviews shall be at intervals of not more than nine hours.

(4) A review may be postponed –

(a) if, having regard to all the circumstances prevailing at the latest time for it specified in subsection (3) above, it is not practicable to carry out the review at that time;

(b) without prejudice to the generality of paragraph (a) above –

(i) if at that time the person in detention is being questioned by a police officer and the review officer is satisfied that an interruption of the questioning for the purpose of carrying out the review would prejudice the investigation in connection with which he is being questioned; or

(ii) if at that time no review officer is readily available.

(5) If a review is postponed under subsection (4) above it shall be carried out as soon as practicable after the latest time specified for it in subsection (3) above.

(6) If a review is carried out after postponement under subsection (4) above, the fact that it was so carried out shall not affect any requirements of this section as to the time at which any subsequent review is to be carried out.

(7) The review officer shall record the reasons for any postponement of a review in the custody record.

(8) Subject to subsection (9) below, where the person whose detention is under review has not been charged before the time of the review, section 37(1) to (6) above shall have effect in relation to him, but with the substitution –

(a) of references to the person whose detention is under review for references to the person arrested; and

(b) of references to the review officer for references to the custody officer.

(9) Where a person has been kept in police detention by virtue of section 37(9) above, section 37(1) to (6) shall not have effect in relation to him but it shall be the duty of the review officer to determine whether he is yet in a fit state.

(10) Where the person whose detention is under review has been charged before the time of the review, section 38(1) to (6) above shall have effect in relation to him, but with the substitution of references to the person whose detention is under review for references to the person arrested.

(11) Where –

(a) an officer of higher rank than the review officer gives directions relating to a person in police detention; and

(b) the directions are at variance –

(i) with any decision made or action taken by the review officer in the performance of a duty imposed on him under this Part of this Act; or

(ii) with any decision or action which would but for the directions have been made or taken by him in the performance of such a duty,

the review officer shall refer the matter at once to an officer of the rank of superintendent or above who is responsible for the police station for which the review officer is acting as review officer in connection with the detention.

(12) Before determining whether to authorise a person's continued detention the review officer shall give –

(a) that person (unless he is asleep); or

(b) any solicitor representing him who is available at the time of the review,

an opportunity to make representations to him about the detention.

(13) Subject to subsection (14) below, the person whose detention is under review or his solicitor may make representations under subsection (12) above either orally or in writing.

(14) The review officer may refuse to hear oral representations from the person whose detention is under review if he considers that he is unfit to make such representations by reason of his condition or behaviour.

41 Limits on period of detention without charge

(1) Subject to the following provisions of this section and to sections

42 and 43 below, a person shall not be kept in police detention for more than 24 hours without being charged.

(2) The time from which the period of detention of a person is to be calculated (in this Act referred to as 'the relevant time') –

(a) in the case of a person to whom this paragraph applies, shall be –

(i) the time at which that person arrives at the relevant police station; or

(ii) the time 24 hours after the time of that person's arrest,

whichever is the earlier;

(b) in the case of a person arrested outside England and Wales, shall be –

(i) the time at which that person arrives at the first police station to which he is taken in the police area in England or Wales in which the offence for which he was arrested is being investigated; or

(ii) the time 24 hours after the time of that person's entry into England and Wales,

whichever is the earlier;

(c) in the case of a person who –

(i) attends voluntarily at a police station; or

(ii) accompanies a constable to a police station without having been arrested,

and is arrested at the police station, the time of his arrest;

(d) in any other case, except where subsection (5) below applies, shall be the time at which the person arrested arrives at the first police station to which he is taken after his arrest.

(3) Subsection (2)(a) above applies to a person if –

(a) his arrest is sought in one police area in England and Wales;

(b) he is arrested in another police area; and

(c) he is not questioned in the area in which he is arrested in order to obtain evidence in relation to an offence for which he is arrested;

and in sub-paragraph (i) of that paragraph 'the relevant police station' means the first police station to which he is taken in the police area in which his arrest was sought.

(4) Subsection (2) above shall have effect in relation to a person arrested under section 31 above as if every reference in it to his arrest or his being arrested were a reference to his arrest or his being arrested for the offence for which he was originally arrested.

(5) If –

(a) a person is in police detention in a police area in England and Wales ('the first area'); and

(b) his arrest for an offence is sought in some other police area in England and Wales ('the second area'); and

(c) he is taken to the second area for the purposes of investigating that offence, without being questioned in the first area in order to obtain evidence in relation to it,

the relevant time shall be –

(i) the time 24 hours after he leaves the place where he is detained in the first area; or

(ii) the time at which he arrives at the first police station to which he is taken in the second area,

whichever is the earlier.

(6) When a person who is in police detention is removed to hospital because he is in need of medical treatment, any time during which he is being questioned in hospital or on the way there or back by a police officer for the purpose of obtaining evidence relating to an offence shall be included in any period which falls to be calculated for the purposes of this Part of this Act, but any other time while he is in hospital or on his way there or back shall not be so included.

(7) Subject to subsection (8) below, a person who at the expiry of 24 hours after the relevant time is in police detention and has not been charged shall be released at that time either on bail or without bail.

(8) Subsection (7) above does not apply to a person whose detention for more than 24 hours after the relevant time has been authorised or is otherwise permitted in accordance with section 42 or 43 below.

(9) A person released under subsection (7) above shall not be re-arrested without a warrant for the offence for which he was previously arrested unless new evidence justifying a further arrest has come to light since his release.

42 Authorisation of continued detention

(1) Where a police officer of the rank of superintendent or above who is responsible for the police station at which a person is detained has reasonable grounds for believing that –

(a) the detention of that person without charge is necessary to secure or preserve evidence relating to an offence for which he is under arrest or to obtain such evidence by questioning him;

(b) an offence for which he is under arrest is a serious arrestable offence; and

(c) the investigation is being conducted diligently and expeditiously,

he may authorise the keeping of that person in police detention for a period expiring at or before 36 hours after the relevant time.

(2) Where an officer such as is mentioned in subsection (1) above has authorised the keeping of a person in police detention for a period expiring less than 36 hours after the relevant time, such an officer may authorise the keeping of that person in police detention for a further period expiring not more than 36 hours after that time if the conditions specified in subsection (1) above are still satisfied when he gives the authorisation.

(3) If it is proposed to transfer a person in police detention to another police area, the officer determining whether or not to authorise keeping him in detention under subsection (1) above shall have regard to the distance and the time the journey would take.

(4) No authorisation under subsection (1) above shall be given in respect of any person –

(a) more than 24 hours after the relevant time; or

(b) before the second review of his detention under section 40 above has been carried out.

(5) Where an officer authorises the keeping of a person in police detention under subsection (1) above, it shall be his duty –

(a) to inform that person of the grounds for his continued detention; and

(b) to record the grounds in that person's custody record.

(6) Before determining whether to authorise the keeping of a person in detention under subsection (1) or (2) above, an officer shall give –

(a) that person; or

(b) any solicitor representing him who is available at the time when it falls to the officer to determine whether to give the authorisation,

an opportunity to make representations to him about the detention.

(7) Subject to subsection (8) below, the person in detention or his solicitor may make representations under subsection (6) above either orally or in writing.

(8) The officer to whom it falls to determine whether to give the authorisation may refuse to hear oral representations from the person in detention if he considers that he is unfit to make such representations by reason of his condition or behaviour.

(9) Where –

(a) an officer authorises the keeping of a person in detention under subsection (1) above; and

(b) at the time of the authorisation he has not yet exercised a right conferred on him by section 56 or 58 below,

the officer –

(i) shall inform him of that right;

(ii) shall decide whether he should be permitted to exercise it;

(iii) shall record the decision in his custody record; and

(iv) if the decision is to refuse to permit the exercise of the right, shall also record the grounds for the decision in that record.

(10) Where an officer has authorised the keeping of a person who has not been charged in detention under subsection (1) or (2) above, he shall be released from detention, either on bail or without bail, not later than 36 hours after the relevant time, unless –

(a) he has been charged with an offence; or

(b) his continued detention is authorised or otherwise permitted in accordance with section 43 below.

(11) A person released under subsection (10) above shall not be re-arrested without a warrant for the offence for which he was previously arrested unless new evidence justifying a further arrest has come to light since his release.

43   Warrants of further detention

(1) Where, on an application on oath made by a constable and supported by an information, a magistrates' court is satisfied that there are reasonable grounds for believing that the further detention of the person to whom the application relates is justified, it may issue a warrant of further detention authorising the keeping of that person in police detention.

(2) A court may not hear an application for a warrant of further detention unless the person to whom the application relates –

   (a) has been furnished with a copy of the information; and

   (b) has been brought before the court for the hearing.

(3) The person to whom the application relates shall be entitled to be legally represented at the hearing and, if he is not so represented but wishes to be so represented –

   (a) the court shall adjourn the hearing to enable him to obtain representation; and

   (b) he may be kept in police detention during the adjournment.

(4) A person's further detention is only justified for the purposes of this section or section 44 below if –

   (a) his detention without charge is necessary to secure or preserve evidence relating to an offence for which he is under arrest or to obtain such evidence by questioning him;

   (b) an offence for which he is under arrest is a serious arrestable offence; and

   (c) the investigation is being conducted diligently and expeditiously.

(5) Subject to subsection (7) below, an application for a warrant of further detention may be made –

   (a) at any time before the expiry of 36 hours after the relevant time; or

   (b) in a case where –

      (i) it is not practicable for the magistrates' court to which the application will be made to sit at the expiry of 36 hours after the relevant time; but

      (ii) the court will sit during the six hours following the end of that period,

   at any time before the expiry of the said six hours.

(6) In a case to which subsection (5)(b) above applies –

(a) the person to whom the application relates may be kept in police detention until the application is heard; and

(b) the custody officer shall make a note in that person's custody record –

(i) of the fact that he was kept in police detention for more than 36 hours after the relevant time; and

(ii) of the reason why he was so kept.

(7) If –

(a) an application for a warrant of further detention is made after the expiry of 36 hours after the relevant time; and

(b) it appears to the magistrates' court that it would have been reasonable for the police to make it before the expiry of that period,

the court shall dismiss the application.

(8) Where on an application such as is mentioned in subsection (1) above a magistrates' court is not satisfied that there are reasonable grounds for believing that the further detention of the person to whom the application relates is justified, it shall be its duty –

(a) to refuse the application; or

(b) to adjourn the hearing of it until a time not later than 36 hours after the relevant time.

(9) The person to whom the application relates may be kept in police detention during the adjournment.

(10) A warrant of further detention shall –

(a) state the time at which it is issued;

(b) authorise the keeping in police detention of the person to whom it relates for the period stated in it.

(11) Subject to subsection (12) below, the period stated in a warrant of further detention shall be such period as the magistrates' court thinks fit, having regard to the evidence before it.

(12) The period shall not be longer than 36 hours.

(13) If it is proposed to transfer a person in police detention to a police area other than that in which he is detained when the application for a warrant of further detention is made, the court

hearing the application shall have regard to the distance and the time the journey would take.

(14) Any information submitted in support of an application under this section shall state –

(a) the nature of the offence for which the person to whom the application relates has been arrested;

(b) the general nature of the evidence on which that person was arrested;

(c) what inquiries relating to the offence have been made by the police and what further inquiries are proposed by them;

(d) the reasons for believing the continued detention of that person to be necessary for the purposes of such further inquiries.

(15) Where an application under this section is refused, the person to whom the application relates shall forthwith be charged or, subject to subsection (16) below, released, either on bail or without bail.

(16) A person need not be released under subsection (15) above –

(a) before the expiry of 24 hours after the relevant time; or

(b) before the expiry of any longer period for which his continued detention is or has been authorised under section 42 above.

(17) Where an application under this section is refused, no further application shall be made under this section in respect of the person to whom the refusal relates, unless supported by evidence which has come to light since the refusal.

(18) Where a warrant of further detention is issued, the person to whom it relates shall be released from police detention, either on bail or without bail, upon or before the expiry of the warrant unless he is charged.

(19) A person released under subsection (18) above shall not be re-arrested without a warrant for the offence for which he was previously arrested unless new evidence justifying a further arrest has come to light since his release.

44   Extension of warrants of further detention

(1) On an application on oath made by a constable and supported by an information a magistrates' court may extend a warrant of

further detention issued under section 43 above if it is satisfied that there are reasonable grounds for believing that the further detention of the person to whom the application relates is justified.

(2) Subject to subsection (3) below, the period for which a warrant of further detention may be extended shall be such period as the court thinks fit, having regard to the evidence before it.

(3) The period shall not –

(a) be longer than 36 hours; or
(b) end later than 96 hours after the relevant time.

(4) Where a warrant of further detention has been extended under subsection (1) above, or further extended under this subsection, for a period ending before 96 hours after the relevant time, on an application such as is mentioned in that subsection a magistrates' court may further extend the warrant if it is satisfied as there mentioned; and subsections (2) and (3) above apply to such further extensions as they apply to extensions under subsection (1) above.

(5) A warrant of further detention shall, if extended or further extended under this section, be endorsed with a note of the period of the extension.

(6) Subsections (2), (3) and (14) of section 43 above shall apply to an application made under this section as they apply to an application made under that section.

(7) Where an application under this section is refused, the person to whom the application relates shall forthwith be charged or, subject to subsection (8) below, released, either on bail or without bail.

(8) A person need not be released under subsection (7) above before the expiry of any period for which a warrant of further detention issued in relation to him has been extended or further extended on an earlier application made under this section.

45   Detention before charge – supplementary

(1) In sections 43 and 44 of this Act 'magistrates' court' means a court consisting of two or more justices of the peace sitting otherwise than in open court.

(2) Any reference in this Part of this Act to a period of time or a time of day is to be treated as approximate only.

46 Detention after charge

(1) Where a person –

(a) is charged with an offence; and
(b) after being charged –

(i) is kept in police detention; or
(ii) is detained by a local authority in pursuance of arrangements made under section 38(6) above,

he shall be brought before a magistrates' court in accordance with the provisions of this section.

(2) If he is to be brought before a magistrates' court for the petty sessions area in which the police station at which he was charged is situated, he shall be brought before such a court as soon as is practicable and in any event not later than the first sitting after he is charged with the offence.

(3) If no magistrates' court for that area is due to sit either on the day on which he is charged or on the next day, the custody officer for the police station at which he was charged shall inform the clerk to the justices for the area that there is a person in the area to whom subsection (2) above applies.

(4) If the person charged is to be brought before a magistrates' court for a petty sessions area other than that in which the police station at which he was charged is situated, he shall be removed to that area as soon as is practicable and brought before such a court as soon as is practicable after his arrival in the area and in any event not later than the first sitting of a magistrates' court for that area after his arrival in the area.

(5) If no magistrates' court for that area is due to sit either on the day on which he arrives in the area or on the next day –

(a) he shall be taken to a police station in the area; and
(b) the custody officer at that station shall inform the clerk to the justices for the area that there is a person in the area to whom subsection (4) applies.

(6) Subject to subsection (8) below, where a clerk to the justices for a petty sessions area has been informed –

(a) under subsection (3) above that there is a person in the area to whom subsection (2) above applies; or

(b) under subsection (5) above that there is a person in the area to whom subsection (4) above applies,

the clerk shall arrange for a magistrates' court to sit not later than the day next following the relevant day.

(7) In this section 'the relevant day' –

(a) in relation to a person who is to be brought before a magistrates' court for the petty sessions area in which the police station at which he was charged is situated, means the day on which he was charged; and

(b) in relation to a person who is to be brought before a magistrates' court for any other petty sessions area, means the day on which he arrives in the area.

(8) Where the day next following the relevant day is Christmas Day, Good Friday or a Sunday, the duty of the clerk under subsection (6) above is a duty to arrange for a magistrates' court to sit not later than the first day after the relevant day which is not one of those days.

(9) Nothing in this section requires a person who is in hospital to be brought before a court if he is not well enough.

47   Bail after arrest

(1) Subject to subsection (2) below, a release on bail of a person under this Part of this Act shall be a release on bail granted in accordance with the Bail Act 1976.

(2) Nothing in the Bail Act 1976 shall prevent the re-arrest without warrant of a person released on bail subject to a duty to attend at a police station if new evidence justifying a further arrest has come to light since his release.

(3) Subject to subsection (4) below, in this Part of this Act references to 'bail' are references to bail subject to a duty –

(a) to appear before a magistrates' court at such time and such place; or

(b) to attend at such police station at such time,

as the custody officer may appoint.

(4) Where a custody officer has granted bail to a person subject to a duty to appear at a police station, the custody officer may give notice in writing to that person that his attendance at the police station is not required.

(5) Where a person arrested for an offence who was released on bail subject to a duty to attend at a police station so attends, he may be detained without charge in connection with that offence only if the custody officer at the police station has reasonable grounds for believing that his detention is necessary –

(a) to secure or preserve evidence relating to the offence; or

(b) to obtain such evidence by questioning him.

(6) Where a person is detained under subsection (5) above, any time during which he was in police detention prior to being granted bail shall be included as part of any period which falls to be calculated under this Part of this Act.

(7) Where a person who was released on bail subject to a duty to attend at a police station is re-arrested, the provisions of this Part of this Act shall apply to him as they apply to a person arrested for the first time.

51 Savings

Nothing in this Part of this Act shall affect –

(a) the powers conferred on immigration officers by section 4 of and Schedule 2 to the Immigration Act 1971 (administrative provisions as to control on entry, etc);

(b) the powers conferred by or by virtue of section 14 of the Prevention of Terrorism (Temporary Provisions) Act 1989 or Schedule 2 or 5 to that Act (powers of arrest and detention and control of entry and procedure for removal);

(c) any duty of a police officer under –

(i) sections 129, 190 or 202 of the Army Act 1955 (duties of governors of prisons and others to receive prisoners, deserters, absentees and persons under escort);

(ii) sections 129, 190 or 202 of the Air Force Act 1955 (duties of governors of prisons and others to receive prisoners, deserters, absentees and persons under escort);

(iii) section 107 of the Naval Discipline Act 1957 (duties of governors of civil prisons, etc); or

(iv) paragraph 5 of Schedule 5 to the Reserve Forces Act 1980 (duties of governors of civil prisons); or

(d) any right of a person in police detention to apply for a writ of habeas corpus or other prerogative remedy.

PART V

QUESTIONING AND TREATMENT OF PERSONS BY POLICE

53   Abolition of certain powers of constables to search persons

(1) Subject to subsection (2) below, there shall cease to have effect any Act (including a local Act) passed before this Act in so far as it authorises –

(a) any search by a constable of a person in police detention at a police station; or

(b) an intimate search of a person by a constable;

and any rule of common law which authorises a search such as is mentioned in paragraph (a) or (b) above is abolished.

54   Searches of detained persons

(1) The custody officer at a police station shall ascertain and record or cause to be recorded everything which a person has with him when he is –

(a) brought to the station after being arrested elsewhere or after being committed to custody by an order or sentence of a court; or

(b) arrested at the station or detained there under section 47(5) above.

(2) In the case of an arrested person the record shall be made as part of his custody record.

(3) Subject to subsection (4) below, a custody officer may seize and retain any such thing or cause any such thing to be seized and retained.

(4) Clothes and personal effects may only be seized if the custody officer –

(a) believes that the person from whom they are seized may use them –

(i) to cause physical injury to himself or any other person;

(ii) to damage property;

(iii) to interfere with evidence; or

(iv) to assist him to escape; or

(b) has reasonable grounds for believing that they may be evidence relating to an offence.

(5) Where anything is seized, the person from whom it is seized shall be told the reason for the seizure unless he is –

(a) violent or likely to become violent; or

(b) incapable of understanding what is said to him.

(6) Subject to subsection (7) below, a person may be searched if the custody officer considers it necessary to enable him to carry out his duty under subsection (1) above and to the extent that the custody officer considers necessary for that purpose.

(6A) A person who is in custody at a police station or is in police detention otherwise than at a police station may at any time be searched in order to ascertain whether he has with him anything which he could use for the purposes specified in subsection (4)(a) above.

(6B) Subject to subsection (6C) below, a constable may seize and retain, or cause to be seized and retained, anything found on such a search.

(6C) A constable may only seize clothes and personal effects in the circumstances specified in subsection (4) above.

(7) An intimate search may not be conducted under this section.

(8) A search under this section shall be carried out by a constable.

(9) The constable carrying out a search shall be of the same sex as the person searched.

55 Intimate searches

(1) Subject to the following provisions of this section, if an officer of at least the rank of superintendent has reasonable grounds for believing –

(a) that a person who has been arrested and is in police detention may have concealed on him anything which –

(i) he could use to cause physical injury to himself or others; and
(ii) he might so use while he is in police detention or in the custody of a court; or

(b) that such a person –

(i) may have a Class A drug concealed on him; and
(ii) was in possession of it with the appropriate criminal intent before his arrest,

he may authorise an intimate search of that person.

(2) An officer may not authorise an intimate search of a person for anything unless he has reasonable grounds for believing that it cannot be found without his being intimately searched.

(3) An officer may give an authorisation under subsection (1) above orally or in writing but, if he gives it orally, he shall confirm it in writing as soon as is practicable.

(4) An intimate search which is only a drug offence search shall be by way of examination by a suitably qualified person.

(5) Except as provided by subsection (4) above, an intimate search shall be by way of examination by a suitably qualified person unless an officer of at least the rank of superintendent considers that this is not practicable.

(6) An intimate search which is not carried out as mentioned in subsection (5) above shall be carried out by a constable.

(7) A constable may not carry out an intimate search of a person of the opposite sex.

(8) No intimate search may be carried out except –

(a) at a police station;

(b) at a hospital;

(c) at a registered medical practitioner's surgery; or

(d) at some other place used for medical purposes.

(9) An intimate search which is only a drug offence search may not be carried out at a police station.

(10) If an intimate search of a person is carried out, the custody record relating to him shall state –

(a) which parts of his body were searched; and

(b) why they were searched.

(11) The information required to be recorded by subsection (10) above shall be recorded as soon as practicable after the completion of the search.

(12) The custody officer at a police station may seize and retain anything which is found on an intimate search of a person, or cause any such thing to be seized and retained –

(a) if he believes that the person from whom it is seized may use it –

(i)   to cause physical injury to himself or any other person;

(ii) to damage property;

(iii) to interfere with evidence; or

(iv) to assist him to escape; or

(b) if he has reasonable grounds for believing that it may be evidence relating to an offence.

(13) Where anything is seized under this section, the person from whom it is seized shall be told the reason for the seizure unless he is –

(a) violent or likely to become violent; or

(b) incapable of understanding what is said to him ...

(17) In this section –

'the appropriate criminal intent' means an intent to commit an offence under –

(a) section 5(3) of the Misuse of Drugs Act 1971 (possession of controlled drug with intent to supply to another); or

(b) section 68(2) of the Customs and Excise Management Act 1979 (exportation etc with intent to evade a prohibition of restriction);

'Class A drug' has the meaning assigned to it by section 2(1)(b) of the Misuse of Drugs Act 1971;

'drug offence search' means an intimate search for a Class A drug which an officer has authorised by virtue of subsection (1)(b) above; and

'suitably qualified person' means –

(a) a registered medical practitioner; or

(b) a registered nurse.

56 Right to have someone informed when arrested

(1) Where a person has been arrested and is being held in custody in a police station or other premises, he shall be entitled, if he so requests, to have one friend or relative or other person who is known to him or who is likely to take an interest in his welfare told, as soon as is practicable except to the extent that delay is permitted by this section, that he has been arrested and is being detained there.

(2) Delay is only permitted –

(a) in the case of a person who is in police detention for a serious arrestable offence; and

(b) if an officer of at least the rank of superintendent authorises it.

(3) In any case the person in custody must be permitted to exercise the right conferred by subsection (1) above within 36 hours from the relevant time, as defined in section 41(2) above.

(4) An officer may give an authorisation under subsection (2) above orally or in writing but, if he gives it orally, he shall confirm it in writing as soon as is practicable.

(5) Subject to subsection (5A) below, an officer may only authorise delay where he has reasonable grounds for believing that telling the named person of the arrest –

(a) will lead to interference with or harm to evidence connected with a serious arrestable offence or interference with or physical injury to other persons; or

(b) will lead to the alerting of other persons suspected of having committed such an offence but not yet arrested for it; or

(c) will hinder the recovery of any property obtained as a result of such an offence.

(5A) An officer may also authorise delay where the serious arrestable offence is a drug trafficking offence or an offence to which Part VI of the Criminal Justice Act 1988 applies (offences in respect of which confiscation orders under that Part may be made) and the officer has reasonable grounds for believing –

(a) where the offence is a drug trafficking offence, that the detained person has benefited from drug trafficking and that the recovery of the value of that person's proceeds of drug trafficking will be hindered by telling the named person of the arrest; and

(b) where the offence is one to which Part VI of the Criminal Justice Act 1988 applies, that the detained person has benefited from the offence and that the recovery of the value of the property obtained by that person from or in connection with the offence or of the pecuniary advantage derived by him from or in connection with it will be hindered by telling the named person of the arrest.

(6) If a delay is authorised –

(a) the detained person shall be told the reason for it; and

(b) the reason shall be noted on his custody record.

(7) The duties imposed by subsection (6) above shall be performed as soon as is practicable.

(8) The rights conferred by this section on a person detained at a police station or other premises are exercisable whenever he is transferred from one place to another; and this section applies to each subsequent occasion on which they are exercisable as it applies to the first such occasion.

(9) There may be no further delay in permitting the exercise of the right conferred by subsection (1) above once the reason for authorising delay ceases to subsist.

(10) In the foregoing provisions of this section references to a person who has been arrested include references to a person who has been detained under the terrorism provisions and 'arrest' includes detention under those provisions.

(11) In its application to a person who has been arrested or detained under the terrorism provisions –

(a) subsection (2)(a) above shall have effect as if for the words 'for a serious arrestable offence' there were substituted the words 'under the terrorism provisions';

(b) subsection (3) above shall have effect as if for the words from 'within' onwards there were substituted the words 'before the end of the period beyond which he may no longer be detained without the authority of the Secretary of State'; and

(c) subsection (5) above shall have effect as if at the end there were added 'or

(d) will lead to interference with the gathering of information about the commission, preparation or instigation of acts of terrorism; or

(e) by alerting any person, will make it more difficult –

(i) to prevent an act of terrorism; or

(ii) to secure the apprehension, prosecution or conviction of any person in connection with the commission, preparation or instigation of an act of terrorism.'.

58 Access to legal advice

(1) A person arrested and held in custody in a police station or other premises shall be entitled, if he so requests, to consult a solicitor privately at any time.

(2) Subject to subsection (3) below, a request under subsection (1) above and the time at which it was made shall be recorded in the custody record.

(3) Such a request need not be recorded in the custody record of a person who makes it at a time while he is at a court after being charged with an offence.

(4) If a person makes such a request, he must be permitted to consult a solicitor as soon as is practicable except to the extent that delay is permitted by this section.

(5) In any case he must be permitted to consult a solicitor within 36 hours from the relevant time, as defined in section 41(2) above.

(6) Delay in compliance with a request is only permitted –

(a) in the case of a person who is in police detention for a serious arrestable offence; and

(b) if an officer of at least the rank of superintendent authorises it.

(7) An officer may give an authorisation under subsection (6) above orally or in writing but, if he gives it orally, he shall confirm it in writing as soon as is practicable.

(8) Subject to subsection (8A) below, an officer may only authorise delay where he has reasonable grounds for believing that the exercise of the right conferred by subsection (1) above at the time when the person detained desires to exercise it –

(a) will lead to interference with or harm to evidence connected with a serious arrestable offence or interference with or physical injury to other persons; or

(b) will lead to the alerting of other persons suspected of having committed such an offence but not yet arrested for it; or

(c) will hinder the recovery of any property obtained as a result of such an offence.

(8A) An officer may also authorise delay where the serious arrestable offence is a drug trafficking offence or an offence to which Part VI of the Criminal Justice Act 1988 applies and the officer has reasonable grounds for believing –

(a) where the offence is a drug trafficking offence, that the detained person has benefited from drug trafficking and that the recovery of the value of that person's proceeds of drug trafficking will be hindered by the exercise of the right conferred by subsection (1) above; and

(b) where the offence is one to which Part VI of the Criminal Justice Act 1988 applies, that the detained person has benefited from the offence and that the recovery of the value of the property obtained by that person from or in connection with the offence or of the pecuniary advantage derived by him from or in connection with it will be hindered by the exercise of the right conferred by subsection (1) above.

(9) If delay is authorised –

(a) the detained person shall be told the reason for it; and

(b) the reason shall be noted on his custody record.

(10) The duties imposed by subsection (9) above shall be performed as soon as is practicable.

(11) There may be no further delay in permitting the exercise of the

right conferred by subsection (1) above once the reason for authorising delay ceases to subsist.

(12) The reference in subsection (1) above to a person arrested includes a reference to a person who has been detained under the terrorism provisions.

(13) In the application of this section to a person who has been arrested or detained under the terrorism provisions –

(a) subsection (5) above shall have effect as if for the words from 'within' onwards there were substituted the words 'before the end of the period beyond which he may no longer be detained without the authority of the Secretary of State';

(b) subsection (6)(a) above shall have effect as if for the words 'for a serious arrestable offence' there were substituted the words 'under the terrorism provisions'; and

(c) subsection (8) above shall have effect as if at the end there were added 'or

(d) will lead to interference with the gathering of information about the commission, preparation or instigation of acts of terrorism; or

(e) by alerting any person, will make it more difficult –

(i) to prevent an act of terrorism; or

(ii) to secure the apprehension, prosecution or conviction of any person in connection with the commission, preparation or instigation of an act of terrorism.'.

(14) If an officer of appropriate rank has reasonable grounds for believing that, unless he gives a direction under subsection (15) below, the exercise by a person arrested or detained under the terrorism provisions of the right conferred by subsection (1) above will have any of the consequences specified in subsection (8) above (as it has effect by virtue of subsection (13) above), he may give a direction under that subsection.

(15) A direction under this subsection is a direction that a person desiring to exercise the right conferred by subsection (1) above may only consult a solicitor in the sight and hearing of a qualified officer of the uniformed branch of the force of which the officer giving the direction is a member.

(16) An officer is qualified for the purpose of subsection (15) above if –

(a) he is of at least the rank of inspector; and

(b) in the opinion of the officer giving the direction he has no connection with the case.

(17) An officer is of appropriate rank to give a direction under subsection (15) above if he is of at least the rank of Commander or Assistant Chief Constable.

(18) A direction under subsection (15) above shall cease to have effect once the reason for giving it ceases to subsist.

61   Fingerprinting

(1) Except as provided by this section no person's fingerprints may be taken without the appropriate consent.

(2) Consent to the taking of a person's fingerprints must be in writing if it is given at a time when he is at a police station.

(3) The fingerprints of a person detained at a police station may be taken without the appropriate consent –

(a) if an officer of at least the rank of superintendent authorises them to be taken; or

(b) if –

(i) he has been charged with a recordable offence or informed that he will be reported for such an offence; and

(ii) he has not had his fingerprints taken in the course of the investigation of the offence by the police.

(4) An officer may only give an authorisation under subsection (3)(a) above if he has reasonable grounds –

(a) for suspecting the involvement of the person whose fingerprints are to be taken in a criminal offence; and

(b) for believing that his fingerprints will tend to confirm or disprove his involvement.

(5) An officer may give an authorisation under subsection (3)(a) above orally or in writing but, if he gives it orally, he shall confirm it in writing as soon as is practicable.

(6) Any person's fingerprints may be taken without the appropriate consent if he has been convicted of a recordable offence.

(7) In a case where by virtue of subsection (3) or (6) above a person's fingerprints are taken without the appropriate consent –

(a) he shall be told the reason before his fingerprints are taken; and

(b) the reason shall be recorded as soon as is practicable after the fingerprints are taken.

(8) If he is detained at a police station when the fingerprints are taken, the reason for taking them shall be recorded on his custody record.

(9) Nothing in this section –

(a) affects any power conferred by paragraph 18(2) of Schedule 2 to the Immigration Act 1971; or

(b) except as provided in section 15(10) of, and paragraph 7(6) of Schedule 5 to, the Prevention of Terrorism (Temporary Provisions) Act 1989, applies to a person arrested or detained under the terrorism provisions.

62 Intimate samples

(1) An intimate sample may be taken from a person in police detention only –

(a) if a police officer of at least the rank of superintendent authorises it to be taken; and

(b) if the appropriate consent is given.

(2) An officer may only give an authorisation if he has reasonable grounds –

(a) for suspecting the involvement of the person from whom the sample is to be taken in a serious arrestable offence; and

(b) for believing that the sample will tend to confirm or disprove his involvement.

(3) An officer may give an authorisation under subsection (1) above orally or in writing but, if he gives it orally, he shall confirm it in writing as soon as is practicable.

(4) The appropriate consent must be given in writing.

(5) Where –

(a) an authorisation has been given; and

(b) it is proposed that an intimate sample shall be taken in pursuance of the authorisation,

an officer shall inform the person from whom the sample is to be taken –

(i) of the giving of the authorisation; and
(ii) of the grounds for giving it.

(6) The duty imposed by subsection (5)(ii) above includes a duty to state the nature of the offence in which it is suspected that the person from whom the sample is to be taken has been involved.

(7) If an intimate sample is taken from a person –

(a) the authorisation by virtue of which it was taken;
(b) the grounds for giving the authorisation; and
(c) the fact that the appropriate consent was given,

shall be recorded as soon as is practicable after the sample is taken.

(8) If an intimate sample is taken from a person detained at a police station, the matters required to be recorded by subsection (7) above shall be recorded in his custody record.

(9) An intimate sample, other than a sample of urine or saliva, may only be taken from a person by a registered medical practitioner.

(10) Where the appropriate consent to the taking of an intimate sample from a person was refused without good cause, in any proceedings against that person for an offence –

(a) the court, in determining –

(i) whether to commit that person for trial; or
(ii) whether there is a case to answer; and

(b) the court or jury, in determining whether that person is guilty of the offence charged,

may draw such inferences from the refusal as appear proper; and the refusal may, on the basis of such inferences, be treated as, or as capable of amounting to, corroboration of any evidence against the person in relation to which the refusal is material.

(11) Nothing in this section affects sections 4 to 11 of the Road Traffic Act 1988.

63 Other samples

(1) Except as provided by this section, a non-intimate sample may not be taken from a person without the appropriate consent.

(2) Consent to the taking of a non-intimate sample must be given in writing.

(3) A non-intimate sample may be taken from a person without the appropriate consent if –

(a) he is in police detention or is being held in custody by the police on the authority of a court; and

(b) an officer of at least the rank of superintendent authorises it to be taken without the appropriate consent.

(4) An officer may only give an authorisation under subsection (3) above if he has reasonable grounds –

(a) for suspecting the involvement of the person from whom the sample is to be taken in a serious arrestable offence; and

(b) for believing that the sample will tend to confirm or disprove his involvement.

(5) An officer may give an authorisation under subsection (3) above orally or in writing but, if he gives it orally, he shall confirm it in writing as soon as is practicable.

(6) Where –

(a) an authorisation has been given; and

(b) it is proposed that a non-intimate sample shall be taken in pursuance of the authorisation,

an officer shall inform the person from whom the sample is to be taken –

(i) of the giving of the authorisation; and

(ii) of the grounds for giving it.

(7) The duty imposed by subsection (6)(ii) above includes a duty to state the nature of the offence in which it is suspected that the person from whom the sample is to be taken has been involved.

(8) If a non-intimate sample is taken from a person by virtue of subsection (3) above –

(a) the authorisation by virtue of which it was taken; and

(b) the grounds for giving the authorisation,

shall be recorded as soon as is practicable after the sample is taken.

(9) If a non-intimate sample is taken from a person detained at a police station, the matters required to be recorded by subsection (8) above shall be recorded in his custody record.

64   Destruction of fingerprints and samples

(1) If –

(a) fingerprints or samples are taken from a person in connection with the investigation of an offence; and

(b) he is cleared of that offence,

they must be destroyed as soon as is practicable after the conclusion of the proceedings.

(2) If –

(a) fingerprints or samples are taken from a person in connection with such an investigation; and

(b) it is decided that he shall not be prosecuted for the offence and he has not admitted it and been dealt with by way of being cautioned by a constable,

they must be destroyed as soon as is practicable after that decision is taken.

(3) If –

(a) fingerprints or samples are taken from a person in connection with the investigation of an offence; and

(b) that person is not suspected of having committed the offence,

they must be destroyed as soon as they have fulfilled the purpose for which they were taken.

(4) Proceedings which are discontinued are to be treated as concluded for the purposes of this section.

(5) If fingerprints are destroyed –

(a) any copies of the fingerprints shall also be destroyed; and

(b) any chief officer of police controlling access to computer data relating to the fingerprints shall make access to the data impossible, as soon as it is practicable to do so.

(6) A person who asks to be allowed to witness the destruction of his fingerprints or copies of them shall have a right to witness it.

(6A) If –

(a) subsection (5)(b) above falls to be complied with; and

(b) the person to whose fingerprints the data relate asks for a certificate that it has been complied with,

such a certificate shall be issued to him, not later than the end of the period of three months beginning with the day on which he asks for it, by the responsible chief officer of police or a person authorised by him or on his behalf for the purposes of this section.

(6B) In this section –

'chief officer of police' means the chief officer of police for an area mentioned in Schedule 8 to the Police Act 1964; and

'the responsible chief officer of police' means the chief officer of police in whose area the computer data were put on to the computer.

(7) Nothing in this section –

(a) affects any power conferred by paragraph 18(2) of Schedule 2 to the Immigration Act 1971; or

(b) applies to a person arrested or detained under the terrorism provisions.

65   Part V – supplementary

In this Part of this Act –

'appropriate consent' means –

(a) in relation to a person who has attained the age of 17 years, the consent of that person;

(b) in relation to a person who has not attained that age but has attained the age of 14 years, the consent of that person and his parent or guardian; and

(c) in relation to a person who has not attained the age of 14 years, the consent of his parent or guardian;

'drug trafficking' and 'drug trafficking offence' have the same meaning as in the Drug Trafficking Offences Act 1986;

'fingerprints' includes palm prints;

'intimate sample' means a sample of blood, semen or any other tissue fluid, urine, saliva or pubic hair, or a swab taken from a person's body orifices;

'non-intimate sample' means –

(a) a sample of hair other than pubic hair;

(b) a sample taken from a nail or from under a nail;

(c) a swab taken from any part of a person's body other than a body orifice;

(d) a footprint or a similar impression of any part of a person's body other than a part of his hand;

'the terrorism provisions' means section 14(1) of the Prevention of Terrorism (Temporary Provisions) Act 1989 and any provision of Schedule 2 or 5 to that Act conferring a power of arrest or detention; and

'terrorism' has the meaning assigned to it by section 20(1) of that Act.

References in this Part to any person's proceeds of drug trafficking are to be construed in accordance with the Drug Trafficking Offences Act 1986.

PART VI

CODES OF PRACTICE – GENERAL

66 Codes of practice

The Secretary of State shall issue codes of practice in connection with –

(a) the exercise by police officers of statutory powers –

(i) to search a person without first arresting him; or

(ii) to search a vehicle without making an arrest;

(b) the detention, treatment, questioning and identification of persons by police officers;

(c) searches of premises by police officers; and

(d) the seizure of property found by police officers on persons or premises.

67 Codes of practice – supplementary

(1) When the Secretary of State proposes to issue a code of practice to which this section applies, he shall prepare and publish a draft of that code, shall consider any representations made to him about the draft and may modify the draft accordingly.

(2) This section applies to a code of practice under section 60 or 66 above.

(3) The Secretary of State shall lay before both Houses of Parliament a draft of any code of practice prepared by him under this section.

(4) When the Secretary of State has laid the draft of a code before Parliament, he may bring the code into operation by order made by statutory instrument.

(5) No order under subsection (4) above shall have effect until approved by a resolution of each House of Parliament.

(6) An order bringing a code of practice into operation may contain such transitional provisions or savings as appear to the Secretary of State to be necessary or expedient in connection with the code of practice thereby brought into operation.

(7) The Secretary of State may from time to time revise the whole or any part of a code of practice to which this section applies and issue that revised code; and the foregoing provisions of this section shall apply (with appropriate modifications) to such a revised code as they apply to the first issue of a code.

(8) A police officer shall be liable to disciplinary proceedings for a failure to comply with any provision of such a code, unless such proceedings are precluded by section 104 below.

(9) Persons other than police officers who are charged with the duty of investigating offences or charging offenders shall in the discharge of that duty have regard to any relevant provision of such a code.

(10) A failure on the part –

(a) of a police officer to comply with any provision of such a code; or

(b) of any person other than a police officer who is charged with the duty of investigating offences or charging offenders to have regard to any relevant provision of such a code in the discharge of that duty,

shall not of itself render him liable to any criminal or civil proceedings.

(11) In all criminal and civil proceedings any such code shall be admissible in evidence; and if any provision of such a code appears to the court or tribunal conducting the proceedings to be relevant to any question arising in the proceedings it shall be taken into account in determining that question.

(12) In this section 'criminal proceedings' includes –

(a) proceedings in the United Kingdom or elsewhere before a court-martial constituted under the Army Act 1955, the Air Force Act 1955 or the Naval Discipline Act 1957 or a disciplinary court constituted under section 50 of the said Act of 1957;

(b) proceedings before the Courts-Martial Appeal Court; and

(c) proceedings before a Standing Civilian Court.

PART VIII

EVIDENCE IN CRIMINAL PROCEEDINGS – GENERAL

76 Confessions

(1) In any proceedings a confession made by an accused person may be given in evidence against him in so far as it is relevant to any matter in issue in the proceedings and is not excluded by the court in pursuance of this section.

(2) If, in any proceedings where the prosecution proposes to give in evidence a confession made by an accused person, it is represented to the court that the confession was or may have been obtained –

(a) by oppression of the person who made it; or

(b) in consequence of anything said or done which was likely, in the circumstances existing at the time, to render unreliable any confession which might be made by him in consequence thereof,

the court shall not allow the confession to be given in evidence against him except in so far as the prosecution proves to the court beyond reasonable doubt that the confession (notwithstanding that it may be true) was not obtained as aforesaid.

(3) In any proceedings where the prosecution proposes to give in evidence a confession made by an accused person, the court may of its own motion require the prosecution, as a condition of allowing it to do so, to prove that the confession was not obtained as mentioned in subsection (2) above.

(4) The fact that a confession is wholly or partly excluded in pursuance of this section shall not affect the admissibility in evidence –

(a) of any facts discovered as a result of the confession; or

(b) where the confession is relevant as showing that the accused speaks, writes or expresses himself in a particular way, of so much of the confession as is necessary to show that he does so.

(5) Evidence that a fact to which this subsection applies was discovered as a result of a statement made by an accused person shall not be admissible unless evidence of how it was discovered is given by him or on his behalf.

(6) Subsection (5) above applies –

(a) to any fact discovered as a result of a confession which is wholly excluded in pursuance of this section; and

(b) to any fact discovered as a result of a confession which is partly so excluded, if the fact is discovered as a result of the excluded part of the confession.

(7) Nothing in Part VII of this Act shall prejudice the admissibility of a confession made by an accused person.

(8) In this section 'oppression' includes torture, inhuman or degrading treatment, and the use or threat of violence (whether or not amounting to torture).

77 Confessions by mentally handicapped persons

(1) Without prejudice to the general duty of the court at a trial on indictment to direct the jury on any matter on which it appears to the court appropriate to do so, where at such a trial –

(a) the case against the accused depends wholly or substantially on a confession by him; and

(b) the court is satisfied –

(i) that he is mentally handicapped; and

(ii) that the confession was not made in the presence of an independent person,

the court shall warn the jury that there is special need for caution before convicting the accused in reliance on the confession, and shall explain that the need arises because of the circumstances mentioned in paragraphs (a) and (b) above.

(2) In any case where at the summary trial of a person for an offence it appears to the court that a warning under subsection (1) above would be required if the trial were on indictment, the court shall treat the case as one in which there is a special need for caution before convicting the accused on his confession.

(3) In this section –

'independent person' does not include a police officer or a person employed for, or engaged on, police purposes;

'mentally handicapped', in relation to a person, means that he is in a state of arrested or incomplete development of mind which includes significant impairment of intelligence and social functioning; and

'police purposes' has the meaning assigned to it by section 64 of the Police Act 1964.

78   Exclusion of unfair evidence

(1) In any proceedings the court may refuse to allow evidence on which the prosecution proposes to rely to be given if it appears to the court that, having regard to all the circumstances, including the circumstances in which the evidence was obtained, the admission of the evidence would have such an adverse effect on the fairness of the proceedings that the court ought not to admit it.

(2) Nothing in this section shall prejudice any rule of law requiring a court to exclude evidence.

82   Part VIII – interpretation

(1) In this Part of this Act –

'confession' includes any statement wholly or partly adverse to the person who made it, whether made to a person in authority or not and whether made in words or otherwise;

'court-martial' means a court-martial constituted under the Army Act 1955, the Air Force Act 1955 or the Naval Discipline Act 1957 or a disciplinary court constituted under section 50 of the said Act of 1957;

'proceedings' means criminal proceedings, including –

(a) proceedings in the United Kingdom or elsewhere before a court-martial constituted under the Army Act 1955 or the Air Force Act 1955;

(b) proceedings in the United Kingdom or elsewhere before the Courts-Martial Appeal Court –

(i) on an appeal from a court-martial so constituted or from a court-martial constituted under the Naval Discipline Act 1957; or

(ii) on a reference under section 34 of the Courts-Martial (Appeals) Act 1968; and

(b) proceedings before a Standing Civilian Court; and

'Service court' means a court-martial or a Standing Civilian Court.

(2) In this Part of this Act references to conviction before a Service court are references –

(a) as regards a court-martial constituted under the Army Act 1955 or the Air Force Act 1955, to a finding of guilty which is, or falls to be treated as, a finding of the court duly confirmed;

(b) as regards –

(i) a court-martial; or

(ii) a disciplinary court,

constituted under the Naval Discipline Act 1957, to a finding of guilty which is, or falls to be treated as, the finding of the court;

and 'convicted' shall be construed accordingly.

(3) Nothing in this Part of this Act shall prejudice any power of a court to exclude evidence (whether by preventing questions from being put or otherwise) at its discretion.

PART XI

MISCELLANEOUS AND SUPPLEMENTARY

116 Meaning of 'serious arrestable offence'

(1) This section has effect for determining whether an offence is a serious arrestable offence for the purposes of this Act.

(2) The following arrestable offences are always serious –

    (a) an offence (whether at common law or under any enactment) specified in Part I of Schedule 5 to this Act; and

    (aa) any of the offences mentioned in paragraphs (a) to (d) of the definition of 'drug trafficking offence' in section 38(1) of the Drug Trafficking Offences Act 1986; and

    (b) an offence under an enactment specified in Part II of that Schedule.

(3) Subject to subsections (4) and (5) below, any other arrestable offence is serious only if its commission –

    (a) has led to any of the consequences specified in subsection (6) below; or

    (b) is intended or is likely to lead to any of those consequences.

(4) An arrestable offence which consists of making a threat is serious if carrying out the threat would be likely to lead to any of the consequences specified in subsection (6) below.

(5) An offence under section 2, 8, 9, 10 or 11 of the Prevention of Terrorism (Temporary Provisions) Act 1989 is always a serious arrestable offence for the purposes of section 56 or 58 above, and an attempt or conspiracy to commit any such offence is also always a serious arrestable offence for those purposes.

(6) The consequences mentioned in subsections (3) and (4) above are –

    (a) serious harm to the security of the State or to public order;

    (b) serious interference with the administration of justice or with the investigation of offences or of a particular offence;

    (c) the death of any person;

    (d) serious injury to any person;

    (e) substantial financial gain to any person; and

    (f) serious financial loss to any person.

(7) Loss is serious for the purposes of this section if, having regard to all the circumstances, it is serious for the person who suffers it.

(8) In this section 'injury' includes any disease and any impairment of a person's physical or mental condition.

117 Power of constable to use reasonable force

Where any provision of this Act –

(a) confers a power on a constable; and
(b) does not provide that the power may only be exercised with the consent of some person, other than a police officer,

the officer may use reasonable force, if necessary, in the exercise of the power.

118 General interpretation

(1) In this Act –

'arrestable offence' has the meaning assigned to it by section 24 above;

'designated police station' has the meaning assigned to it by section 35 above;

'document' has the same meaning as in Part I of the Civil Evidence Act 1968;

'intimate search' means a search which consists of the physical examination of a person's body orifices;

'item subject to legal privilege' has the meaning assigned to it by section 10 above;

'parent or guardian' means –

(a) in the case of a child or young person in the care of a local authority, that authority;

'premises' has the meaning assigned to it by section 23 above;

'recordable offence' means any offence to which regulations under section 27 above apply;

'vessel' includes any ship, boat, raft or other apparatus constructed or adapted for floating on water.

(2) A person is in police detention for the purposes of this Act if –

(a) he has been taken to a police station after being arrested for an offence or after being arrested under section 14 of the Prevention of Terrorism (Temporary Provisions) Act 1989 or under paragraph 6 of Schedule 5 to that Act by an examining officer who is a constable; or

(b) he is arrested at a police station after attending voluntarily at the station or accompanying a constable to it,

and is detained there or is detained elsewhere in the charge of a constable, except that a person who is at a court after being charged is not in police detention for those purposes.

SCHEDULE 1

SPECIAL PROCEDURE

1. If on an application made by a constable a circuit judge is satisfied that one or other of the sets of access conditions is fulfilled, he may make an order under paragraph 4 below.

2. The first set of access conditions is fulfilled if –

(a) there are reasonable grounds for believing –

(i) that a serious arrestable offence has been committed;

(ii) that there is material which consists of special procedure material or includes special procedure material and does not also include excluded material on premises specified in the application;

(iii) that the material is likely to be of substantial value (whether by itself or together with other material) to the investigation in connection with which the application is made; and

(iv) that the material is likely to be relevant evidence;

(b) other methods of obtaining the material –

(i) have been tried without success; or

(ii) have not been tried because it appeared that they were bound to fail; and

(c) it is in the public interest, having regard –

(i) to the benefit likely to accrue to the investigation if the material is obtained; and

(ii) to the circumstances under which the person in possession of the material holds it,

that the material should be produced or that access to it should be given.

3. The second set of access conditions is fulfilled if –

(a) there are reasonable grounds for believing that there is material which consists of or includes excluded material or special procedure material on premises specified in the application;

(b) but for section 9(2) above a search of the premises for that material could have been authorised by the issue of a warrant to a constable under an enactment other than this Schedule; and

(c) the issue of such a warrant would have been appropriate.

4. An order under this paragraph is an order that the person who appears to the circuit judge to be in possession of the material to which the application relates shall –

(a) produce it to a constable for him to take away; or

(b) give a constable access to it,

not later than the end of the period of seven days from the date of the order or the end of such longer period as the order may specify.

5. Where the material consists of information contained in a computer –

(a) an order under paragraph 4(a) above shall have effect as an order to produce the material in a form in which it can be taken away and in which it is visible and legible; and

(b) an order under paragraph 4(b) above shall have effect as an order to give a constable access to the material in a form in which it is visible and legible.

6. For the purposes of sections 21 and 22 above material produced in pursuance of an order under paragraph 4(a) above shall be treated as if it were material seized by a constable ...

11. Where notice of an application for an order under paragraph 4 above has been served on a person, he shall not conceal, destroy, alter or dispose of the material to which the application relates except –

(a) with the leave of a judge; or

(b) with the written permission of a constable,

until –

(i) the application is dismissed or abandoned; or
(ii) he has complied with an order under paragraph 4 above made on the application.

12. If on an application made by a constable a circuit judge –

(a) is satisfied –

(i) that either set of access conditions is fulfilled; and
(ii) that any of the further conditions set out in paragraph 14 below is also fulfilled; or

(b) is satisfied –

(i) that the second set of access conditions is fulfilled; and
(ii) that an order under paragraph 4 above relating to the material has not been complied with,

he may issue a warrant authorising a constable to enter and search the premises.

13. A constable may seize and retain anything for which a search has been authorised under paragraph 12 above.

14. The further conditions mentioned in paragraph 12(a)(ii) above are –

(a) that it is not practicable to communicate with any person entitled to grant entry to the premises to which the application relates;
(b) that it is practicable to communicate with a person entitled to grant entry to the premises but it is not practicable to communicate with any person entitled to grant access to the material;
(c) that the material contains information which –

(i) is subject to a restriction or obligation such as is mentioned in section 11(2)(b) above; and
(ii) is likely to be disclosed in breach of it if a warrant is not issued;

(d) that service of notice of an application for an order under paragraph 4 above may seriously prejudice the investigation.

15. (1) If a person fails to comply with an order under paragraph 4 above, a circuit judge may deal with him as if he had committed a contempt of the Crown Court.

(2) Any enactment relating to contempt of the Crown Court shall have effect in relation to such a failure as if it were such a contempt.

16. The costs of any application under this Schedule and of anything done or to be done in pursuance of an order made under it shall be in the discretion of the judge.

SCHEDULE 2

PRESERVED POWERS OF ARREST

Section 17(2) of the Military Lands Act 1892.

Section 12(1) of the Protection of Animals Act 1911.

Section 2 of the Emergency Powers Act 1920.

Section 7(3) of the Public Order Act 1936.

Section 49 of the Prison Act 1952.

Section 13 of the Visiting Forces Act 1952.

Sections 186 and 190B of the Army Act 1955.

Section 186 and 190B of the Air Force Act 1955.

Sections 104 and 105 of the Naval Discipline Act 1957.

Section 1(3) of the Street Offences Act 1959.

Section 32 of the Children and Young Persons Act 1969.

Section 24(2) of the Immigration Act 1971 and paragraphs 17, 24 and 33 of Schedule 2 and paragraph 7 of Schedule 3 to that Act.

Section 7 of the Bail Act 1976.

Sections 6(6), 7(11), 8(4), 9(7) and 10(5) of the Criminal Law Act 1977.

Schedule 5 to the Reserve Forces Act 1980.

Sections 60(5) and 61(1) of the Animal Health Act 1981.

Rule 36 in Schedule 1 to the Representation of the People Act 1983.

Sections 18, 35(10), 36(8), 38(7), 136(1) and 138 of the Mental Health Act 1983.

Section 5(5) of the Repatriation of Prisoners Act 1984.

SCHEDULE 5

SERIOUS ARRESTABLE OFFENCES

PART I

OFFENCES MENTIONED IN SECTION 116(2)(a)

1. Treason.

2. Murder.

3. Manslaughter.

4. Rape.

5. Kidnapping.

6. Incest with a girl under the age of 13.

7. Buggery with –

    (a) a boy under the age of 16; or
    (b) a person who has not consented.

8. Indecent assault which constitutes an act of gross indecency.

PART II

OFFENCES MENTIONED IN SECTION 116(2)(b)

Explosive Substances Act 1883 (c 3)

Section 2 (causing explosion likely to endanger life or property).

Sexual Offences Act 1956 (c 69)

Section 5 (intercourse with a girl under the age of 13).

Firearms Act 1968 (c 27)

Section 16 (possession of firearms with intent to injure).

Section 17(1) (use of firearms and imitation firearms to resist arrest).

Section 18 (carrying firearms with criminal intent).

Taking of Hostages Act 1982 (c 28)

Section 1 (hostage-taking).

Aviation Security Act 1982 (c 36)

Section 1 (hi-jacking).

Road Traffic Act 1988 (c 52)

Section 1 (causing death by dangerous driving).

Section 3A (causing death by careless driving when under the influence of drink or drugs).

Criminal Justice Act 1988 (c 33)

Section 134 (torture).

As amended by the Sexual Offences Act 1985, s5(3), Schedule; Representation of the People Act 1985, s25(1); Public Order Act 1986, s40(2), (3), Schedule 2, para 7, Schedule 3; Drug Trafficking Offences Act 1986, ss32(1), (3), 36; Criminal Justice Act 1988, ss99(1), (2), 140(1), 147, 148, 170, Schedule 15, paras 97, 98, 99, 100, 102, Schedule 16; Road Traffic (Consequential Provisions) Act 1988, ss3, 4, Schedules 1, 3, para 27(1), (3), (4), (5); Children Act 1989, s108(5), (7), Schedule 13, paras 53, 54, 55, Schedule 15; Official Secrets Act 1989, s11(1); Prevention of Terrorism (Temporary Provisions) Act 1989, s25(1), Schedule 8, para 6(1), (2), (3), (4), (5), (6), (7), (8); Football (Offences) Act 1991, s5(1); Criminal Justices Act 1991, s59; Road Traffic Act 1991, s48, Schedule 4, para 39.

PROSECUTION OF OFFENCES ACT 1985
(1985 c 23)

1 The Crown Prosecution Service

(1) There shall be a prosecuting service for England and Wales (to be known as the 'Crown Prosecution Service'), consisting of –

(a) the Director of Public Prosecutions, who shall be head of the Service;

(b) the Chief Crown Prosecutors, designated under subsection (4) below, each of whom shall be the member of the Service responsible to the Director for supervising the operation of the Service in his area; and

(c) the other staff appointed by the Director under this section.

(2) The director shall appoint such staff for the Service as, with the approval of the Treasury as to numbers, remuneration and other terms and conditions of service, he considers necessary for the discharge of his functions.

(3) The Director may designate any member of the Service who has a general qualification (within the meaning of section 71 of the Courts and Legal Services Act 1990) for the purposes of this subsection, and any person so designated shall be known as a Crown Prosecutor.

(4) The Director shall divide England and Wales into areas and, for each of those areas, designate a Crown Prosecutor for the purposes of this subsection and any person so designated shall be known as a Chief Crown Prosecutor.

(5) The Director may, from time to time, vary the division of England and Wales made for the purposes of subsection (4) above.

(6) Without prejudice to any functions which may have been assigned to him in his capacity as a member of the Service, every Crown Prosecutor shall have all the powers of the Director as to

the institution and conduct of proceedings but shall exercise those powers under the direction of the Director.

(7) Where any enactment (whenever passed) –

(a) prevents any step from being taken without the consent of the Director or without his consent or the consent of another; or

(b) requires any step to be taken by or in relation to the Director;

any consent given by or, as the case may be, step taken by or in relation to, a Crown Prosecutor shall be treated, for the purposes of that enactment, as given by or, as the case may be, taken by or in relation to the Director.

2 The Director of Public Prosecutions

(1) The Director of Public Prosecutions shall be appointed by the Attorney General.

(2) The Director must be a person who has a ten year general qualification, within the meaning of section 71 of the Courts and Legal Services Act 1990.

(3) There shall be paid to the Director such remuneration as the Attorney General may, with the approval of the Treasury, determine.

3 Functions of the Director

(1) The Director shall discharge his functions under this or any other enactment under the superintendence of the Attorney General.

(2) It shall be the duty of the Director, subject to any provisions contained in the Criminal Justice Act 1987 –

(a) to take over the conduct of all criminal proceedings, other than specified proceedings, instituted on behalf of a police force (whether by a member of that force or by any other person);

(b) to institute and have the conduct of criminal proceedings in any case where it appears to him that –

(i) the importance or difficulty of the case makes it appropriate that proceedings should be instituted by him; or

(ii) it is otherwise appropriate for proceedings to be instituted by him;

(c) to take over the conduct of all binding over proceedings instituted on behalf of a police force (whether by a member of that force or by any other person);

(d) to take over the conduct of all proceedings begun by summons issued under section 3 of the Obscene Publications Act 1959 (forfeiture of obscene articles);

(e) to give, to such extent as he considers appropriate, advice to police forces on all matters relating to criminal offences;

(f) to appear for the prosecution, when directed by the court to do so, on any appeal under –

(i) section 1 of the Administration of Justice Act 1960 (appeal from the High Court in criminal cases);

(ii) Part I or Part II of the Criminal Appeal Act 1968 (appeals from the Crown Court to the criminal division of the Court of Appeal and thence to the House of Lords); or

(iii) section 108 of the Magistrates' Courts Act 1980 (right of appeal to Crown Court) as it applies, by virtue of subsection (5) of section 12 of the Contempt of Court Act 1981, to orders made under section 12 (contempt of magistrates' courts); and

(g) to discharge such other functions as may from time to time be assigned to him by the Attorney General in pursuance of this paragraph.

(3) In this section –

'the court' means –

(a) in the case of an appeal to or from the criminal division of the Court of Appeal, that division;

(b) in the case of an appeal from a Divisional Court of the Queen's Bench Division, the Divisional Court; and

(c) in the case of an appeal against an order of a magistrates' court, the Crown Court.

'police force' means any police force maintained by a police authority under the Police Act 1964 and any other body of constables for the time being specified by order made by the Secretary of State for the purposes of this section; and

'specified proceedings' means proceedings which fall within any category for the time being specified by order made by the Attorney General for the purposes of this section.

4   Crown Prosecutors

(1) Crown Prosecutors shall continue to have the same rights of audience, in any court, as they had immediately before the coming into force of the Courts and Legal Services Act 1990.

(2) Subsection (1) is not to be taken as preventing those rights being varied or added to in accordance with the provisions of that Act.

(3) The Lord Chancellor may at any time direct, as respects one or more specified places where the Crown Court sits, that Crown Prosecutors, or such category of Crown Prosecutors as may be specified in the direction, may have rights of audience in the Crown Court.

(3A) Any such direction may be limited to apply only in relation to proceedings of a description specified in the direction.

(3B) In considering whether to exercise his powers under this section the Lord Chancellor shall have regard, in particular, to the need to secure the availability of persons with rights of audience in the court or proceedings in question.

(3C) Any direction under this section may be revoked by direction of the Lord Chancellor.

(3D) Any direction under this section may be subject to such conditions and restrictions as appear to the Lord Chancellor to be necessary or expedient.

(3E) Any exercise by the Lord Chancellor of his powers to give a direction under this section shall be with the concurrence of the Lord Chief Justice, the Master of the Rolls, the President of the Family Division and the Vice-Chancellor.

5   Conduct of prosecutions on behalf of the Service

(1) The Director may at any time appoint a person who is not a Crown Prosecutor but who has a general qualification (within the meaning of section 71 of the Courts and Legal Services Act 1990) to institute or take over the conduct of such criminal proceedings as the Director may assign to him.

(2) Any person conducting proceedings assigned to him under this section shall have all the powers of a Crown Prosecutor but shall exercise those powers subject to any instructions given to him by a Crown Prosecutor.

6 Prosecutions instituted and conducted otherwise than by the Service

(1) Subject to subsection (2) below, nothing in this Part shall preclude any person from instituting any criminal proceedings or conducting any criminal proceedings to which the Director's duty to take over the conduct of proceedings does not apply.

(2) Where criminal proceedings are instituted in circumstances in which the Director is not under a duty to take over their conduct, he may nevertheless do so at any stage.

As amended by the Criminal Justice Act 1987, s15, Schedule 2, para 13; Courts and Legal Services Act 1990, ss71(2), 125(3), Schedule 10, paras 60, 61(1), (2), Schedule 18, para 51.

CORONERS ACT 1988
(1988 c 13)

2   Qualifications for appointment as coroner

(1) No person shall be qualified to be appointed as coroner unless –

(a) he has a five year general qualification, within the meaning of section 71 of the Courts and Legal Services Act 1990; or

(b) he is a legally qualified medical practitioner of not less than five years' standing.

(2) A person shall, so long as he is a councillor of a metropolitan district or London borough, and for six months after he ceases to be one, be disqualified for being a coroner for a coroner's district which consists of, includes or is included in that metropolitan district or London borough.

(3) A person shall, so long as he is an alderman or a councillor of a non-metropolitan county, and for six months after he ceases to be one, be disqualified for being a coroner for that county.

(4) A person shall, so long as he is an alderman of the City or a common councillor, and for six months after he ceases to be one, be disqualified for being a coroner for the City.

8   Duty to hold inquest

(1) Where a coroner is informed that the body of a person ('the deceased') is lying within his district and there is reasonable cause to suspect that the deceased –

(a) has died a violent or an unnatural death;

(b) has died a sudden death of which the cause is unknown; or

(c) has died in prison or in such a place or in such circumstances as to require an inquest under any other Act,

then, whether the cause of death arose within his district or not, the coroner shall as soon as practicable hold an inquest into the death of the deceased either with or, subject to subsection (3) below, without a jury.

(2) In the case of an inquest with a jury –

(a) the coroner shall summon by warrant not less than seven nor more than 11 persons to appear before him at a specified time and place, there to inquire as jurors into the death of the deceased; and

(b) when not less than seven jurors are assembled, they shall be sworn by or before the coroner diligently to inquire into the death of the deceased and to give a true verdict according to the evidence.

(3) If it appears to a coroner, either before he proceeds to hold an inquest or in the course of an inquest begun without a jury, that there is reason to suspect –

(a) that the death occurred in prison or in such a place or in such circumstances as to require an inquest under any other Act;

(b) that the death occurred while the deceased was in police custody, or resulted from an injury caused by a police officer in the purported execution of his duty;

(c) that the death was caused by an accident, poisoning or disease notice of which is required to be given under any Act to a government department, to any inspector or other officer of a government department or to an inspector appointed under section 19 of the Health and Safety at Work, etc Act 1974; or

(d) that the death occurred in circumstances the continuance or possible recurrence of which is prejudicial to the health or safety of the public or any section of the public,

he shall proceed to summon a jury in the manner required by subsection (2) above.

(4) If it appears to a coroner, either before he proceeds to hold an inquest or in the course of an inquest begun without a jury, that there is any reason for summoning a jury, he may proceed to summon a jury in the manner required by subsection (2) above.

(5) In the case of an inquest or any part of an inquest held without a jury, anything done by or before the coroner alone shall be as validly done as if it had been done by or before the coroner and a jury.

(6) Where an inquest is held into the death of a prisoner who dies within a prison, neither a prisoner in the prison nor any person

engaged in any sort of trade or dealing with the prison shall serve as a juror at the inquest.

9 Qualifications of jurors

(1) A person shall not be qualified to serve as a juror at an inquest held by a coroner unless he is for the time being qualified to serve as a juror in the Crown Court, the High Court and county courts in accordance with section 1 of the Juries Act 1974 ...

12 Failure of jury to agree

(1) This section applies where, in the case of an inquest held with a jury, the jury fails to agree on a verdict.

(2) If the minority consists of not more than two, the coroner may accept the verdict of the majority ...

(3) In any other case of disagreement the coroner may discharge the jury and issue a warrant for summoning another jury and, in that case, the inquest shall proceed in all respects as if the proceedings which terminated in the disagreement had not taken place.

30 Treasure trove

A coroner shall continue to have jurisdiction –

(a) to inquire into any treasure which is found in his district; and
(b) to inquire who were, or are suspected of being, the finders;

and the provisions of this Act shall, so far as applicable, apply to every such inquest.

As amended by the Courts and Legal Services Act 1990, ss71(2), 125(7), Schedule 10, para 70, Schedule 20.

LEGAL AID ACT 1988
(1988 c 34)

1 Purpose of this Act

The purpose of this Act is to establish a framework for the provision under Parts II, III, IV, V and VI of advice, assistance and representation which is publicly funded with a view to helping persons who might otherwise be unable to obtain advice, assistance or representation on account of their means.

3 The Legal Aid Board

(1) There shall be established a body to be known as the Legal Aid Board (in this Act referred to as 'the Board').

(2) Subject to subsections (3) and (4) below, the Board shall have the general function of securing that advice, assistance and representation are available in accordance with this Act and of administering this Act.

(3) Subsection (2) above does not confer on the Board any functions with respect to the grant of representation under Part VI for the purposes of proceedings for contempt.

(4) Subsection (2) above does not confer on the Board any of the following functions unless the Lord Chancellor so directs by order and then only to the extent specified in the order.

The functions referred to are –

    (a) determination of the costs of representation under Part IV;
    (b) functions as respects representation under Part V other than determination of the costs of representation for the purposes of proceedings in magistrates' courts;
    (d) determination of the financial resources of persons for the purposes of this Act.

(5) Subject to subsection (6) below, the Board shall consist of no

fewer than 11 and no more than 17 members appointed by the Lord Chancellor; and the Lord Chancellor shall appoint one of the members to be chairman.

(6) The Lord Chancellor may, by order, substitute, for the number for the time being specified in subsection (5) above as the maximum or minimum membership of the Board, such other number as he thinks appropriate.

(7) The Board shall include at least two solicitors appointed after consultation with the Law Society.

(8) The Lord Chancellor shall consult the General Council of the Bar with a view to the inclusion on the Board of at least two barristers.

(9) In appointing persons to be members of the Board the Lord Chancellor shall have regard to the desirability of securing that the Board includes persons having expertise in or knowledge of –

(a) the provision of legal services;

(b) the work of the courts and social conditions; and

(c) management.

(10) Schedule 1 to this Act shall have effect with respect to the Board.

5 Duties of the Board

(1) The Board shall, from time to time, publish information as to the discharge of its functions in relation to advice, assistance and representation including the forms and procedures and other matters connected therewith.

(2) The Board shall, from time to time, furnish to the Lord Chancellor such information as he may require relating to its property and to the discharge or proposed discharge of its functions.

(3) It shall be the duty of the Board to provide to the Lord Chancellor, as soon as possible after 31 March in each year, a report on the discharge of its functions during the preceding 12 months.

(4) The Board shall deal in any report under subsection (3) above with such matters as the Lord Chancellor may from time to time direct.

(5) The Board shall have regard, in discharging its functions, to such guidance as may from time to time be given by the Lord Chancellor.

(6) Guidance under subsection (5) above shall not relate to the consideration or disposal, in particular cases, of –

(a) applications for advice, assistance or representation;

(b) supplementary or incidental applications or requests to the Board in connection with any case where advice, assistance or representation has been made available.

(7) For the purposes of subsection (2) above the Board shall permit any person authorised by the Lord Chancellor for the purpose to inspect and make copies of any accounts or documents of the Board and shall furnish such explanations of them as that person or the Lord Chancellor may require.

6   Board to have separate legal aid fund

(1) The Board shall establish and maintain a separate legal aid fund.

(2) Subject to regulations, there shall be paid out of the fund –

(a) such sums as are, by virtue of any provision of or made under this Act, due from the Board in respect of remuneration and expenses properly incurred in connection with the provision, under this Act, of advice, assistance or representation;

(b) costs awarded to any unassisted party under section 13 or 18;

(c) any part of a contribution repayable by the Board under section 16(4) or 23(7); and

(d) such other payments for the purposes of this Act as the Lord Chancellor may, with the concurrence of the Treasury, determine.

(3) Subject to regulations, there shall be paid into the fund –

(a) any contribution payable to the Board by any person in respect of advice, assistance or representation under this Act;

(b) any sum awarded under an order of a court or agreement as to costs in any proceedings in favour of any legally assisted party which is payable to the Board;

(c) any sum which is to be paid out of property recovered or preserved for any legally assisted party to any proceedings;

(d) any sum in respect of the costs of an unassisted party awarded under section 13 or 18 which is repaid to the Board under that section;

(e) the sums to be paid by the Lord Chancellor in pursuance of section 42(1)(a); and

(f) such other receipts of the Board as the Lord Chancellor may, with the concurrence of the Treasury, determine.

As amended by the Children Act 1989, s108(7), Schedule 15.

COURTS AND LEGAL SERVICES ACT 1990
(1990 c 41)

PART I

PROCEDURE, ETC IN CIVIL COURTS

1 Allocation of business between High Court and county courts

(1) The Lord Chancellor may by order make provision –

(a) conferring jurisdiction on the High Court in relation to proceedings in which county courts have jurisdiction;

(b) conferring jurisdiction on county courts in relation to proceedings in which the High Court has jurisdiction;

(c) allocating proceedings to the High Court or to county courts;

(d) specifying proceedings which may be commenced only in the High Court;

(e) specifying proceedings which may be commenced only in a county court;

(f) specifying proceedings which may be taken only in the High Court;

(g) specifying proceedings which may be taken only in a county court.

(2) Without prejudice to the generality of section 120(2), any such order may differentiate between categories of proceedings by reference to such criteria as the Lord Chancellor sees fit to specify in the order.

(3) The criteria so specified may, in particular, relate to –

(a) the value of an action (as defined by the order);

(b) the nature of the proceedings;

(c) the parties to the proceedings;

(d) the degree of complexity likely to be involved in any aspect of the proceedings; and

(e) the importance of any question likely to be raised by, or in the course of, the proceedings.

(4) An order under subsection (1)(b), (e) or (g) may specify one or more particular county courts in relation to the proceedings so specified.

(5) Any jurisdiction exercisable by a county court, under any provision made by virtue of subsection (4), shall be exercisable throughout England and Wales.

(6) Rules of court may provide for a matter –

(a) which is pending in one county court; and

(b) over which that court has jurisdiction under any provision made by virtue of subsection (4),

to be heard and determined wholly or partly in another county court which also has jurisdiction in that matter under any such provision.

(7) Any such order may –

(a) amend or repeal any provision falling within subsection (8) and relating to –

(i) the jurisdiction, practice or procedure of the Supreme Court; or

(ii) the jurisdiction, practice or procedure of any county court,

so far as the Lord Chancellor considers it to be necessary, or expedient, in consequence of any provision made by the order; or

(b) make such incidental or transitional provision as the Lord Chancellor considers necessary, or expedient, in consequence of any provision made by the order.

(8) A provision falls within this subsection if it is made by any enactment other than this Act or made under any enactment.

(9) Before making any such order the Lord Chancellor shall consult the Lord Chief Justice, the Master of the Rolls, the President of the Family Division, the Vice-Chancellor and the Senior Presiding Judge (appointed under section 72).

(10) No such order shall be made so as to confer jurisdiction on any county court to hear any application for judicial review.

(11) For the purposes of this section the commencement of proceedings may include the making of any application in anticipation of any proceedings or in the course of any proceedings.

(12) The Lord Chancellor shall, within one year of the coming into force of the first order made under this section, and annually thereafter, prepare and lay before both Houses of Parliament a report as to the business of the Supreme Court and county courts.

8   Powers of Court of Appeal to award damages

(1) In this section 'case' means any case where the Court of Appeal has power to order a new trial on the ground that damages awarded by a jury are excessive or inadequate.

(2) Rules of court may provide for the Court of Appeal, in such classes of case as may be specified in the rules, to have power, in place of ordering a new trial, to substitute for the sum awarded by the jury such sum as appears to the court to be proper.

(3) This section is not to be read as prejudicing in any way any other power to make rules of court.

9   Allocation of family proceedings which are within the jurisdiction of county courts

(1) The Lord Chancellor may, with the concurrence of the President of the Family Division, give directions that, in such circumstances as may be specified –

   (a) any family proceedings which are within the jurisdiction of county courts; or
   (b) any specified description of such proceedings,

shall be allocated to specified judges or to specified descriptions of judge.

(2) Any such direction shall have effect regardless of any rules of court.

(3) Where any directions have been given under this section allocating any proceedings to specified judges, the validity of anything done by a judge in, or in relation to, the proceedings shall not be called into question by reason only of the fact that he was not a specified judge.

(4) For the purposes of subsection (1) 'county court' includes the principal registry of the Family Division of the High Court in so far as it is treated as a county court.

(5) In this section –

'family proceedings' has the same meaning as in the Matrimonial and Family Proceedings Act 1984 and also includes any other proceedings which are family proceedings for the purposes of the Children Act 1989;

'judge' means any person who –

(a) is capable of sitting as a judge for a county court district;

(b) is a district judge, an assistant district judge or a deputy district judge; or

(c) is a district judge of the principal registry of the Family Division of the High Court; and

'specified' means specified in the directions.

11   Representation in certain county court cases

(1) The Lord Chancellor may by order provide that there shall be no restriction on the persons who may exercise rights of audience, or rights to conduct litigation, in relation to proceedings in a county court of such a kind as may be specified in the order.

(2) The power to make an order may only be exercised in relation to proceedings –

(a) for the recovery of amounts due under contracts for the supply of goods or services;

(b) for the enforcement of any judgment or order of any court or the recovery of any sum due under such judgment or order;

(c) on any application under the Consumer Credit Act 1974;

(d) in relation to domestic premises; or

(e) referred to arbitration in accordance with county court rules made under section 64 of the County Court Act 1984 (small claims)

or any category (determined by reference to such criteria as the Lord Chancellor considers appropriate) of such proceedings.

(3) Where an order is made under this section, section 20 of the Solicitors Act 1974 (unqualified person not to act as solicitor) shall

cease to apply in relation to proceedings of the kind specified in the order.

(4) Where a county court is of the opinion that a person who would otherwise have a right of audience by virtue of an order under this section is behaving in an unruly manner in any proceedings, it may refuse to hear him in those proceedings.

(5) Where a court exercises its power under subsection (4), it shall specify the conduct which warranted its refusal.

(6) Where, in any proceedings in a county court –

(a) a person is exercising a right of audience or a right to conduct litigation;

(b) he would not be entitled to do so were it not for an order under this section; and

(c) the judge has reason to believe that (in those or any other proceedings in which he has exercised a right of audience or a right to conduct litigation) that person has intentionally misled the court, or otherwise demonstrated that he is unsuitable to exercise that right,

the judge may order that person's disqualification from exercising any right of audience or any right to conduct litigation in proceedings in any county court.

(7) Where a judge makes an order under subsection (6) he shall give his reasons for so doing.

(8) Any person against whom such an order is made may appeal to the Court of Appeal.

(9) Any such order may be revoked at any time by any judge of a county court.

(10) Before making any order under this section the Lord Chancellor shall consult the Senior Presiding Judge.

(11) In this section 'domestic premises' means any premises which are wholly or mainly used as a private dwelling.

PART II

LEGAL SERVICES

17 The statutory objective and the general principle

(1) The general objective of this Part is the development of legal services in England and Wales (and in particular the development of advocacy, litigation, conveyancing and probate services) by making provision for new or better ways of providing such services and a wider choice of persons providing them, while maintaining the proper and efficient administration of justice.

(2) In this Act that objective is referred to as 'the statutory objective'.

(3) As a general principle the question whether a person should be granted a right of audience, or be granted a right to conduct litigation in relation to any court or proceedings, should be determined only by reference to –

(a) whether he is qualified in accordance with the educational and training requirements appropriate to the court or proceedings;

(b) whether he is a member of a professional or other body which –

(i) has rules of conduct (however described) governing the conduct of its members;

(ii) has an effective mechanism for enforcing the rules of conduct; and

(iii) is likely to enforce them;

(c) whether, in the case of a body whose members are or will be providing advocacy services, the rules of conduct make satisfactory provision in relation to the court or proceedings in question requiring any such member not to withhold those services –

(i) on the ground that the nature of the case is objectionable to him or to any section of the public;

(ii) on the ground that the conduct, opinions or beliefs of the prospective client are unacceptable to him or to any section of the public;

(iii) on any ground relating to the source of any financial support which may properly be given to the prospective client for the proceedings in question (for example, on the ground that such support will be available under the Legal Aid Act 1988); and

(d) whether the rules of conduct are, in relation to the court or proceedings, appropriate in the interest of the proper and efficient administration of justice.

(4) In this Act that principle is referred to as 'the general principle'.

(5) Rules of conduct which allow a member of the body in question to withhold his services if there are reasonable grounds for him to consider that, having regard to –

(a) the circumstances of the case;

(b) the nature of his practice; or

(c) his experience and standing,

he is not being offered a proper fee, are not on that account to be taken as being incompatible with the general principle.

18   The statutory duty

(1) Where any person is called upon to exercise any functions which are conferred by this Part with respect to –

(a) the granting of rights of audience;

(b) the granting of rights to conduct litigation;

(c) the approval of qualification regulations or rules of conduct; or

(d) the giving of advice with respect to any matter mentioned in paragraphs (a) to (c),

it shall be the duty of that person to exercise those functions as soon as is reasonably practicable and consistent with the provisions of this Part.

(2) A person exercising any such functions shall act in accordance with the general principle and, subject to that, shall –

(a) so far as it is possible to do so in the circumstances of the case, act to further the statutory objective; and

(b) not act in any way which would be incompatible with the statutory objective.

19   The Lord Chancellor's Advisory Committee on Legal Education and Conduct

(1) There shall be a body corporate to be known as the Lord

Chancellor's Advisory Committee on Legal Education and Conduct (in this Act referred to as 'the Advisory Committee').

(2) The Advisory Committee shall consist of a Chairman, and 16 other members, appointed by the Lord Chancellor.

(3) The Chairman shall be a Lord of Appeal in Ordinary or a judge of the Supreme Court of England and Wales.

(4) Of the 16 other members of the Advisory Committee –

(a) one shall be a judge who is or has been a Circuit judge;

(b) two shall be practising barristers appointed after consultation with the General Council of the Bar;

(c) two shall be practising solicitors appointed after consultation with the Law Society;

(d) two shall be persons with experience in the teaching of law, appointed after consultation with such institutions concerned with the teaching of law and such persons representing teachers of law as the Lord Chancellor considers appropriate; and

(e) nine shall be persons other than –

(i) salaried judges of any court;

(ii) practising barristers;

(iii) practising solicitors; or

(iv) teachers of law,

appointed after consultation with such organisations as the Lord Chancellor considers appropriate.

(5) In appointing any member who falls within subsection (4)(e), the Lord Chancellor shall have regard to the desirability of appointing persons who have experience in, or knowledge of –

(a) the provision of legal services;

(b) civil or criminal proceedings and the working of the courts;

(c) the maintenance of professional standards among barristers or solicitors;

(d) social conditions;

(e) consumer affairs;

(f) commercial affairs; or

(g) the maintenance of professional standards in professions other than the legal profession.

(6) The Advisory Committee shall not be regarded as the servant or agent of the Crown, or as enjoying any status, immunity or privilege of the Crown.

(7) The Advisory Committee's property shall not be regarded as property of, or held on behalf of, the Crown.

(8) In this section 'practising' means –

(a) in relation to a barrister, one who is in independent practice or is employed wholly or mainly for the purpose of providing legal services to his employer;

(b) in relation to a solicitor, one who has a practising certificate in force or is employed wholly or mainly for the purpose of providing legal services to his employer.

(9) The provisions of Schedule 1 shall have effect with respect to the constitution, procedure and powers of the Advisory Committee and with respect to connected matters.

20   Duties of the Advisory Committee

(1) The Advisory Committee shall have the general duty of assisting in the maintenance and development of standards in the education, training and conduct of those offering legal services.

(2) The Advisory Committee shall carry out that general duty by performing the functions conferred on it by Schedule 2.

(3) In discharging its functions the Advisory Committee shall –

(a) where it considers it appropriate, have regard to the practices and procedures of other member States in relation to the provision of legal services;

(b) have regard to the desirability of equality of opportunity between persons seeking to practise any profession, pursue any career or take up any employment, in connection with the provision of legal services.

21   The Legal Services Ombudsman

(1) The Lord Chancellor shall appoint a person for the purpose of conducting investigations under this Act.

(2) The person appointed shall be known as 'the Legal Services Ombudsman'.

(3) The Legal Services Ombudsman –

(a) shall be appointed for a period of not more than three years; and

(b) shall hold and vacate office in accordance with the terms of his appointment.

(4) At the end of his term of appointment the Legal Services Ombudsman shall be eligible for re-appointment.

(5) The Legal Services Ombudsman shall not be an authorised advocate, authorised litigator, licensed conveyancer, authorised practitioner or notary.

(6) Schedule 3 shall have effect with respect to the Legal Services Ombudsman.

22   Ombudsman's functions

(1) Subject to the provisions of this Act, the Legal Services Ombudsman may investigate any allegation which is properly made to him and which relates to the manner in which a complaint made to a professional body with respect to –

(a) a person who is or was an authorised advocate, authorised litigator, licensed conveyancer, registered foreign lawyer, recognised body or duly certificated notary public and a member of that professional body; or

(b) any employee of such a person,

has been dealt with by that professional body.

(2) If the Ombudsman investigates an allegation he may investigate the matter to which the complaint relates.

(3) If the Ombudsman begins to investigate an allegation he may at any time discontinue his investigation.

(4) If the Ombudsman decides not to investigate an allegation which he would be entitled to investigate, or discontinues an investigation which he has begun, he shall notify the following of the reason for his decision –

(a) the person making the allegation;

(b) any person with respect to whom the complaint was made; and

(c) the professional body concerned.

(5) The Ombudsman shall not investigate an allegation while –

(a) the complaint is being investigated by the professional body concerned;

(b) an appeal is pending against the determination of the complaint by that body; or

(c) the time within which such an appeal may be brought by any person has not expired.

(6) Subsection (5) does not apply if –

(a) the allegation is that the professional body –

(i) has acted unreasonably in failing to start an investigation into the complaint; or

(ii) having started such an investigation, has failed to complete it within a reasonable time; or

(b) the Ombudsman is satisfied that, even though the complaint is being investigated by the professional body concerned, an investigation by him is justified.

(7) The Ombudsman shall not investigate –

(a) any issue which is being or has been determined by –

(i) a court;

(ii) the Solicitors Disciplinary Tribunal;

(iii) the Disciplinary Tribunal of the Council of the Inns of Court; or

(iv) any tribunal specified in an order made by the Lord Chancellor for the purposes of this subsection; or

(b) any allegation relating to a complaint against any person which concerns an aspect of his conduct in relation to which he has immunity from any action in negligence or contract.

(8) The Ombudsman may –

(a) if so requested by the Scottish ombudsman, investigate an allegation relating to a complaint made to a professional body in Scotland; and

(b) arrange for the Scottish ombudsman to investigate an allegation relating to a complaint made to a professional body in England and Wales.

(9) For the purposes of this section, an allegation is properly made if it is made –

(a) in writing; and

(b) by any person affected by what is alleged in relation to the complaint concerned or, where that person has died or is unable to act for himself, by his personal representative or by any relative or other representative of his.

(10) The Ombudsman may investigate an allegation even though –

(a) the complaint relates to a matter which arose before the passing of this Act; or

(b) the person making the complaint may be entitled to bring proceedings in any court with respect to the matter complained of.

(11) In this section –

'professional body' means any body which, or the holder of any office who –

(a) has disciplinary powers in relation to any person mentioned in subsection (1)(a); and

(b) is specified in an order made by the Lord Chancellor for the purposes of this subsection;

'recognised body' means any body recognised under section 9 of the Administration of Justice Act 1985 (incorporated practices) or under section 32 of that Act (incorporated bodies carrying on business of provision of conveyancing services); and

'the Scottish ombudsman' means any person appointed to carry out functions in relation to the provision of legal services in Scotland which are similar to those of the Ombudsman.

23   Recommendations

(1) Where the Legal Services Ombudsman has completed an investigation under this Act he shall send a written report of his conclusions to –

(a) the person making the allegation;

(b) the person with respect to whom the complaint was made;

(c) any other person with respect to whom the Ombudsman makes a recommendation under subsection (2); and

(d) the professional body concerned.

(2) In reporting his conclusions, the Ombudsman may recommend –

(a) that the complaint be reconsidered by the professional body concerned;

(b) that the professional body concerned or any other relevant disciplinary body consider exercising its powers in relation to –

(i) the person with respect to whom the complaint was made; or

(ii) any person who, at the material time, was connected with him;

(c) that –

(i) the person with respect to whom the complaint was made; or

(ii) any person who, at the material time, was connected with him,

pay compensation of an amount specified by the Ombudsman to the complainant for loss suffered by him, or inconvenience or distress caused to him, as a result of the matter complained of;

(d) that the professional body concerned pay compensation of an amount specified by the Ombudsman to the person making the complaint for loss suffered by him, or inconvenience or distress caused to him, as a result of the way in which the complaint was handled by that body;

(e) that the person or professional body to which a recommendation under paragraph (c) or (d) applies make a separate payment to the person making the allegation of an amount specified by the Ombudsman by way of reimbursement of the cost, or part of the cost, of making the allegation.

(3) More than one such recommendation may be included in a report under this section.

(4) Where the Ombudsman includes any recommendation in a report under this section, the report shall give his reasons for making the recommendation.

(5) For the purposes of the law of defamation the publication of any report of the Ombudsman under this section and any publicity given under subsection (9) shall be absolutely privileged.

(6) It shall be the duty of any person to whom a report is sent by the Ombudsman under subsection (1)(b) or (c) to have regard to the conclusions and recommendations set out in the report, so far as they concern that person.

(7) Where –

(a) a report is sent to any person under this section; and

(b) the report includes a recommendation directed at him,

he shall, before the end of the period of three months beginning with the date on which the report was sent, notify the Ombudsman of the action which he has taken, or proposes to take, to comply with the recommendation.

(8) Any person who fails to comply (whether wholly or in part) with a recommendation under subsection (2) shall publicise that failure, and the reasons for it, in such manner as the Ombudsman may specify.

(9) Where a person is required by subsection (8) to publicise any failure, the Ombudsman may take such steps as he considers reasonable to publicise that failure if –

(a) the period mentioned in subsection (7) has expired and that person has not complied with subsection (8); or

(b) the Ombudsman has reasonable cause for believing that that person will not comply with subsection (8) before the end of that period.

(10) Any reasonable expenses incurred by the Ombudsman under subsection (9) may be recovered by him (as a civil debt) from the person whose failure he has publicised.

(11) For the purposes of this section, the person with respect to whom a complaint is made ('the first person') and another person ('the second person') are connected if –

(a) the second person –

(i) employs the first person; and

(ii) is an authorised advocate, authorised litigator, duly certified notary public, licensed conveyancer or partnership;

(b) they are both partners in the same partnership; or

(c) the second person is a recognised body which employs the first person or of which the first person is an officer.

24 Advisory functions

(1) The Legal Services Ombudsman may make recommendations to any professional body about the arrangements which that body

has in force for the investigation of complaints made with respect to persons who are subject to that body's control.

(2) It shall be the duty of any professional body to whom a recommendation is made under this section to have regard to it.

(3) The Ombudsman may refer to the Advisory Committee any matters which come to his notice in the exercise of his functions and which appear to him to be relevant to the Committee's functions.

25 Procedure and offences

(1) Where the Legal Services Ombudsman is conducting an investigation under this Act he may require any person to furnish such information or produce such documents as he considers relevant to the investigation.

(2) For the purposes of any such investigation, the Ombudsman shall have the same powers as the High Court in respect of the attendance and examination of witnesses (including the administration of oaths or affirmations and the examination of witnesses abroad) and in respect of the production of documents.

(3) No person shall be compelled, by virtue of subsection (2), to give evidence or produce any document which he could not be compelled to give or produce in civil proceedings before the High Court.

(4) If any person is in contempt of the Ombudsman in relation to any investigation conducted under section 22, the Ombudsman may certify that contempt to the High Court.

(5) For the purposes of this section a person is in contempt of the Ombudsman if he acts, or fails to act, in any way which would constitute contempt if the investigation being conducted by the Ombudsman were civil proceedings in the High Court.

(6) Where a person's contempt is certified under subsection (4), the High Court may enquire into the matter.

(7) Where the High Court conducts an inquiry under subsection (6) it may, after –

(a) hearing any witness produced against, or on behalf of, the person concerned; and
(b) considering any statement offered in his defence,

deal with him in any manner that would be available to it had he been in contempt of the High Court.

26 Extension of Ombudsman's remit

(1) The Lord Chancellor may by regulation extend the jurisdiction of the Legal Services Ombudsman by providing for the provisions of sections 21 to 25 to have effect, with such modifications (if any) as he thinks fit, in relation to the investigation by the Ombudsman of allegations –

(a) which relate to complaints of a prescribed kind concerned with the provision of probate services; and

(b) which he would not otherwise be entitled to investigate.

(2) Without prejudice to the generality of the power given to the Lord Chancellor by subsection (1), the regulations may make provision for the investigation only of allegations relating to complaints –

(a) made to prescribed bodies; or

(b) with respect to prescribed categories of person.

27 Rights of audience

(1) The question whether a person has a right of audience before a court, or in relation to any proceedings, shall be determined solely in accordance with the provisions of this Part.

(2) A person shall have a right of audience before a court in relation to any proceedings only in the following cases –

(a) where –

(i) he has a right of audience before that court in relation to those proceedings granted by the appropriate authorised body; and

(ii) that body's qualification regulations and rules of conduct have been approved for the purposes of this section, in relation to the granting of that right;

(b) where paragraph (a) does not apply but he has a right of audience before that court in relation to those proceedings granted by or under any enactment;

(c) where paragraph (a) does not apply but he has a right of audience granted by that court in relation to those proceedings;

(d) where he is a party to those proceedings and would have had a right of audience, in his capacity as such a party, if this Act had not been passed; or

(e) where –

(i) he is employed (whether wholly or in part), or is otherwise engaged, to assist in the conduct of litigation and is doing so under instructions given (either generally or in relation to the proceedings) by a qualified litigator; and

(ii) the proceedings are being heard in chambers in the High Court or a county court and are not reserved family proceedings.

(3) No person shall have a right of audience as a barrister by virtue of subsection (2)(a) above unless he has been called to the Bar by one of the Inns of Court and has not been disbarred or temporarily suspended from practice by order of an Inn of Court.

(4) Nothing in this section affects the power of any court in any proceedings to refuse to hear a person (for reasons which apply to him as an individual) who would otherwise have a right of audience before the court in relation to those proceedings.

(5) Where a court refuses to hear a person as mentioned in subsection (4) it shall give its reasons for refusing.

(6) Nothing in this section affects any provision made by or under any enactment which prevents a person from exercising a right of audience which he would otherwise be entitled to exercise.

(7) Where, immediately before the commencement of this section, no restriction was placed on the persons entitled to exercise any right of audience in relation to any particular court or in relation to particular proceedings, nothing in this section shall be taken to place any such restriction on any person.

(8) Where –

(a) immediately before the commencement of this section; or

(b) by virtue of any provision made by or under an enactment passed subsequently,

a court does not permit the appearance of advocates, or permits the appearance of advocates only with leave, no person shall have a right of audience before that court, in relation to any proceedings, solely by virtue of the provisions of this section.

(9) In this section –

'advocate', in relation to any proceedings, means any person exercising a right of audience as a representative of, or on behalf of, any party to the proceedings;

'authorised body' means –

(a) the General Council of the Bar;

(b) the Law Society; and

(c) any professional or other body which has been designated by Order in Council as an authorised body for the purposes of this section.

'appropriate authorised body', in relation to any person claiming to be entitled to any right of audience by virtue of subsection (2)(a), means the authorised body –

(a) granting that right; and

(b) of which that person is a member;

'family proceedings' has the same meaning as in the Matrimonial and Family Proceedings Act 1984 and also includes any other proceedings which are family proceedings for the purposes of the Children Act 1989;

'qualification regulations', in relation to an authorised body, means regulations (however they may be described) as to the education and training which members of that body must receive in order to be entitled to any right of audience granted by it;

'qualified litigator' means –

(i) any practising solicitor ('practising' having the same meaning as in section 19(8)(b));

(ii) any recognised body; and

(iii) any person who is exempt from the requirement to hold a practising certificate by virtue of section 88 of the Solicitors Act 1974 (saving for solicitors to public departments and the City of London);

'recognised body' means any body recognised under section 9 of the Administration of Justice Act 1985 (incorporated practices);

'reserved family proceedings' means such category of family proceedings as the Lord Chancellor may, after consulting the President of the Law Society and with the concurrence of the President of the Family Division, by order prescribe; and 'rules of conduct', in relation to an authorised body, means rules (however they may be described) as to the conduct required of members of that body in exercising any right of audience granted by it.

(10) Section 20 of the Solicitors Act 1974 (unqualified person not to act as a solicitor), section 22 of that Act (unqualified person not to prepare certain documents etc) and section 25 of that Act (costs where an unqualified person acts as a solicitor), shall not apply in relation to any act done in the exercise of a right of audience.

28   Rights to conduct litigation

(1) The question whether a person has a right to conduct litigation, or any category of litigation, shall be determined solely in accordance with the provisions of this Part.

(2) A person shall have a right to conduct litigation in relation to any proceedings only in the following cases –

(a) where –

(i) he has a right to conduct litigation in relation to those proceedings granted by the appropriate authorised body; and

(ii) that body's qualification regulations and rules of conduct have been approved for the purposes of this section, in relation to the granting of that right;

(b) where paragraph (a) does not apply but he has a right to conduct litigation in relation to those proceedings granted by or under any enactment;

(c) where paragraph (a) does not apply but he has a right to conduct litigation granted by that court in relation to those proceedings;

(d) where he is a party to those proceedings and would have had a right to conduct the litigation, in his capacity as such a party, if this Act had not been passed.

(3) Nothing in this section affects any provisions made by or under any enactment which prevents a person from exercising a right to conduct litigation which he would otherwise be entitled to exercise.

(4) Where, immediately before the commencement of this section, no restriction was placed on the persons entitled to exercise any right to conduct litigation in relation to a particular court, or in relation to particular proceedings, nothing in this section shall be taken to place any such restriction on any person.

(5) In this section –

'authorised body' means

(a) the Law Society; and

(b) any professional or other body which has been designated by Order in Council as an authorised body for the purposes of this section;

'appropriate authorised body', in relation to any person claiming to be entitled to any right to conduct litigation by virtue of subsection (2)(a), means the authorised body –

(a) granting that right; and

(b) of which that person is a member;

'qualification regulations', in relation to an authorised body, means regulations (however they may be described) as to the education and training which members of that body must receive in order to be entitled to any right to conduct litigation granted by it; and

'rules of conduct', in relation to any authorised body, means rules (however they may be described) as to the conduct required of members of that body in exercising any right to conduct litigation granted by it.

(6) Section 20 of the Solicitors Act 1974 (unqualified person not to act as a solicitor), section 22 of that Act (unqualified person not to prepare certain documents, etc) and section 25 of that Act (costs where unqualified person acts as a solicitor) shall not apply in relation to any act done in the exercise of a right to conduct litigation.

29 Authorised bodies: designation and approval of regulations and rules

(1) In order to be designated as an authorised body for the purposes of section 27 or 28 a professional or other body must –

(a) apply to the Lord Chancellor under this section, specifying the purposes for which it is seeking authorisation; and

(b) comply with the provisions of Part I of Schedule 4 as to the approval of qualification regulations and rules of conduct and other matters.

(2) Where –

(a) an application has been made to the Lord Chancellor under this section;

(b) the requirements of Part I of Schedule 4 have been satisfied; and

(c) the application has not failed,

the Lord Chancellor may recommend to Her Majesty that an Order in Council be made designating that body as an authorised body for the purposes of section 27 or (as the case may be) section 28.

(3) Where an authorised body alters –

(a) any of its qualification regulations; or

(b) any of its rules of conduct,

those alterations shall not have effect, so far as they relate to any right of audience or any right to conduct litigation granted by that body, unless they have been approved under Part II of Schedule 4.

(4) Where an authorised body makes any alteration to the rights of audience or rights to conduct litigation granted by it (including the grant of a new right), the qualification regulations and rules of conduct of that body must be approved under Part II of Schedule 4.

(5) Where the Lord Chancellor or any of the designated judges considers that it might be appropriate for an authorised body to alter –

(a) any of its qualification regulations or rules of conduct; or

(b) any right of audience, or right to conduct litigation, which it is entitled to grant,

he may advise that body accordingly.

(6) Where –

(a) the Lord Chancellor gives any advice under subsection (5), he shall inform the designated judges; and

(b) where a designated judge gives any such advice, he shall inform the Lord Chancellor and the other designated judges.

(7) Where an authorised body has been given any such advice it shall, in the light of that advice, consider whether to make the recommended alteration.

30   Revocation of authorised body's designation

(1) Where an Order in Council has been made under section 29 designating a body as an authorised body, the Lord Chancellor may recommend to Her Majesty that an Order in Council be made revoking that designation.

(2) An Order under this section may only be made if –

(a) the authorised body has made a written request to the Lord Chancellor asking for it to be made;

(b) that body has agreed (in writing) to its being made; or

(c) the Lord Chancellor is satisfied that the circumstances at the time when he is considering the question are such that, had that body then been applying to become an authorised body, its application would have failed.

(3) The provisions of Part III of Schedule 4 shall have effect with respect to the revocation of designations under this section.

(4) An Order made under this section may make such transitional and incidental provision as the Lord Chancellor considers necessary or expedient.

(5) Where such an order is made, any right of audience or right to conduct litigation granted to any person by the body with respect to whom the Order is made shall cease to have effect, subject to any transitional provision made by the Order.

(6) Where such an Order is made, the Lord Chancellor shall –

(a) give the body with respect to whom the Order is made written notice of the making of the Order;

(b) take such steps as are reasonably practicable to bring the making of the Order to the attention of the members of that body; and

(c) publish notice of the making of the Order in such manner as he considers appropriate for bringing it to the attention of persons (other than those members) who, in his opinion, are likely to be affected by the Order.

31   The General Council of the Bar

(1) On the coming into force of section 27 –

(a) barristers shall be deemed to have been granted by the General Council of the Bar the rights of audience exercisable by barristers (in their capacity as such) immediately before 7 December 1989; and

(b) the General Council of the Bar shall be deemed to have in force qualification regulations and rules of conduct which have been properly approved for the purposes of section 27.

(2) Those qualification regulations and rules of conduct shall be deemed to have been approved only –

(a) in relation to the rights of audience mentioned in subsection (1)(a); and

(b) so far as they relate to those rights of audience.

(3) If any particular provision of those regulations or rules would not have been approved for the purposes of section 27 had it been submitted for approval under Part I of Schedule 4 it (but no other such provision) shall not be deemed to have been approved.

(4) In the event of any question arising as to whether any provision is deemed to have been approved, subsection (5) shall apply in relation to that question if the Lord Chancellor so directs.

(5) Where a direction is given under subsection (4) –

(a) the Lord Chancellor shall seek the advice of the Advisory Committee and the Director;

(b) the Lord Chancellor and each of the designated judges shall consider, in the light of that advice, whether the provision in question is deemed to have been so approved; and

(c) that provision shall not be deemed to have been so approved unless the Lord Chancellor and each of the designated judges are satisfied that it has been.

(6) In the event of any question arising as to whether any provision of the qualification regulations or rules of conduct of the General Council of the Bar requires to be approved by virtue of section 29(3) or (4), subsection (7) shall apply in relation to that question if the Lord Chancellor so directs.

(7) Where a direction is given under subsection (6) –

(a) the Lord Chancellor shall seek the advice of the Advisory Committee and the Director;

(b) the Lord Chancellor and each of the designated judges shall consider, in the light of that advice, whether the provision in question requires approval; and

(c) it shall require approval unless the Lord Chancellor and each of the designated judges are satisfied that it does not require approval.

(8) Where, by virtue of subsection (5)(c), any provision is not deemed to have been approved –

(a) it shall cease to have effect, so far as it relates to any right of audience deemed to have been granted by the General Council of the Bar; and

(b) the regulations and rules which are deemed, by virtue of subsection (1)(b), to have been properly approved shall be taken not to include that provision.

(9) Nothing in this section shall affect the validity of anything done in reliance on any provision of regulations or rules at any time before –

(a) it is determined in accordance with subsection (5)(c) that that provision is not deemed to have been approved; or

(b) it is determined in accordance with subsection (7)(c) that that provision requires approval.

32 The Law Society: rights of audience

(1) On the coming into force of section 27 –

(a) solicitors shall be deemed to have been granted by the Law Society the rights of audience exercisable by solicitors (in their capacity as such) immediately before 7 December 1989; and

(b) the Law Society shall be deemed to have in force qualification regulations and rules of conduct which have been properly approved for the purposes of section 27.

(2) Those qualification regulations and rules of conduct shall be deemed to have been approved only –

(a) in relation to the rights of audience mentioned in subsection (1)(a); and

(b) so far as they relate to those rights of audience.

(3) If any particular provision of those regulations or rules would not have been approved for the purposes of section 27 had it been

submitted for approval under Part I of Schedule 4 it (but no other such provision) shall not be deemed to have been approved.

(4) In the event of any question arising as to whether any provision is deemed to have been approved, subsection (5) shall apply in relation to that question if the Lord Chancellor so directs.

(5) Where a direction is given under subsection (4) –

(a) the Lord Chancellor shall seek the advice of the Advisory Committee and the Director;

(b) the Lord Chancellor and each of the designated judges shall consider, in the light of that advice, whether the provision in question is deemed to have been so approved; and

(c) that provision shall not be deemed to have been so approved unless the Lord Chancellor and each of the designated judges are satisfied that it has been.

(6) In the event of any question arising as to whether any provision of the qualification regulations or rules of conduct of the Law Society requires to be approved by virtue of section 29(3) or (4), subsection (7) shall apply in relation to that question if the Lord Chancellor so directs.

(7) Where a direction is given under subsection (6) –

(a) the Lord Chancellor shall seek the advice of the Advisory Committee and the Director;

(b) the Lord Chancellor and each of the designated judges shall consider, in the light of that advice, whether the provision in question requires approval; and

(c) it shall require approval unless the Lord Chancellor and each of the designated judges are satisfied that it does not require approval.

(8) Where, by virtue of subsection (5)(c), any provision is not deemed to have been approved –

(a) it shall cease to have effect, so far as it relates to any right of audience deemed to have been granted by the Law Society; and

(b) the regulations and rules which are deemed, by virtue of subsection (1)(b), to have been properly approved shall be taken not to include that provision.

(9) Nothing in this section shall affect the validity of anything done in reliance on any provision of regulations or rules at any time before –

(a) it is determined in accordance with subsection (5)(c) that that provision is not deemed to have been approved; or

(b) it is determined in accordance with subsection (7)(c) that that provision requires approval.

33   The Law Society: rights to conduct litigation

(1) On the coming into force of section 28 –

(a) solicitors shall be deemed to have been granted by the Law Society the rights to conduct litigation exercisable by solicitors (in their capacity as such) immediately before 7 December 1989; and

(b) the Law Society shall be deemed to have in force qualification regulations and rules of conduct which have been properly approved for the purposes of section 28.

(2) Those qualification regulations and rules of conduct shall be deemed to have been approved only –

(a) in relation to the rights to conduct litigation mentioned in subsection (1)(a); and

(b) so far as they relate to those rights to conduct litigation.

(3) If any particular provision of those regulations or rules would not have been approved for the purposes of section 28 had it been submitted for approval under Part I of Schedule 4 it (but no other such provision) shall not be deemed to have been approved.

(4) In the event of any question arising as to whether any provision is deemed to have been approved, subsection (5) shall apply in relation to that question if the Lord Chancellor so directs.

(5) Where a direction is given under subsection (4) –

(a) the Lord Chancellor shall seek the advice of the Advisory Committee and the Director;

(b) the Lord Chancellor and each of the designated judges shall consider, in the light of that advice, whether the provision in question is deemed to have been so approved; and

(c) that provision shall not be deemed to have been so approved unless the Lord Chancellor and each of the designated judges are satisfied that it has been.

(6) In the event of any question arising as to whether any provision requires to be approved by virtue of section 29(3) or (4), subsection

(7) shall apply in relation to that question if the Lord Chancellor so directs.

(7) Where a direction is given under subsection (6) –

(a) the Lord Chancellor shall seek the advice of the Advisory Committee and the Director;

(b) the Lord Chancellor and each of the designated judges shall consider in the light of that advice, whether the provision in question requires approval; and

(c) it shall require approval unless the Lord Chancellor and each of the designated judges are satisfied that it does not require approval.

(8) Where, by virtue of subsection (5)(c), any provision is not deemed to have been approved –

(a) it shall cease to have effect, so far as it relates to any right to conduct litigation deemed to have been granted by the Law Society; and

(b) the regulations and rules which are deemed, by virtue of subsection (1)(b), to have been properly approved shall be taken not to include that provision.

(9) Nothing in this section shall affect the validity of anything done in reliance on any provision of regulations or rules at any time before –

(a) it is determined in accordance with subsection (5)(c) that that provision is not deemed to have been approved; or

(b) it is determined in accordance with subsection (7)(c) that that provision requires approval.

34 The Authorised Conveyancing Practitioners Board

(1) There shall be a body corporate to be known as the Authorised Conveyancing Practitioners Board (in this Act referred to as 'the Board').

(2) The Board shall consist of a Chairman and at least four, and at most eight, other members appointed by the Lord Chancellor.

(3) In appointing any member, the Lord Chancellor shall have regard to the desirability of –

(a) appointing persons who have experience in, or knowledge of –

(i) the provision of conveyancing services;
(ii) financial arrangements associated with conveyancing;
(iii) consumer affairs; or
(iv) commercial affairs; and

(b) securing, so far as is reasonably practicable, that the composition of the Board is such as to provide a proper balance between the interests of authorised practitioners and those who make use of their services.

(4) The Board shall not be regarded as the servant or agent of the Crown, or as enjoying any status, immunity or privilege of the Crown.

(5) The Board's property shall not be regarded as property of, or held on behalf of, the Crown.

(6) Neither the Board nor any of its staff or members shall be liable in damages for anything done or omitted in the discharge or purported discharge of any of its functions.

(7) Subsection (6) does not apply where the act or omission is shown to have been in bad faith.

(8) The provisions of Schedule 5 shall have effect with respect to the constitution, procedure and powers of the Board and with respect to connected matters.

35   Functions of the Board and financial provisions

(1) It shall be the general duty of the Board –

(a) to seek to develop competition in the provision of conveyancing services;
(b) to supervise the activities of authorised practitioners in connection with the provision by them of conveyancing services.

(2) In discharging the duty imposed on it by subsection (1)(b) the Board shall, in particular, make arrangements designed to enable it to ascertain whether authorised practitioners are complying with regulations made by the Lord Chancellor under section 40.

(3) The Board shall have the specific functions conferred on it by or under this Act.

(4) Where the Lord Chancellor refers to the Board any matter connected with –

(a) the provision of conveyancing services by authorised practitioners; or

(b) the organisation or practice of authorised practitioners,

it shall be the duty of the Board to consider the matter and to report its conclusions to the Lord Chancellor.

(5) Any report made under subsection (4) may be published by the Lord Chancellor in such manner as he thinks fit.

(6) A copy of any guidance for authorised practitioners issued by the Board shall be sent by the Board to the Lord Chancellor.

(7) Where it appears to the Lord Chancellor that there are grounds for believing that the Board has failed in any way to carry out any of its duties under this Act, he may give such directions to the Board as he considers appropriate ...

40 Regulations about competence and conduct, etc of authorised practitioners

(1) The Lord Chancellor may by regulation make such provision as he considers expedient with a view to securing –

(a) that authorised practitioners maintain satisfactory standards of competence and conduct in connection with the provision by them of conveyancing services;

(b) that in providing such services (and in particular in fixing their charges) they act in a manner which is consistent with the maintenance of fair competition between authorised practitioners and others providing conveyancing services; and

(c) that the interests of their clients are satisfactorily protected.

(2) The regulations may, in particular, make provisions –

(a) designed to –

(i) provide for the efficient transaction of business;

(ii) avoid unnecessary delays;

(b) as to the supervision, by persons with such qualifications as may be prescribed, of such descriptions of work as may be prescribed;

(c) requiring authorised practitioners to arrange, so far as is reasonably practicable, for each transaction to be under the overall control of one individual;

(d) designed to avoid conflicts of interest;

(e) as to the terms and conditions on which authorised practitioners may provide conveyancing services;

(f) as to the information to be given to prospective clients, the manner in which or person by whom it is to be given and the circumstances in which it is to be given free of charge;

(g) as to the handling by authorised practitioners of their clients' money;

(h) as to the disclosure of and accounting for commissions.

56 Administration of oaths, etc by justices in certain probate business

(1) Every justice shall have power to administer any oath or take any affidavit which is required for the purposes of an application for a grant of probate or letters of administration made in any non-contentious or common form probate business.

(2) A justice before whom any oath or affidavit is taken or made under this section shall state in the jurat or attestation at which place and on what date the oath or affidavit is taken or made.

(3) No justice shall exercise the powers conferred by this section in any proceedings in which he is interested.

(4) A document purporting to be signed by a justice administering an oath or taking an affidavit shall be admitted in evidence without proof of the signature and without proof that he is a justice.

(5) In this section –

'affidavit' has the same meaning as in the Commissioners for Oaths Act 1889;

'justice' means a justice of the peace;

'letters of administration' includes all letters of administration of the effects of deceased persons, whether with or without a will annexed, and whether granted for general, special or limited purposes; and

'non-contentious or common form probate business' has the same meaning as in section 128 of the Supreme Court Act 1981.

57 Notaries

(1) Public notaries shall no longer be appointed to practise only within particular districts in England, or particular districts in Wales.

(2) It shall no longer be necessary to serve a period of apprenticeship before being admitted as a public notary ...

(4) The Master may by rules make provision –

> (a) as to the educational and training qualifications which must be satisfied before a person may be granted a faculty to practise as a public notary;
>
> (b) as to further training which public notaries are to be required to undergo;
>
> (c) for regulating the practice, conduct and discipline of public notaries;
>
> (d) supplementing the provision made by subsections (8) and (9);
>
> (e) as to the keeping by public notaries of records and accounts;
>
> (f) as to the handling by public notaries of clients' money;
>
> (g) as to the indemnification of public notaries against losses arising from claims in respect of civil liability incurred by them;
>
> (h) as to compensation payable for losses suffered by persons in respect of dishonesty on the part of public notaries or their employees; and
>
> (i) requiring the payment, in such circumstances as may be prescribed, of such reasonable fees as may be prescribed, including in particular fees for –
>
>> (i) the grant of a faculty;
>>
>> (ii) the issue of a practising certificate by the Court of Faculties of the Archbishop of Canterbury; or
>>
>> (iii) the entering in that court of a practising certificate issued under the Solicitors Act 1974 ...

(8) With effect from the operative date, any restriction placed on a qualifying district notary, in terms of the district within which he may practise as a public notary, shall cease to apply.

(9) In this section –

> 'Master' means the Master of the Faculties;
>
> 'the operative date' means the date on which subsection (1)

comes into force or, if on that date the notary concerned is not a qualifying district notary (having held his faculty for less than five years) –

(a) the date on which he becomes a qualifying district notary; or

(b) such earlier date, after the commencement of subsection (1), as the Master may by rules prescribe for the purpose of this subsection;

'prescribed' means prescribed by rules made under this section; and

'qualifying district notary' means a person who –

(a) holds a faculty as a notary appointed under section 2 of the Act of 1833 or section 37 of the Act of 1914; and

(b) has held it for a continuous period of at least five years ...

(11) Nothing in this section shall be taken –

(a) to authorise any public notary to practise as a notary or to perform or certify any notarial act within the jurisdiction of the Incorporated Company of Scriveners of London or to affect the jurisdiction or powers of the Company; or

(b) to restrict the power of the Company to require a person seeking to become a public notary within its jurisdiction to serve a period of apprenticeship.

59   Representation under the Legal Aid Act 1988

(1) Nothing in this Part shall affect the right of a person who is represented in proceedings in the Supreme Court or the House of Lords under the Legal Aid Act 1988 to select his legal representative.

(2) The power to make regulations with respect to representation under section 2(7) or 32(8) of that Act shall not be exercised so as to provide that representation in any such proceedings may only be by a single barrister, solicitor or other legal representative (but that is not to be taken as restricting the power to make regulations under section 34(2)(e) of that Act).

61 Right of barrister to enter into contract for the provision of his services

(1) Any rule of law which prevents a barrister from entering into a contract for the provision of his services as a barrister is hereby abolished.

(2) Nothing in subsection (1) prevents the General Council of the Bar from making rules (however described) which prohibit barristers from entering into contracts or restrict their right to do so.

62 Immunity of advocates from actions in negligence and for breach of contract

(1) A person –

(a) who is not a barrister; but

(b) who lawfully provides any legal services in relation to any proceedings,

shall have the same immunity from liability for negligence in respect of his acts or omissions as he would have if he were a barrister lawfully providing those services.

(2) No act or omission on the part of any barrister or other person which is accorded immunity from liability for negligence shall give rise to an action for breach of any contract relating to the provision by him of the legal services in question.

63 Legal professional privilege

(1) This section applies to any communication made to or by a person who is not a barrister or solicitor at any time when that person is –

(a) providing advocacy or litigation services as an authorised advocate or authorised litigator; ...

(2) Any such communication shall in any legal proceedings be privileged from disclosure in like manner as if the person in question had at all material times been acting as his client's solicitor ...

66 Multi-disciplinary and multi-national practices

(1) Section 39 of the Solicitors Act 1974 (which, in effect, prevents

solicitors entering into partnership with persons who are not solicitors) shall cease to have effect.

(2) Nothing in subsection (1) prevents the Law Society making rules which prohibit solicitors from entering into any unincorporated association with persons who are not solicitors, or restrict the circumstances in which they may do so.

(3) Section 10 of the Public Notaries Act 1801 (which, in effect, prevents notaries entering into partnership with persons who are not notaries) shall cease to have effect.

(4) Nothing in subsection (3) prevents the Master of the Faculties making rules which prohibit notaries from entering into any unincorporated association with persons who are not notaries, or restrict the circumstances in which they may do so.

(5) It is hereby declared that no rule of common law prevents barristers from entering into any unincorporated association with persons who are not barristers.

(6) Nothing in subsection (5) prevents the General Council of the Bar from making rules which prohibit barristers from entering into any such unincorporated association, or restrict the circumstances in which they may do so.

69 Exemption from liability for damages, etc

(1) Neither the Lord Chancellor nor any of the designated judges shall be liable in damages for anything done or omitted in the discharge or purported discharge of any of their functions under this Part.

(2) For the purposes of the law of defamation, the publication by the Lord Chancellor, a designated judge or the Director of any advice or reasons given by or to him in the exercise of functions under this Part shall be absolutely privileged.

70 Offences

(1) If any person does any act in the purported exercise of a right of audience, or right to conduct litigation, in relation to any proceedings or contemplated proceedings when he is not entitled to exercise that right he shall be guilty of an offence ...

(6) A person guilty of an offence under this section, by virtue of

subsection (1), shall also be guilty of contempt of the court concerned and may be punished accordingly ...

PART III

JUDICIAL AND OTHER OFFICES AND JUDICIAL PENSIONS

71 Qualification for judicial and certain other appointments

(3) For the purposes of this section, a person has –

(a) a 'Supreme Court qualification' if he has a right of audience in relation to all proceedings in the Supreme Court;

(b) a 'High Court qualification' if he has a right of audience in relation to all proceedings in the High Court;

(c) a 'general qualification' if he has a right of audience in relation to any class of proceedings in any part of the Supreme Court, or all proceedings in county courts or magistrates' courts;

(d) a 'Crown Court qualification' if he has a right of audience in relation to all proceedings in the Crown Court;

(e) a 'county court qualification' if he has a right of audience in relation to all proceedings in county courts;

(f) a 'magistrates' court qualification' if he has a right of audience in relation to all proceedings in magistrates' courts.

(4) References in subsection (3) to a right of audience are references to a right of audience granted by an authorised body.

(5) Any reference in any enactment, measure or statutory instrument to a person having such a qualification of a particular number of years' length shall be construed as a reference to a person who –

(a) for the time being has that qualification, and

(b) has had it for a period (which need not be continuous) of at least that number of years.

(6) Any period during which a person had a right of audience but was not entitled to exercise it shall count towards the period mentioned in subsection (5)(b) unless he was prevented by the authorised body concerned from exercising that right of audience as a result of disciplinary proceedings.

(7) For the purposes of subsection (5)(a), a solicitor who does not

have a right of audience, by reason only of not having a practising certificate in force, shall be deemed to have such a right, unless his not having a practising certificate in force is the result of disciplinary proceedings.

(8) For the purposes of subsection (5)(b), any period during which a solicitor did not have a right of audience, by reason only of not having a practising certificate in force, shall be deemed to be a period during which he had such a right, unless his not having a practising certificate in force was the result of disciplinary proceedings.

72 Presiding Judges

(1) For each of the Circuits there shall be at least two Presiding Judges, appointed from among the puisne judges of the High Court.

(2) There shall be a Senior Presiding Judge for England and Wales, appointed from among the Lords Justices of Appeal.

(3) Any appointment under subsection (1) or (2) shall be made by the Lord Chief Justice with the agreement of the Lord Chancellor.

(4) In this section 'the Circuits' means –

(a) the Midland and Oxford Circuit;
(b) the North Eastern Circuit;
(c) the Northern Circuit;
(d) the South Eastern Circuit;
(e) the Western Circuit; and
(f) the Wales and Chester Circuit,

or such other areas of England and Wales as the Lord Chancellor may from time to time, after consulting the Lord Chief Justice, direct.

(5) A person appointed as a Presiding Judge or as the Senior Presiding Judge shall hold that office in accordance with the terms of his appointment ...

73 Delegation of certain administrative functions of Master of the Rolls

(1) Where the Master of the Rolls expects to be absent at a time when it may be appropriate for any relevant functions of his to be exercised, he may appoint a judge of the Supreme Court to exercise those functions on his behalf.

(2) Where the Master of the Rolls considers that it would be inappropriate for him to exercise any such functions in connection with a particular matter (because of a possible conflict of interests or for any other reason), he may appoint a judge of the Supreme Court to exercise those functions on his behalf in connection with that matter.

(3) Where the Master of the Rolls is incapable of exercising his relevant functions, the Lord Chancellor may appoint a judge of the Supreme Court to exercise, on behalf of the Master of the Rolls, such of those functions as the Lord Chancellor considers appropriate ...

(5) In this section 'relevant functions' means any functions of the Master of the Rolls under –

(a) section 144A of the Law of Property Act 1922 (functions in relation to manorial documents);

(b) section 7(1) of the Public Records Act 1958 (power to determine where records of the Chancery of England are to be deposited);

(c) the Solicitors Act 1974 (which gives the Master of the Rolls various functions in relation to solicitors);

(d) section 9 of, and Schedule 2 to, the Administration of Justice Act 1985 (functions in relation to incorporated practices).

74   District judges

(1) The offices of –

(a) registrar, assistant registrar and deputy registrar for each county court district; and

(b) district registrar, assistant district registrar and deputy district registrar for each district registry of the High Court,

shall become the offices of district judge, assistant district judge and deputy district judge respectively.

(2) The office of registrar of the principal registry of the Family Division of the High Court shall become the office of district judge of the principal registry of the Family Division ...

75   Judges, etc barred from legal practice

No person holding as a full-time appointment any of the offices listed in Schedule 11 shall –

(a) provide any advocacy or litigation services (in any jurisdiction);

(b) provide any conveyancing or probate services;

(c) practise as a barrister, solicitor, public notary or licensed conveyancer, or be indirectly concerned in any such practice;

(d) practise as an advocate or solicitor in Scotland, or be indirectly concerned in any such practice; or

(e) act for any remuneration to himself as an arbitrator or umpire.

76 Judicial oaths

(1) A person holding any of the following offices –

(a) district judge, including district judge of the principal registry of the Family Division;

(b) Master of the Queen's Bench Division;

(c) Master of the Chancery Division;

(d) Registrar in Bankruptcy of the High Court;

(e) Taxing Master of the Supreme Court;

(f) Admiralty Registrar,

shall take the oath of allegiance and the judicial oath before a judge of the High Court or a Circuit judge ...

113 Administration of oaths and taking of affidavits

(1) In this section –

'authorised person' means –

(a) any authorised advocate or authorised litigator, other than one who is a solicitor (in relation to whom provision similar to that made by this section is made by section 81 of the Solicitors Act 1974); or

(b) any person who is a member of a professional or other body prescribed by the Lord Chancellor for the purposes of this section; and

'general notary' means any public notary other than –

(a) an ecclesiastical notary; or

(b) one who is a member of the Incorporated Company of

Scriveners (in relation to whom provision similar to that made by this section is made by section 65 of the Administration of Justice Act 1985).

(2) Section 1(1) of the Commissioners for Oaths Act 1889 (appointment of commissioners by Lord Chancellor) shall cease to have effect.

(3) Subject to the provisions of this section, every authorised person shall have the powers conferred on a commissioner for oaths by the Commissioners for Oaths Acts 1889 and 1891 and section 24 of the Stamp Duties Management Act 1891; and any reference to such a commissioner in an enactment or instrument (including an enactment passed or instrument made after the commencement of this Act) shall include a reference to an authorised person unless the context otherwise requires.

(4) Subject to the provisions of this section, every general notary shall have the powers conferred on a commissioner for oaths by the Commissioners for Oaths Acts 1889 and 1891; and any reference to such a commissioner in an enactment or instrument (including an enactment passed or instrument made after the commencement of this Act) shall include a reference to a general notary unless the context otherwise requires.

(5) No person shall exercise the powers conferred by this section in any proceedings in which he is interested.

(6) A person exercising such powers and before whom any oath or affidavit is taken or made shall state in the jurat or attestation at which place and on what date the oath or affidavit is taken or made.

(7) A document containing such a statement and purporting to be sealed or signed by an authorised person or general notary shall be admitted in evidence without proof of the seal or signature, and without proof that he is an authorised person or general notary.

(8) The Lord Chancellor may, with the concurrence of the Lord Chief Justice and the Master of the Rolls, by order prescribe the fees to be charged by authorised persons exercising the powers of commissioners for oaths by virtue of this section in respect of the administration of an oath or the taking of an affidavit.

(9) In this section 'affidavit' has the same meaning as in the Commissioners for Oaths Act 1889.

(10) Every –

(a) solicitor who holds a practising certificate which is in force;

(b) authorised person;

(c) general notary; and

(d) member of the Incorporated Company of Scriveners ('the Company') who has been admitted to practise as a public notary within the jurisdiction of the Company,

shall have the right to use the title 'Commissioner for Oaths'.

115 Law reports

A report of a case made by a person who is not a barrister but who is a solicitor or has a Supreme Court qualification (within the meaning of section 71) shall have the same authority as if it had been made by a barrister.

119 Interpretation

(1) In this Act –

'administration', in relation to letters of administration, has the same meaning as in section 128 of the Supreme Court Act 1981;

'advocacy services' means any services which it would be reasonable to expect a person who is exercising, or contemplating exercising, a right of audience in relation to any proceedings, or contemplated proceedings, to provide;

'authorised advocate' means any person (including a barrister or solicitor) who has a right of audience granted by an authorised body in accordance with the provisions of this Act;

'authorised body' and 'appropriate authorised body' –

(a) in relation to any right of audience or proposed right of audience, have the meanings given in section 27; and

(b) in relation to any right to conduct litigation or proposed right to conduct litigation, have the meanings given in section 28;

'authorised litigator' means any person (including a solicitor) who has a right to conduct litigation granted by an authorised body in accordance with the provisions of this Act;

'authorised practitioner' has the same meaning as in section 37;

'conveyancing services' means the preparation of transfers, conveyances, contracts and other documents in connection with, and other services ancillary to, the disposition or acquisition of estates or interests in land;

'court' includes –

(a) any tribunal which the Council on Tribunals is under a duty to keep under review;

(b) any court-martial; and

(c) a statutory inquiry within the meaning of section 16(1) of the Tribunals and Inquiries Act 1992;

'designated judge' means the Lord Chief Justice, the Master of the Rolls, the President of the Family Division or the Vice-Chancellor;

'the Director' means the Director General of Fair Trading;

'duly certificated notary public' has the same meaning as it has in the Solicitors Act 1974 by virtue of section 87(1) of that Act;

'the general principle' has the meaning given in section 17(4);

'licensed conveyancer' has the same meaning as it has in the Administration of Justice Act 1985 by virtue of section 11 of that Act;

'litigation services' means any services which it would be reasonable to expect a person who is exercising, or contemplating exercising, a right to conduct litigation in relation to any proceedings, or contemplated proceedings, to provide;

'member', in relation to any professional or other body (other than any body established by this Act), includes any person who is not a member of that body but who may be subject to disciplinary sanctions for failure to comply with any of that body's rules;

'multi-national partnership' has the meaning given by section 89(9);

'probate services' means the drawing or preparation of any papers on which to found or oppose a grant of probate or a grant of letters of administration and the administration of the estate of a deceased person;

'prescribed' means prescribed by regulations under this Act.

'proceedings' means proceedings in any court;

'qualification regulations' and 'rules of conduct' –

(a) in relation to any right of audience or proposed right of audience, have the meanings given in section 27; and

(b) in relation to any right to conduct litigation or proposed right to conduct litigation, have the meanings given in section 28;

'qualified person' has the meaning given in section 36(6);

'registered foreign lawyer' has the meaning given by section 89(9);

'right of audience' means the right to exercise any of the functions of appearing before and addressing a court including the calling and examining of witnesses;

'right to conduct litigation' means the right –

(a) to exercise all or any of the functions of issuing a writ or otherwise commencing proceedings before any court; and

(b) to perform any ancillary functions in relation to proceedings (such as entering appearances to actions);

'solicitor' means solicitor of the Supreme Court; and

'the statutory objective' has the meaning given in section 17(2).

(2) For the purposes of the definition of 'conveyancing services' in subsection (1) –

'disposition'

(i) does not include a testamentary disposition or any disposition in the case of such a lease as is referred to in section 54(2) of the Law of Property Act 1925 (short leases); but

(ii) subject to that, includes in the case of leases both their grant and their assignment; and

'acquisition' has a corresponding meaning.

(3) In this Act any reference (including those in sections 27(9) and 28(5)) to rules of conduct includes a reference to rules of practice.

120 Regulations and orders

(1) Any power to make orders or regulations conferred by this Act shall be exercisable by statutory instrument.

(2) Any such regulations or order may make different provisions for different cases or classes of case.

(3) Any such regulations or order may contain such incidental, supplemental or transitional provisions or savings as the person making the regulations or order considers expedient.

(4) No instrument shall be made under section 1(1), 26(1), 37(10), 40(1), 58, 60, 89(5) or (7), 125(4) or paragraph 4 or 6 of Schedule 9 or paragraph 9(c) of Schedule 14 unless a draft of the instrument has been approved by both Houses of Parliament.

(5) An Order in Council shall not be made in pursuance of a recommendation made under section 29(2) or 30(1) unless a draft of the Order has been approved by both Houses of Parliament.

(6) Any other statutory instrument made under this Act other than one under section 124(3) shall be subject to annulment in pursuance of a resolution of either House of Parliament.

SCHEDULE 1

THE ADVISORY COMMITTEE

1. (1) Every member of the Advisory Committee –

(a) shall be appointed for such term, not exceeding five years, as the Lord Chancellor may specify; and

(b) shall hold and vacate office in accordance with the terms of his appointment.

(2) Any person who ceases to be a member of the Advisory Committee shall be eligible for re-appointment.

(3) A member of the Advisory Committee may at any time resign his office by giving notice in writing to the Lord Chancellor.

(4) The Lord Chancellor may remove a member of the Advisory Committee if satisfied –

(a) that he has been absent from meetings of the Advisory Committee for a period of more than six consecutive months without the permission of the Advisory Committee;

(b) that a bankruptcy order has been made against him or that this estate has been sequestrated or that he has made a composition or arrangement with, or granted a trust deed for, his creditors; or

(c) that he is otherwise unable or unfit to discharge the functions of a member of the Advisory Committee ...

12. For the purposes of the law of defamation, the publication of any advice or report by the Advisory Committee in the exercise of any of its functions shall be absolutely privileged ...

SCHEDULE 2

SPECIFIC FUNCTIONS OF THE ADVISORY COMMITTEE

1. (1) The Advisory Committee shall –

(a) keep under review the education and training of those who offer to provide legal services;

(b) consider the need for continuing education and training for such persons and the form it should take; and

(c) consider the steps which professional and other bodies should take to ensure that their members benefit from such continuing education and training.

(2) The Advisory Committee shall give such advice as it thinks appropriate with a view to ensuring that the education and training of those who offer to provide legal services is relevant to the needs of legal practice and to the efficient delivery of legal services to the public.

(3) The Advisory Committee's duties under this paragraph shall extend to all stages of legal education and training ...

7. In discharging its functions under this Schedule, the Advisory Committee shall have regard to the need for the efficient provision of legal services for persons who face special difficulties in making use of those services, including in particular special difficulties in expressing themselves or in understanding.

SCHEDULE 3

THE LEGAL SERVICES OMBUDSMAN

1. (1) The Lord Chancellor may give general directions concerning the discharge of the functions of the Legal Services Ombudsman ...

2. (1) The Ombudsman may delegate any of his functions to such members of his staff as he thinks fit.

(2) All recommendations and reports prepared by or on behalf of the Ombudsman must be signed by him ...

5. (1) The Ombudsman shall make an annual report to the Lord Chancellor on the discharge of his functions during the year to which the report relates.

(2) The Ombudsman may, in addition, report to the Lord Chancellor at any time on any matter relating to the discharge of the Ombudsman's functions.

(3) The Ombudsman shall provide the Lord Chancellor with such information relating to the discharge of his functions as the Lord Chancellor may see fit to require.

(4) The Lord Chancellor shall lay before each House of Parliament a copy of any annual report made to him under sub-paragraph (1) ...

SCHEDULE 4

AUTHORISATION AND APPROVAL

PART I

AUTHORISATION OF BODIES

1. (1) Any professional or other body which wishes to become an authorised body for the purposes of section 27 or 28 ('the applicant') shall send to the Advisory Committee –

(a) a draft of the qualification regulations which it proposes to apply to those of its members to whom it wishes to grant –

(i) any right of audience; or
(ii) any right to conduct litigation,

(b) a draft of the rules of conduct which it proposes to apply to those of its members exercising any such right granted by it; and

(c) a statement of the rights which it proposes to grant ('the proposed rights') and in relation to which it wishes to have those regulations and rules approved ...

(4) It shall be the duty of the Advisory Committee to consider the applicant's draft qualification regulations and rules of conduct in relation to the proposed rights.

(5) When it has completed its consideration, the Advisory Committee shall advise the applicant of the extent to which (if at all)

the draft regulations or rules should, in the Committee's opinion, be amended in order to make them better designed –

(a) to further the statutory objective; or

(b) to comply with the general principle.

(6) In subsequently making its qualification regulations and rules of conduct, with a view to applying for authorisation for the purposes of section 27 or 28, the applicant shall have regard to any advice given to it by the Advisory Committee under this paragraph.

2. (1) Where the applicant has complied with paragraph 1 and wishes to proceed with its application for authorisation, it shall apply to the Lord Chancellor for its qualification regulations and rules of conduct to be approved in relation to the proposed rights ...

(4) On receipt of such an application, the Lord Chancellor shall –

(a) send a copy of the application and of any documents provided under sub-paragraph (2)(c) or (3) to the Advisory Committee and to each of the designated judges; and

(b) ask the Committee for advice as to whether the regulations and rules should be approved for the purposes of section 27 or 28.

3. (1) The Lord Chancellor shall also send copies of the documents mentioned in paragraph 2(4)(a) to the Director ...

5. (1) When he has received the advice of the Advisory Committee and that of the Director, the Lord Chancellor shall send a copy of the advice to the applicant.

(2) The applicant shall be allowed a period of 28 days, beginning with the day on which the copy is sent to him, to make representations about the advice –

(a) to the Lord Chancellor; or

(b) where the Lord Chancellor appoints a person for the purposes of this sub-paragraph, to that person.

(3) When the period of 28 days has expired the Lord Chancellor shall consider, in the light of the advice and of any representations duly made by the applicant under sub-paragraph (2) –

(a) whether the regulations and rules should be approved for the purposes of section 27 or 28; and

(b) whether the application should be approved.

(4) When the Lord Chancellor has complied with sub-paragraph (3) he shall –

(a) send to each designated judge a copy of –

(i) the advice; and

(ii) any representations duly made by the applicant under sub-paragraph (2); and

(b) inform each of those judges of the answers which he proposes to give to the questions which he has considered under sub-paragraph (3).

(5) It shall then be the duty of each designated judge to consider the regulations and rules and, in the light of the other material sent to him by the Lord Chancellor under sub-paragraph (4), to consider the questions considered by the Lord Chancellor under sub-paragraph (3) ...

(10) If the Lord Chancellor or any of the designated judges has refused to approve the application it shall fail ...

PART II

APPROVAL REQUIRED BY SECTION 29

6. (1) Where an authorised body proposes to make any alterations to its qualification regulations or rules of conduct which is required by section 29(3) to be approved under this Part of this Schedule, it shall send to the Advisory Committee a copy of –

(a) its qualification regulations;

(b) its rules of conduct; and

(c) the proposed amending regulations or rules.

(2) Where an authorised body proposes to make any alteration in the rights granted by it which calls for its qualification regulations and rules of conduct to be approved under section 29(4), it shall send to the Advisory Committee a copy of –

(a) its qualification regulations;

(b) its rules of conduct; and

(c) a statement of the proposed alteration to the rights in question ...

7. (1) It shall be the duty of the Advisory Committee to consider the applicant's regulations and rules and the proposed alteration.

(2) When it has completed its consideration, the Advisory Committee shall advise the applicant of the extent to which (if at all) its qualification regulations or rules of conduct should, in the Committee's opinion, be amended in order better to –

    (a) further the statutory objective; or

    (b) comply with the general principle.

8. (1) If, after –

    (a) receiving the Advisory Committee's advice; and

    (b) making the alteration in question,

the applicant wishes the approval required by section 29(3) or (as the case may be) (4) to be given, it shall apply to the Lord Chancellor under this paragraph ...

(4) On receipt of such an application, the Lord Chancellor shall –

    (a) send a copy of the application and of any documents provided under sub-paragraph (2)(c) or (3) to the Advisory Committee and to each of the designated judges; and

    (b) refer the application to the Committee for advice.

9. (1) The Lord Chancellor shall also send a copy of the documents mentioned in paragraph 8(4)(a) to the Director ...

11. (1) When he has received the advice of the Advisory Committee and that of the Director, the Lord Chancellor shall send a copy of the advice to the applicant.

(2) The applicant shall be allowed a period of 28 days, beginning with the day on which the copy is sent to him, to make representations about the advice –

    (a) to the Lord Chancellor; or

    (b) where the Lord Chancellor appoints a person for the purposes of this sub-paragraph, to that person.

(3) When the period of 28 days has expired the Lord Chancellor shall consider, in the light of the advice and of any representations duly made by the applicant under sub-paragraph (2) whether the approval required by section 29(3) or (4) should be given.

(4) When the Lord Chancellor has complied with sub-paragraph (3) he shall –

    (a) send to each designated judge a copy of –

        (i) the advice; and

        (ii) any representations duly made by the applicant under sub-paragraph (2);

    (b) inform each designated judge as to whether he proposes to give the required approval; and

    (c) where he proposes to withhold that approval, inform each designated judge of his reason for doing so.

(5) It shall then be the duty of each designated judge to consider, in the light of the material sent to him by the Lord Chancellor under sub-paragraph (4), whether the required approval should be given ...

(7) If the Lord Chancellor, or any of the designated judges, is satisfied that the alteration is incompatible with the statutory objective or the general principle, he shall refuse to give the required approval ...

PART III

REVOCATION OF DESIGNATION OF AUTHORISED BODY

12. (1) Where the Lord Chancellor is considering whether to recommend the making of a revoking Order by virtue of section 30(2)(c) or is advised by one or more of the designated judges that there are grounds for making such a recommendation, he shall seek the advice of the Advisory Committee.

(2) The Advisory Committee shall carry out such investigations with respect to the authorised body concerned as it considers appropriate.

(3) Where –

    (a) the Lord Chancellor has not sought the advice of the Advisory Committee under sub-paragraph (1); but

    (b) the Committee has reason to believe that there may be grounds for recommending that an Order be made under section 30(2)(c) with respect to an authorised body, it may carry out such investigations with respect to the authorised body as it considers appropriate.

(4) On concluding any investigation carried out under sub-paragraph (2) or (3), the Advisory Committee shall –

(a) advise the Lord Chancellor as to whether or not there appear to be grounds for recommending the making of an Order under section 30 with respect to the authorised body concerned; and

(b) if its advice is that there appear to be such grounds, advise the Lord Chancellor as to the transitional and incidental provision (if any) which it considers should be made under section 30(4) with respect to the authorised body concerned ...

16. (4) No Order under section 30 shall be made with respect to the authorised body unless the Lord Chancellor and each of the designated judges have decided that it should be made.

SCHEDULE 5

THE AUTHORISED CONVEYANCING PRACTITIONERS BOARD

1. (1) Every member of the Board –

(a) shall be appointed for such term, not exceeding three years, as the Lord Chancellor may specify; and

(b) shall hold and vacate office in accordance with the terms of his appointment.

(2) Any person who ceases to be a member of the Board shall be eligible for re-appointment.

(3) A member of the Board may at any time resign his office by giving notice in writing to the Lord Chancellor.

(4) The Lord Chancellor may remove a member of the Board if satisfied –

(a) that he has failed to carry out his duties;

(b) that a bankruptcy order has been made against him or that his estate has been sequestrated or that he has made a composition or arrangement with, or granted a trust deed for, his creditors; or

(c) that he is otherwise unable or unfit to discharge the functions of a member of the Board ...

10. (1) The Board shall submit to the Lord Chancellor an annual report on the discharge of its functions.

(2) The Lord Chancellor shall lay the Board's annual report before Parliament ...

SCHEDULE 11

JUDGES, ETC BARRED FROM LEGAL PRACTICE

The following are the offices for the purposes of section 75 –

Lord of Appeal in Ordinary
Lord Justice of Appeal
Puisne judge of the High Court
Circuit judge
District judge, including district judge of the principal registry of the Family Division
Master of the Queen's Bench Division
Queen's Coroner and Attorney and Master of the Crown Office and Registrar of Criminal Appeals
Admiralty Registrar
Master of the Chancery Division
Registrar in Bankruptcy of the High Court
Taxing Master of the Supreme Court
Registrar of Civil Appeals
Master of the Court of Protection
District probate registrar
Judge Advocate General
Vice Judge Advocate General
Assistant or Deputy Judge Advocate General
Stipendiary Magistrate
Social Security Commissioner
President of social security appeal tribunals, medical appeal tribunals and disability appeal tribunals or regional or other full-time chairman of such tribunals

President of Industrial Tribunals or chairman of such a tribunal appointed under the Industrial Tribunals (England and Wales) Regulations 1965

President or member of the Immigration Appeal Tribunal appointed under Schedule 5 to the Immigration Act 1971

Member of the Lands Tribunal appointed under section 2 of the Lands Tribunal Act 1949

President of Value Added Tax Tribunals or chairman of such a tribunal appointed under Schedule 8 to the Value Added Tax Act 1983

Special Commissioner appointed under section 4 of the Taxes Management Act 1970

Charity Commissioner appointed as provided in Schedule 1 to the Charities Act 1993

Coroner appointed under section 2 of the Coroners Act 1988.

As amended by the Disability Living Allowance and Disability Working Allowance Act 1991, s4(2), Schedule 2, para 22; Tribunals and Inquiries Act 1992, s18(1), Schedule 3, para 35; Social Security (Consequential Provisions) Act 1992, s3(1), Schedule 1; Charities Act 1993, s98(1), Schedule 6, para 26.

CHILD SUPPORT ACT 1991
(1991 c 48)

48 Right of audience

(1) Any person authorised by the Secretary of State for the purposes of this section shall have, in relation to any proceedings under this Act before a magistrates' court, a right of audience and the right to conduct litigation.

(2) In this section 'right of audience' and 'right to conduct litigation' have the same meaning as in section 119 of the Courts and Legal Services Act 1990.

CRIMINAL JUSTICE ACT 1991
(1991 c 53)

53 Notices of transfer in certain cases involving children

(1) If a person has been charged with an offence to which section 32(2) of the [Criminal Justice Act 1988] applies (sexual offences and offences involving violence or cruelty) and the Director of Public Prosecutions is of the opinion –

(a) that the evidence of the offence would be sufficient for the person charged to be committed for trial;

(b) that a child who is alleged –

(i) to be a person against whom the offence was committed; or

(ii) to have witnessed the commission of the offence,

will be called as a witness at the trial; and

(c) that, for the purpose of avoiding any prejudice to the welfare of the child, the case should be taken over and proceeded with without delay by the Crown Court,

a notice ('notice of transfer') certifying that opinion may be served by or on behalf of the Director on the magistrates' court in whose jurisdiction the offence has been charged.

(2) A notice of transfer shall be served before the magistrates' court begins to inquire into the case as examining justices.

(3) On the service of a notice of transfer the functions of the magistrates' court shall cease in relation to the case except as provided by paragraphs 2 and 3 of Schedule 6 to this Act or by section 20(4) of the Legal Aid Act 1988.

(4) The decision to serve a notice of transfer shall not be subject to appeal or liable to be questioned in any court.

(5) Schedule 6 to this Act (which makes further provision in relation to notices of transfer) shall have effect.

(6) In this section 'child' means a person who –

(a) in the case of an offence falling within section 32(2)(a) or (b) of the 1988 Act, is under 14 years of age or, if he was under that age when any such video recording as is mentioned in section 32A(2) of that Act was made in respect of him, is under 15 years of age; or

(b) in the case of an offence falling within section 32(2)(c) of that Act, is under 17 years of age or, if he was under that age when any such video recording was made in respect of him, is under 18 years of age.

(7) Any reference in subsection (6) above to an offence falling within paragraph (a), (b) or (c) of section 32(2) of that Act includes a reference to an offence which consists of attempting or conspiring to commit, or of aiding, abetting, counselling, procuring or inciting the commission of, an offence falling within that paragraph.

BAIL (AMENDMENT) ACT 1993
(1993 c 26)

1   Prosecution right of appeal

(1) Where a magistrates' court grants bail to a person who is charged with or convicted of –

(a) an offence punishable by a term of imprisonment of five years or more, or

(b) an offence under section 12 (taking a conveyance without authority) or 12A (aggravated vehicle taking) of the Theft Act 1968,

the prosecution may appeal to a judge of the Crown Court against the granting of bail.

(2) Subsection (1) above applies only where the prosecution is conducted –

(a) by or on behalf of the Director of Public Prosecutions; or

(b) by a person who falls within such class or description of person as may be prescribed for the purposes of this section by order made by the Secretary of State.

(3) Such an appeal may be made only if –

(a) the prosecution made representations that bail should not be granted; and

(b) the representations were made before it was granted.

(4) In the event of the prosecution wishing to exercise the right of appeal set out in subsection (1) above, oral notice of appeal shall be given to the magistrates' court at the conclusion of the proceedings in which such bail has been granted and before the release from custody of the person concerned.

(5) Written notice of appeal shall thereafter be served on the magistrates' court and the person concerned within two hours of the conclusion of such proceedings.

(6) Upon receipt from the prosecution of oral notice of appeal from its decision to grant bail the magistrates' court shall remand in custody the person concerned, until the appeal is determined or otherwise disposed of.

(7) Where the prosecution fails, within the period of two hours mentioned in subsection (5) above, to serve one or both of the notices required by that subsection, the appeal shall be deemed to have been disposed of.

(8) The hearing of an appeal under subsection (1) above against a decision of the magistrates' court to grant bail shall be commenced within 48 hours, excluding weekends and any public holiday (that is to say, Christmas Day, Good Friday or a bank holiday), from the date on which oral notice of appeal is given.

(9) At the hearing of any appeal by the prosecution under this section, such appeal shall be by way of re-hearing, and the judge hearing any such appeal may remand the person concerned in custody or may grant bail subject to such conditions (if any) as he thinks fit.

(10) In relation to a child or young person (within the meaning of the Children and Young Persons Act 1969) –

(a) the reference in subsection (1) above to an offence punishable by a term of imprisonment is to be read as a reference to an offence which would be so punishable in the case of an adult; and

(b) the reference in subsection (5) above to remand in custody is to be read subject to the provisions of section 23 of the Act of 1969 (remands to local authority accommodation).

(11) The power to make an order under subsection (2) above shall be exercisable by statutory instrument and any instrument shall be subject to annulment in pursuance of a resolution of either House of Parliament.

Note. This section was not in force on 1 October 1993 and no date had then been appointed for its commencement.